Advertising and the Community

Advertising and the Community

Edited by
Alexander Wilson

Manchester University Press

© 1968 Manchester University Press

Published by the University of Manchester
at the University Press
316-324 Oxford Road
Manchester 13

GB SBN 7190 0336 9

Printed in Great Britain by
Butler & Tanner Ltd, Frome and London

Contents

Acknowledgements

The text of Professor Hoggart's chapter was published in similar form in the *Advertisers Weekly* in November 1965. We are indebted to the editor for permitting us to reprint it.

We are also grateful to the editor of the *Spectator* for his permission to make use of a lengthy quotation from an article by Mr Peter Goldman 'Consuming Interest—Viennese Counter-Offensive', published in the *Spectator* of 30 September 1966.

Contributors

Elizabeth Ackroyd
Director of the Consumer Council

J C Braun
Secretary of the Advertising Standards Authority

John Cohen
Professor of Psychology, University of Manchester

Michael Finley
Editor, *The Sheffield Morning Telegraph*

Archie Graham
Head of Advertising Control, Independent Television Authority

Richard Hoggart
Director of Centre for Contemporary Cultural Studies, University of Birmingham

Murray Leask
Group Director, Masius, Wynne-Williams Ltd

Bruce McConnach
Head of Information, Consumers' Association

W McMillan
Advertisement Director, the *Guardian*

Francis Noel-Baker
Member of Parliament, Chairman of the Advertising Inquiry Council

James P O'Connor
Director of the Institute of Practitioners in Advertising

Kenneth Simmonds
Professor of Marketing, Manchester Business School

Harry Street
Professor of Law, University of Manchester

J M Wood
Parliamentary Secretary, Co-operative Union

E G Wedell
Professor of Adult Education, Director of the Department of Extra-Mural Studies, University of Manchester

Maurice Zinkin
Economic Adviser, Unilever Ltd

Alexander Wilson (Editor)
Director of Studies in Management and Industrial Relations, Extra-Mural Department, University of Manchester

Abbreviations used in text

AA   Advertising Association
AIC   Advertising Inquiry Council
AID   Advertising Investigation Department
ASA   Advertising Standards Authority
BBC   British Broadcasting Corporation
BOA   British Optical Association
BMA   British Medical Association
BSI   British Standards Institution
CA   Consumers' Association
CAB   Citizens Advice Bureaux
CAP   Code of Advertising Practice
CAPC   Code of Advertising Practice Committee
EEC   European Economic Community
FTC   Federal Trade Commission
ICI   Imperial Chemical Industries Ltd
IPA   Institute of Practitioners in Advertising
ISBA   Incorporated Society of British Advertisers
ITA   Independent Television Authority
NCB   National Consumer Board
NHS   National Health Service
NOP   National Opinion Poll
NPA   Newspaper Proprietors' Association
PAGB   Proprietary Association of Great Britain
P & G   Procter and Gamble Ltd
PPA   Periodical Proprietors' Association
RTSA   Retail Trading Standards Association
TAM   Television Audience Measurement

Introduction

It has been a notable feature of affluent societies that there seems to be far more interest now in protecting and educating the consumer than ever before. Possibly in earlier times the consumer needed far more protection against gross exploitation by manufacturer and retailer. In these times the consumer co-operative movements in Britain, Scandinavia and other parts of the world played a useful role both in the provision of decent quality goods and in stimulating legislatures into enacting protective legislation. This covered such matters as food adulteration, shoddy clothing and furniture, electrical safety, branding and labelling, and hire-purchase agreements. For a time it seemed that the education of the consumer in the best use of what was bought might become even more important than assisting the consumer to make wise choices in purchasing.

Over the last fifteen or twenty years, however, there has been a bewildering increase in the number of new materials which modern technology enables us to use. Growing affluence has greatly broadened the range of sophisticated products, such as TV sets, transistor radios, cars, refrigerators, washing machines and other durable goods which have come within the purchasing power of most families. At the same time mass media pressures on the consumer, especially TV commercials, seem to have become more insistent, immediate and effective than ever before.

The consumer finds himself able to spend increasingly more of his income on durable goods rather than on food and basic necessities. He and his wife appear to try to exercise more discrimination in their purchasing. But owing to the complexity of the choices facing them, they still rely to a very large extent on the honesty and acumen of the retailer, though the retailer is often as incompetent as they are to assess the qualities of the goods he stocks. The provision of credit facilities with the minimum of collateral security has been enormously important. And it has not been unusual for the best, or at least easiest, credit terms to be associated with the poorest quality goods. Factors of prestige and conformism also influence consumer choice significantly.

The consumer still needs to be his own best protector. And perhaps his second best should be his salesman. For unless the consumer gets satisfaction, the salesman's future is jeopardized. Ideally consumer and salesman should be in partnership. And often they are. But we don't live in an ideal world, and consumers in many countries in recent years have been building up new forms of information and protection.

Perhaps the outstanding development has been a crop of consumers' associations in Western Europe, Scandinavia and Australasia. These have generally followed in the footsteps of the Consumers' Union of the USA, set up about thirty years ago, to inform subscribers of the results of tests of branded goods and services on the basis of fairly objective criteria. In Britain, the Consumers' Association has been operating for ten years. It has over 450,000 subscribers to its monthly report *Which?* It has tested a very wide range of household goods and various types of services. It produces special assessments of cars for a more limited range of subscribers. Unlike most of its fellow organizations, it tries to select 'best buys' for each commodity tested. Others believe this to be liable to mislead if consumers omit to read the description of the tests and the criteria on which judgement has been based. Perhaps even more seriously, it also assumes a high degree of quality control, without which 'best buys' will still be a gamble.

Parliaments in several countries have concerned themselves with bringing up to date standards of safety, weights and measures, labelling and product testing. Sweden has normally been furthest ahead in this. Some countries have set up Consumer Councils to advise on future legislation affecting the consumer, and to promote consumer education. The Common Market countries have given special consultative status to the European Community Consumers' Contact Committee, so that this committee can give its specialist views on all technical matters which crop up while the EEC Commission is determining policy. At the Hague, there has now been for the last six years, the headquarters of an International Organization of Consumers Unions, while at more local level several of the consumers' unions have promoted local community associations, which discuss reports and make studies of products and services in relation to their own locality. In Britain there are about seventy of these local groups. Several newspapers, including the *Guardian*, have been giving space in recent years to Consumer Affairs with regular columnists, but what they do is comparatively small beside the women's magazines and specialist journals. The BBC has paid more than lip service to the trend for more consumer information. Yet its contribution has been surprisingly small, considering the apparent success of programmes such as *Motoring and the Motorist* and *Choice*, and constant features in *Woman's Hour*.

A new look at Consumer Protection in Britain was taken in 1959, when Parliament appointed the Molony Committee to review the existing legislation relating to merchandise marks and certification trade marks. It was to report on what changes in the law and other measures were desirable for the further protection of consumers. The report was published in 1962. It made recommendations of various kinds, and also indicated what legislative priority should be given to these. The recommendations were:

1. The setting up of a Consumer Council (on the lines of those existing in Norway, Sweden, Netherlands, Eire and Israel).
2. The expansion of the consumer protection activities of the Citizen's Advice Bureaux.
3. Amendment of the Hire Purchase Act, 1938 (to remove unrealistic money limits, and check the activities of doorstep salesmen).
4. Amendment of the law on merchandise marks (to make it clear that all forms of advertising should come under the

control of the Merchandise Marks Acts, and to establish the principle that sales should not be induced or promoted by the making of false or misleading statements of a factual nature.

5. Amendment of the Sale of Goods Act 1893 (to safeguard the purchaser with regard to warranties, etc.).

6. Control of unregistered seals of approval.

There was also a strong suggestion that the practice of resale price maintenance should be prohibited.

Action on these recommendations has been remarkably swift. As a result,

1. The Consumer Council was set up (and had reported on its first year by July 1964).

2. The CAB was given a grant of £27,000.

3. RPM was dealt with in the Resale Prices Act, 1964.

4. The Hire Purchase Act, 1964, amended the law on credit trading.

5. The existing legislation about merchandise marks is being replaced and extended by the Consumers Protection Bill.

In its first report, the Consumer Council was able to point to a wide range of issues on which it had taken prompt, and often effective, action. Its members had taken an active part in Parliamentary consideration of new legislation on hire purchase, resale price maintenance and trading stamps. It had played a leading part (with the *Daily Mail*) in obtaining safety regulations against inflammable nightdresses for children. It secured the provision of non-homogenized milk when most dairies switched over to the more expensive 'homogenized milk'. Since then it has taken steps relating to school uniforms, travel agents, shopping hours, banking hours and doorstep salesmen. It has recently been very concerned with adequate labelling of goods, with misleading advertising and the question of guarantees and warranties (some of which are difficult to understand, and some of which deprive the consumer of his legal rights). The Council has always emphasized that it has not been set up to be against manufacturers, wholesalers and retailers. Its aim is to co-operate with them in protecting the consumer from being exploited in any way. So it has established close links with the British Standards Institute, the Retail Trading Standards Association, and the Advertising Standards Authority.

It is against this rapidly moving background of technical change and sophisticated products, the development of commercial television and discretionary spending power, consumer concern and protective legislation, that one should consider current discussions on advertising and its role in the modern community.

The chapters which follow are based on contributions made at two seminars on advertising, organized by the Extra-Mural Department of Manchester University, and held at Holly Royde College in 1966 and 1967. In them some attention is paid, especially by Maurice Zinkin and Professor Kenneth Simmonds, to the business function and its economic justification in a highly developed economy. Attention is also paid, by Professor John Cohen and others, to the possible psychological justification for advertising in communities where the purchasing of consumer goods is dominated by women's attitudes, aspirations, emotions and choices. But the crux of the matter is the present quality of the advertising of consumer goods. Should it be more informative and revealing than it generally is? How far is it sensible to expect legislation to ensure that the desired level is achieved and maintained? Can self-discipline and self-regulation be relied upon to develop a reasonable sense of social responsibility within the world of advertising? How far is it feasible for consumer organizations to educate the ordinary consumer to protect herself? Inevitably, much of the discussion on these aspects has been concentrated on mass media forms of advertising, especially TV commercials, with a good deal of attention devoted to such topics as the justifiable price for invaluable detergents. The discussion, however, also covers several interesting questions of political and social significance, such as the financial dependence of newspapers on their advertisers, and of the Advertising Standards Authority on the Advertising Association and advertising industry. Several contributors have looked abroad, mainly at the USA, for lessons in the restraint of advertising and in consumer advisory services which might usefully be copied in Britain.

Perhaps it should be admitted at the outset that this collection of essays (arising out of these two confrontation seminars, which were attended by executives and creative people from the advertising industry, the press and broadcasting, along with members of the educational and social services) has not been designed to provide clear-cut solutions to the problems posed, but rather to identify the questions which we must ask ourselves if we are sincerely looking for a common approach to satisfactory solutions—rather than simply seeking publicity and self-advertisement from dramatic gestures and extreme viewpoints.

Several of the contributions have not been translated into a third-person style. This has not been intended to indicate that these are necessarily less objective in approach than the others. It has simply been felt that a personal style seemed more natural in these instances, and that some of the viewpoints expressed might suffer a loss of pungency from any such translation.

Part one

Why advertise?

Psychology and philosophy of advertising

John Cohen

I

Advertising may primarily be regarded as a form of communication. The typical advertising agency occupies itself with devising messages to be sent to the potential consumer who generally receives them through his eyes or ears. These messages are the input to the potential consumer, considered as a channel, while the output is his decision to buy or not to buy.

From this point of view, the effectiveness of the advertiser's communications will depend, in the first place, on his knowledge of the properties of the channel, that is, of the characteristics of the persons whom he is addressing. In the second place, he will need to determine the optimal properties of the message itself. The advertiser's objective, to put it as simply and innocently as possible, is to influence the consumer so that he *either* continues to buy the same article as before *or*, if this is what the advertiser requires, decides to buy a different one.

In this endeavour the advertiser appeals to the consumer's needs and 'wants'. These may be inborn, such as the need to eat or for sexual experience, or they may be acquired, such as the need to smoke or to go to the Bahamas for a winter holiday. The appeal is presented so as to catch the consumer's attention by showing him something that pleases him. His feelings of pleasure thus aroused are supposed to overflow on to the product advertised. Advertisers can be pretty sure that the sexual impulse is highly sensitized and often unsatisfied in their potential customers. They therefore direct their anguished appeal to bring about a transfer of approval from a sexual object to the product they want to sell. The same applies to unsatisfied desires for better health, more strength or greater beauty.

In order to counteract the consumer's habituation, which means his gradual weakening of response to the advertiser's stimulation, there must be introduced, at appropriate intervals, a new slant, so as to arouse the consumer afresh. The consumer's habituation is the advertiser's worst enemy. The task of bringing the consumer to change from one product or brand to another is an application of the theory of habit breaking which involves ethical as well as psychological issues.

Sometimes the advertiser tries to frighten the consumer, playing on his fear of this or that consequence if he fails to buy the particular brand advertised. Here some care must be exercised, for if the advertiser elicits a strong fear, the potential consumer will defend himself by rejecting the information as untrue. Or he will persuade himself that the information only applies to others, as exemplified by the man who feared that he might get lung cancer from smoking and therefore decided to stop reading the newspapers.

When a viewer is absorbing graphic material his reaction can be made more intense if a vital element is omitted from the picture. This is the key to what E. H. Gombrich has called 'suggestive veiling' in the erotic presentation of the semi-naked. The same rule also holds true in art itself. Semi-nakedness is more provocative than nakedness partly because of the so-called barrier effect: other things being equal, we want things more the harder they are to get. During the war, a queue would immediately form once it became known that something, in short supply, had become available, and people joined the queue even if they did not know what it was for. Furthermore, the hunt gives more joy than the disillusioning kill. So long as you have not arrived at your destination you are free to nurse all sorts of illusions about what may in the end turn out to be a mirage.

Accordingly, for anyone who is sexually unsatisfied, even a hint of resemblance between a given object and something which has sexual significance is enough. In this respect there is little to choose between the Victorian and his grandson who lives in a Welfare State. A couple of generations ago, the carved oak legs of pianos, armchairs and tables were (so it is said) decently draped, and the Victorian business man was thrilled to the marrow if a breeze blew up a little of the lace to reveal the wooden leg, just as his descendants wait in queues to see a film which is entitled 'The Half-Naked Lunch'. For similar reasons our dreams allow the widest range of phallic symbols.

How justified is the deliberate exploitation by advertisers of unsatisfied impulses which overflow on to the product advertised?

The advertiser confidently assumes that most potential consumers are anxious to conform. So his message to them tells them how to achieve this security: '90 per cent of men use X shaving cream', or '90 per cent of women use this detergent'. The prestige suggestion that actress so-and-so uses such a soap endows conformity with status. A relatively small proportion, however, take joy in not conforming, in being different from the others. The message to these must therefore be appropriately tailored.

This part of the advertiser's task is very complicated. Take the question of visual presentation in a newspaper, a magazine or a television commercial. The advertiser must consider, among other things, the size of the visual image he wishes to present, the effect of repetition, the difficulty of breaking a long-standing habit and of forming a new one, the advantages which the viewer thinks he will enjoy, whether, say, the additional outlay seems to him to be worth the expected increase in satisfaction. The advertiser must also ask himself how much information he should provide about the product; in what form, for example, in words, pictures or as a leaflet; whether to concentrate on the product as such, or to embed it as one item in a setting which conveys a general mood or atmosphere: for the conjuring up of the atmosphere of, say, a party at the home of the housewife of 1970 may have more impact than a verbal eulogy of the virtues of a particular kind of soap or chocolate. In addition, the advertiser has to decide about inducements: free samples, gifts, prizes, rebates and so on. So much for advertising as an effort to communicate.

II

Ethical considerations introduce a new dimension. They have nothing to do with the question of the efficiency of running a communication system in order to achieve ends laid down in advance. They are concerned rather with the norms or standards of conduct in advertising. To what extent is there conformity with, or violation of, the social code, openly or surreptitiously? This means, to begin with, clearing the air of confusion of *facts* with *values*. To ask, for instance, whether advertising actually has an effect on public taste is quite different from asking whether advertising is a good thing. No amount of knowledge of facts will help to establish our values. Even if we had an encyclopaedic knowledge of the facts of advertising: economic facts, consumer facts, psychological and other facts, we should be no wiser as to whether any particular piece of advertising was good or bad. And *vice versa*: we give no information about advertising when we merely pronounce a moral judgement on it.

The difference between a statement of fact and a value judgement is that the former can be checked in a way that the latter cannot be. If I say 'this parcel weighs half a pound', you can check my statement by placing the parcel on a weighing scale. There is no comparable way of checking my statement that 'this woman is beautiful'. Nevertheless, it is a fact of great psychological importance that we do make, and need to make, value judgements. Indeed, some valuation may be implicit in all our perception of things as well as in our judgements, decisions and actions.

Before we can decide whether advertising is, in our own view, a good or a bad thing, we need to have a yardstick of values by which we can judge goodness or badness. Only when we have such a yardstick, and we are clear about the criteria for distinguishing goodness from badness, can we use our knowledge of the facts to classify the advertisements themselves as good or bad.

It certainly does not make for clarity if we pronounce value judgements disguised as statements of fact. An example of this is the oft-quoted remark of the late Aneurin Bevan that 'advertising is an evil service'. This assertion merely tells us in which of his two private categories 'good' and 'evil' Mr Bevan placed

5

advertising. It adds nothing to our factual knowledge of the subject. It tells us more about Mr Bevan than about advertising. Another illustration is Arnold Toynbee's oracular pronouncement that he 'cannot think of any circumstances in which advertising would not be an evil'. This too only reveals to us the circle within which Mr Toynbee's thoughts move. To the same groups belongs a statement by Mr Galbraith that because of advertising, 'people squander money on "unneeded" things'. There are two points to note here. First, he uses the emotive term 'squander', which means spending more than is justifiable. But who is to decide what is the 'justifiable' amount? Are we all to leave this decision in Mr Galbraith's safe hands? Secondly, there is the reference to 'unneeded' things. Who is to be the judge on what is needed? Is this too to be left to Mr Galbraith?

The spirit of Mr Galbraith's statement is eminently Victorian. Fifty years ago, a British sociologist, J. A. Hobson, pointed out that 'whole generations of economists have accumulated easy virtue by preaching (this) rigorous economy for the working classes'. For it always seemed possible to economists that enough of the 'superfluous' could be squeezed out of the standard of living of the working classes to justify the opinion that most of their misery is their own fault. If they spent their wages rationally, and (for example) never smoked or imbibed alcohol, they could live as decent citizens.

So long as we have economists in our midst, we shall need to be alert to the trick of letting value judgements masquerade as statements of fact. There is yet another use to which the sheep's clothing of fact is put: letting persuasion appear in the guise of information. It is certainly possible to persuade without giving information. Is the converse true? Is it possible to give information without persuading? If the answer is 'Yes', it might be argued that this is the proper thing to do, and that while it is legitimate for advertisers to provide information, so long as it is accurate, in no circumstances should they attempt to persuade, because this would entail manipulation of others.

Whether persuasion is a legitimate role of advertising is sometimes regarded as a political issue. Spokesmen for the USSR claim to be in favour of informative but not of persuasive advertising. Mr A. L. Mikoyan once declared that

The task of Soviet advertising is to give people exact information about the goods that are on sale, (but also) to help to create new demands, to cultivate new tastes, to promote the sale of new kinds of goods and to explain their uses to the consumer.

It seems to me doubtful, however, whether new demands and tastes can be created or cultivated, or the sale of new articles promoted, without persuasion, directly and explicitly or indirectly and implicitly. However, the Russians still (in 1966, according to *Pravda*) insist on the informative aspects in advertising. 'The more goods and products in the shops—the greater the need for advertising, for providing customers with systematic and qualified information on the quality and features of one or another commodity and on where it can be bought.' The largest department store in Moscow, GUM, has an advertising staff of fifty. Inside the store, advertising is accompanied by music, and there are leaflets and posters. But Soviet specialists in advertising declare that they 'have no desire to resort to high pressure salesmanship in advertising'.

Although a knowledge of the facts does not help us to establish values, it may still impose new ethical obligations, and enable us to make more informed value judgements. For example, so long as nothing was known about air-borne, water-borne or milk-borne diseases, no burden of responsibility fell on the public authorities to improve sanitation. Once the origin and transmission of bacterial infection were understood, there was a duty to do something about it. The thalidomide disaster likewise exemplifies a situation in which knowledge of the facts has a bearing on responsibility. It could be argued that the pharmaceutical firm concerned did not have sufficient information about the effects of the drug on pregnant animals to justify putting it on the market. Nevertheless, the marketing of thalidomide was irresponsible in the absence of information that could have been obtained.

Granted that it is almost impossible not to try to persuade, we have another ethical question on our hands. Do advertisers have the *right* to persuade? We know that the world of advertising in Britain (or part of it) is striving earnestly to professionalize itself, like the optical and catering worlds, and that there are written and unwritten codes of good conduct. In practice, it seems, the codes may be disregarded. I refer to such practices as poaching on a competitor's clients or undertaking to advertise goods which the advertiser suspects are below standard. So far as I know there is nothing in the code of advertising which forbids persuasion. In defence of the advertiser, it might be said that so far as persuasion is concerned, advertising is no different in principle from political propaganda or a sermon from the pulpit.

At first sight, therefore, a recent statement by Lord Heyworth, speaking for ICI, that 'freedom of choice includes the freedom to persuade others to your way of thinking', may seem unobjectionable. On second thoughts, such freedom appears to be an illusion. I am free to launch a daily newspaper and to try and persuade others to my way of thinking. In practice I do not have much chance of becoming a press magnate. How many British citizens have the opportunity of persuading others to their way of thinking? But even if we allowed Lord Heyworth's declaration to pass as a harmless fiction, does it necessarily follow, as he claims it does, that advertising 'is a prerequisite to real freedom of choice'? A powerful enough advertiser could soon oust his rivals and limit the consumer's choice to a single product. This is surely the advertiser's goal or, at least, his dream goal.

If advertising were truly 'a prerequisite to real freedom of choice', all advertisements like political party broadcasts, should have equal time and space in the mass media, and all consumers would have to absorb *all* this information before they were permitted to make a choice.

There is a further difficulty. How would Lord Heyworth's formula stand up to the strain if applied to the test case of cigarette advertising on television? Here we have a clash between encouraging freedom of consumer's choice, on the one hand, and State intervention to limit choice in the consumer's interest, on the other. The Ministry of Health, in the name of the Government, intervened to prevent the consumer making a harmful choice. Actually, the intervention does not prevent the consumer from choosing a preferred brand of cigarettes, for they are on sale everywhere. What the Government did was to refuse to allow television to encourage cigarette smoking in any form. The banning of cigarette advertising on TV does not mean limiting the choice as between different brands, but as between cigarette smoking or not smoking.

What seems to me to savour of hypocrisy in this context is the fact that while the Ministry of Health bans the advertisements, the Treasury is not at all keen to lose its revenue from tobacco. From the point of view of the Chancellor of the Exchequer it would be a national disaster if the policy of the Ministry of Health were to prove successful. Indeed, if the viewpoint of the Ministry of Health were shared by the Government as a whole, the import and manufacture of cigarettes would be banned completely, just as the import of hashish is forbidden. Or the price would be made really prohibitive—£100 a packet of ten cigarettes, so that each salaried smoker might afford one puff a month. What the Chancellor hopes when he raises the price of tobacco in his Budget is that the number of smokers who will be deterred by the increase will be more than offset by the number remaining undeterred by it.

As a matter of fact, if the Chancellor's annual increases in the price of cigarettes have any effect on smoking, it is to encourage the smoker to puff away to the bitter end. Since the nicotine accumulates, the consequence is probably to accentuate the hazards from lung cancer. Thus the result achieved by the Chancellor is diametrically opposed to the goal of the Ministry of Health.

We can think of other instances in which a specific piece of persuasion may have far-reaching repercussions. Who would imagine that the purchase of a doll could possibly affect a teenager's way of life and shape her role at home and in society? Yet we cannot rule out this possibility, for there is a celebrated and well-advertised doll, S—y by name, who may be doing just this. She is 'the doll you'll love to dress! S—y is more than a doll, she is a real personality. She is a free-swinging, grown-up girl *who lives her own life and dresses the way she really likes'* (my italics).

State intervention has gone so far as to bar the advertising of cigarettes on television. It has stopped short of barring commercials on holidays abroad. A former Chancellor's (Mr Callaghan) self-confessed obsession with the balance of payments led him not only to clamp down on foreign exchange for travel, but also to influence advertising for holidays abroad. Everyone must have noticed that at the very moment that he was advising everyone (including, presumably, Old Age Pensioners, Widows and Orphans) to invest in a boat for sailing around the coast of Britain, there was a veritable storm of TV 'holiday-abroad' advertising, and questions were subsequently asked in the House of Commons as to the Chancellor's intentions. If his secret aim had been to stimulate holidays abroad he could not have timed his words more carefully.

Evidently the Government's view is that the barring of advertising cannot only be morally justified on the grounds of health. It believes it has the right to intervene whenever it seems in the public interest to do so as, for example, in relation to the problem of balance of payments.

III

Information can be the whole truth or part of the truth. Some advertisers are said by the critics to cultivate their professional work as *the art of telling untruths without actually telling lies*. It is not hard to find illustrations. There are at least two food auxiliaries on the market which are advertised as containing X nutritious ingredients which give physical strength while appealing particularly to the male palate. Yet a hospital food chart for a certain category of patients describes both of them as 'of no food value'. And, as for the beverages which are supposed to induce a deep and dreamless sleep, I personally find that they invariably keep me wide awake all night, far more effectively than a strong black coffee.

Fractionation of truth has enormous scope in the domain of beauty culture. No more potent appeal can be made to the soul of modern woman than the offer of the Goblet of Youth, which holds secrets sought by women for countless centuries. This holy grail is said to bear newly discovered Ingredients of Youth which help the skin recapture its infant flow and prevent dehydration. 'Your skin will drink in the formula thirstily. Soon, wrinkles and lines will begin to fill in and fade. Your skin will be "springier", smoother, brighter. The signs of age will begin to melt away. Your skin will forget its age.'

We must suppose that these claims are not entirely without substance. Yet, can it really be true that the signs of age will 'begin' to melt away? Perhaps the crux of the argument lies in the word *begin*. We are not told how long the entire process will take. What the lady is advised to do is to 'apply it morning and night. Just dip your finger tips into the brimming goblet. Very gently, caress the velvety lotion upward over the face and throat . . . Use it anywhere . . .'

Next of kin to a half-truth is a misguided metaphor. The announcement 'I have a leopard in my tank' is not literally true. No one claims that. In what sense, then, is it true? If different brands of petrol are strictly indistinguishable, as is often alleged, there can be no moral justification for metaphorical advertising which is misleading. The argument that advertising leads to bigger sales and therefore to lower prices is irrelevant at this point. Another objection could be (and has been) raised, namely, that the fictitious leopard could lead to an increase in road accidents. If you believe you have leopard's blood in your veins, you will tend to act like one. With this sort of advertising, our highways could literally become scenes of jungle warfare.

IV

There is an item of expenditure to which I should like to refer at this juncture because it may increasingly attract the attention of advertisers—if we follow the American pattern, as is perhaps likely. I refer to expenditure on funerals. In the first decade of the century, the amount which British working-class families devoted to funerals frequently provoked a storm of moral indignation among the economists to whom I have already referred. The amount spent was described as typical working-class extravagance. Yet, as Hobson remarked, a more human interpretation could be given, for the only time when a working man or woman stands out from his fellows is when he is being buried. 'Is it wholly regrettable that those who care for him should wish to give this narrow, thwarted, obscure personality a moment of dignity and glory?'

This does not mean that we must approve of the elaborate schemes of 'death advertising' customary in the United States (such as 'Die now, and bury yourself at half price'). Miss

Mitford has given us a glowing picture of the pleasures of death from the advertiser's point of view. The catalogue of Practical Burial Footwear (of Columbus, Ohio), she tells us, recommends for the deceased 'soft cushioned soles and warm luxurious slipper comfort, but true shoe smartness'. The women's lingerie department of the same firm supplies 'a de-luxe package with gold-embossed description' of 'pantee, vestee' and nylon hose 'strikingly smart—ultimate in distinction'. Another progressive firm offers 'new Bra-form, Post Mortem Form Restoration, which accomplish so much for so little'. A third company announces that its caskets are equipped with a 'Beauty-rama Adjustable Soft-Foam Bed . . . soft and buoyant, but will hold firm without slipping', and, what is more, a quality mattress which prevents cranking. If it should be thought that American practices have little bearing on English customs Miss Mitford, in her chapter 'Funerals in England', reminds us that the difference between the two countries may only be one of degree.

V

Whether the techniques of advertising are simply to transmit information or whether they are also to manipulate the consumer's values, by persuasion or otherwise, the message tends very often to be addressed to what we popularly call the 'imagination'. A great deal of advertising sustains, nourishes or inspires a train of fantasy. In this sense it assumes the responsibility of stirring or creating a discontent, perhaps a divine discontent, with harsh realities.

The idea of 'imagination' is not well defined. Dr Johnson considered it to be a precious faculty, for without it a man would not be in a position to say whether he is in the arms of a duchess or a chambermaid, and in a society which draws a sacred line between U and non-U, the ability to make this fine distinction is not to be despised. But Dr Johnson might have been in error, for to a man with sufficient imagination a chambermaid might actually seem to be a duchess. Advertising often appears to take upon itself the task of making countless chambermaids imagine that they are duchesses.

Advertising stimulates the fantasy, in the good sense of escapism as well as in the bad sense. It glamorizes the drabness of everyday life. It creates the models which are essential in all societies and civilizations. But it has the responsibility of selecting the models for feeding the National Fantasy and the archetypes of the unconscious.

Thus, the advertiser may use the image of a film star as a model to sustain the cosmetic industry. Countless creams and unguents, innumerable tubes and jars of all shapes and sizes, advertised on a vast scale, are sought by jostling girls at the beauty counters of all large stores. 'Entire laboratories are poured out on the dressing table of the humblest girl.' At the same time the advertisers provide tuition in the techniques of amorous communication: 'charming little pouts, fetching smiles, romantic expressions, far-away looks, words inspired by moonlight and stardust'.

Soap, shampoo and cosmetic advertisements cultivate a profound interest in the narcissistic Body-Image, especially in teenagers. A teenager with money in her pocket is encouraged by advertisers on behalf of the cosmetic industry to believe that she possesses an extraordinary visual acuity in that she can discriminate between eye-lashes which differ by only 3 per cent of an inch in length. There are eye-lash creams on the market that claim to add $\frac{1}{32}$ in. to the length of each hair in each eyelash. It is hard to locate the evidence on which this claim is founded.

VI

One of the chief changes that has taken place since the industrial revolution has been to transform Man the Producer into Man the Consumer, a change which has been intensified by a period of full employment. Now it is in consumption rather than in mass production that we express our taste. Neither the conveyor belt nor automation affords opportunities for individuality. Extended educational opportunities lead to the enrichment, enhancement and diversification of taste. The consequence becomes increasingly apparent in consumption, and the impact will presently be felt in production. Thus the individuality of the consumer will force itself on the attention of the producer. Advertising has an enormous social responsibility in the cultivation of taste. For on this depends the consumer's choice and through him the producer's product.

In a primitive economy people have to buy whatever will feed, clothe and shelter them at the least cost. In a prosperous society people are harder to please. Each basic want becomes a pattern of different wants, and individuals like to satisfy them in their own particular way. Demand becomes as varied as temperament, social background, taste and intelligence. By helping to provide for as many varieties of demand as possible, the advertiser could lead the consumer towards a fuller satisfaction.

2

The advertiser's point of view

Maurice Zinkin

Advertisers are engaged in a very simple task. They are trying to persuade the public to buy something, in most cases a product, occasionally an idea. The product is generally a consumer good, usually a consumer good bought again and again. This places certain very clear restrictions on at least the larger advertiser.

He has to tell the truth. It is useless to advertise a detergent as washing white which does not wash white. The public will buy one packet and never buy a second; the advertiser will lose his money. Disasters of this sort occur to advertisers not infrequently, not because they have deliberately told an untruth but, for example, because that which was true in the laboratory turns out to be not quite so true in the kitchen. The idea that the housewife can be manipulated, that she can be persuaded to see whiteness in a shirt where no whiteness is, or to taste sweetness in a bitter chocolate, is nonsense, the worst sort of intellectual's disrespect for the good sense of the ordinary person.

Advertisers do, of course, occasionally exaggerate.

Sometimes this is because they genuinely believe their product to be better than it really is. The man who makes a particular chocolate or breakfast food is liable to believe it is better than any other. There is no final test of goodness for many products, and the manufacturer may like the taste of his chocolate or the crispness of his cereal more than the housewife does. The right tenderness in a pea, the exact cuddlability of a teddy bear, are matters of subjective judgement.

Sometimes, however, the advertiser is deliberately over-

15

stating his case, as a politician may do in a party political broadcast or a barrister in court. Here the public's protection is that the advertiser cannot get away with very much. The chocolate may not be absolutely the best but it must at least be as good as any other, or the public will be disillusioned. The painkiller may not work quite as well as the commercial claims, but if it does not stop a headache, it will not be bought again. There is perhaps room for regulations which would compel an even higher level of truth than is already prevalent, but it is most unlikely that the effect, either on advertising or on the public's pattern of purchases, would be other than marginal. It would probably be more effective to change the reluctance of advertisers to 'knock' each other's products. Nobody knows his competitors' defects better than another manufacturer. But if advertisers are to knock each other, they will have to be able to sue if they are knocked unfairly. One of the main reasons why there is an element of exaggeration in advertising at present is that the courts refuse to take advertisers' claims seriously; they dismiss them all as puffs, so that no amount of exaggeration gives a competitor a right of action.

Any advertiser who wants to get at the mass of the public with a product which has to be bought frequently, has to face the cost. He must be prepared to spend fairly heavily if he wants his advertising to be effective.

The reason is simple. There are seventeen million housewives in the United Kingdom, and they are not all waiting breathlessly for his message. One can spend a million pounds on a campaign and still find lots of housewives who have never heard of it. In Unilever we have found that even with our most heavily advertised products, products which are household names, only something over a half of all housewives can repeat the point of the advertising message correctly.

Many advertisers are perpetually astonished by this position. They cannot understand why, when their product is so good and their message so convincing, the housewife is so apathetic. But it is not really surprising. The housewife is bombarded with messages of every sort. Mr Heath explains to her the two-facedness of Mr Wilson. Mr Wilson claims that no disaster occurs which he has not foreseen. The sports club wants her to take part in a raffle, the United Nations Association has a bazaar. The baby cries, she has cooking to do, there is something on the BBC, she wants to tell her husband what she said to the neighbour and he wants to tell her what he said to his boss. There are all the other advertisements. If, in the midst of all this welter of competing interests she notices the commercial at all, it is an achievement for the advertiser. If she remembers the message, it is astonishing. If she buys the product, the advertiser must give thanks for a miracle.

The advertiser has to indulge in wearisome repetition. If he is a manufacturer selling on a national scale, he needs a national audience. He is not, however, the Prime Minister delivering a message of portentous import. He can count neither on a national audience, nor on the viewer's (or the reader's) full attention. So he has to go on repeating his message again and again, first, so that everybody will see it at some time or another, and secondly, so that everybody will (more or less) take it in. He has to accept that unless he puts his commercial on once a week, most of the nation will never consciously see it. If he is a small manufacturer, or a local supermarket, this may not matter; one housewife in ten may be a big enough audience, but if he is a large national manufacturer one housewife in ten is not enough. He wants to get at all of them, because if he does not get at them all he cannot achieve the economies of scale of which we shall talk later. This means that he *has* to keep on saying the same old thing week after week. He cannot keep changing what he says, although it would be more interesting and exciting for him if he did, because advertising for him is a way of conveying information. His product has certain advantages and only certain advantages. It is those advantages he wants to get across to the public. It is, therefore, those advantages on which he has to keep insisting. It may be that the regular television viewer, the highly attentive, the very sensitive, get tired of being told that some detergent washes whiter. What the public wants from detergents, however, is precisely that they should wash whiter. It might be amusing for the viewer if the advertiser provided variety by talking of the beauty of his package, the cleanliness of his factory, the modernity of his canteen, or the beauty of his secretaries. This would not sell detergents, because these are not the qualities of his product. They have nothing to do with whether or not the housewife will, at the end of the day, be satisfied with her wash. All that she wants of her wash is that it should be white. If the wash is grey, it is no consolation to her that the advertiser is virtuous, his employees are well paid and his managers went to business school.

The fact that any individual advertiser, any individual product are not central to the housewife's life also has another consequence. It means that the advertiser has to use a certain number of gimmicks in order to get attention. The gimmicks are of every sort, from surrealism to pretty girls, and if there is a certain concentration on pretty girls, this is because their attention value for the middle-aged woman seems to be high. (It is an error to imagine that they have a sexual purpose. There is no reason to think that girls, however pretty and however undressed, have any sexual interest for middle-aged married women, at whom nearly all consumer advertising is necessarily aimed.)

There is nothing peculiar to advertising about this use of gimmicks to get attention. A careful reading of any day's *Hansard* will show that the politician does exactly the same. He learns up jokes, he scores off his opponents, he makes outrageous statements. All of these are gimmicks to make the House listen, and if possible, to hit the headlines and get the notice of the voter, whose attention is just as hard to get as the consumer's. The greatest of all masters of the gimmick are good preachers. Medieval sermons were full of elaborate descriptions of hell, not because devils and torture were essential to doctrine (which they were not) but because an eloquent preacher could guarantee that his audience would be held spell-bound so long as he was describing to them the tortures of the damned, somewhat less spell-bound when he was talking about the blessings of the saved, and not spell-bound at all when he was discussing a difficult point in theology. As every after-dinner speaker knows, one cannot hold the attention of an audience without some gimmicks. An absolutely straightforward presentation of one's case may be intellectually very admirable but it leaves one with too many people asleep in the front rows; and nothing is more demoralizing to a speaker than an audience, half of which is asleep. If the advertiser sometimes seems to go in for even more gimmicks than the after-dinner speaker, this is because the after-dinner speaker can reasonably make the assumption that at least some of his audience may have come to hear him. The advertiser knows that hardly any of his audience is waiting palpitating for his particular message.

Large expenditure is inevitable if one wishes to make some impression on a national audience. The expenditure has to be even larger if the product is one which is bought frequently, as most groceries, for instance, are. If one is advertising motor cars, one can base one's expenditure on the fact that once one has sold a motor car, the customer is likely to go on using that motor car for two or three years. If one is selling margarine, one has no such confidence. The housewife buys margarine every week. She is perpetually under temptation to change to something else, butter, for instance. She therefore needs an equally perpetual reminder of the superiority of one's own product.

This costs money, sometimes as much as 15 per cent or even 20 per cent of the final cost of the product to the consumer, though well under 10 per cent would be much more usual. The consumer may reasonably ask what she gets out of this expenditure except having to pay a higher price for the privilege of being battered by a set of manufacturers between whom she is totally indifferent.

The economist is likely to put a very similar objection in a rather more sophisticated way. In the economist's ideal world the consumer expresses his sovereignty through price. As the relationship between supply and demand shifts, the price changes, and this is an infinitely flexible process. If the world was operating as the economist would desire, prices would shift by infinitesimal amounts in every infinitesimal period of time, each change bringing the economy that little bit nearer to the perfect allocation of resources, though this allocation could never be fully achieved because the ideas of the consumer and the situation of the supplier change all the time. Moreover, the economist simplifies his model by assuming a world in which the transactions take place in markets and products are perfectly substitutable.

The economist then argues that the advertiser upsets this perfection. He differentiates his goods from other goods and thus creates a friction in the working of the price mechanism. People go on buying his product at a given price when there is something else marginally cheaper to which they ought to change.

This criticism would appear to rest on two misapprehensions.

First, there is the belief that before advertising and brands the products were not differentiated. Secondly, there is the belief that the time of the ordinary buyer has no value.

Products never were undifferentiated, except perhaps for a few bulk commodities traded on exchanges, and even then it was the future that never became a commodity rather than the commodity itself which was undifferentiated. With the commodities themselves, it always made a difference whether the wheat was of one quality or another, stored in a warehouse in London or on a farm in Manitoba, in bags or in bulk, offered in cash or for credit, whether the seller was or was not a firm likely to fulfil its contract promptly with bulk supply conforming to sample and without trying to break the contract if the price went up and equally whether the buyer was likely to pay at the due date and not to raise too many quibbles if the price went down.

For consumer goods sold in a shop to a housewife, the differentiation was greater still. It made an enormous difference whether the grocer gave credit and delivered, whether he was polite, whether his shop was clean; whether she suspected him of giving wrong change, of putting sand in the sugar and of always recommending the varieties which gave him the biggest margin. In a market with negligible advertising like an Indian bazaar, the grains and the pulses may all look the same to an economist, but the transactions in them differ almost infinitely in accordance with the way each dealer deals with each customer.

What advertising does is to reduce this infinity of differentiation. It creates a certain number of products that really are the same. A $\frac{1}{2}$-lb of Stork margarine is $\frac{1}{2}$-lb of Stork margarine whoever sells it. All that the customer has to do is to decide whether the particular services offered by one shopkeeper as against another justify any difference in price between the two.

Because advertising reduces differentiation so much, it offers the consumer an enormous saving of time. If one is buying loose ghee in an Indian bazaar, one not merely has to look round the various shops in order to see how prices compare, one also has to try and decide which of the ghees offered is pure and which is adulterated, and to what extent and how dangerously. If one is buying Stork margarine no such expenditure of time is necessary.

What the advertiser does is to offer the consumer a package. If she will buy his product he will guarantee that it will always be the same and always meet the specification suggested by the advertisement. If she in fact finds his quality satisfactory she can save the time she would otherwise have to spend day after day to find the product that meets her needs. Since time is of immense value to housewives, who are on the whole the busiest members of the population, this bargain is a very attractive one. The housewife feels she is making a really worthwhile saving.

The economy as a whole also makes a saving. If every house-wife had to spend the time on every product which the average purchaser in an Indian bazaar spends (if he is not tied by credit to one particular supplier), the third of married women who work would have to stay at home and the husbands would have to have their hours shortened so that they could get home to give the children their tea.

Brand loyalty is the way in which the housewife expresses her desire to save her own time. When she finds a product that she can order with safety even over the telephone, she gives it the benefit of the doubt over other products. The whole of modern mass marketing with all its economies rests upon this 'benefit of the doubt', but it does have a cost. The next advertiser who comes along with an even better bundle of qualities and services wrapped up in his product has to overcome her brand loyalty; he has to advertise on a scale which would not be necessary if she had no loyalties. But this would be very largely true even if there were no advertising. The new Savile Row tailor, in a trade where advertising is very discreet indeed, or the new doctor, in a trade where advertising is not permitted at all, find that the customer's loyalty to his old supplier is stronger than anything on which a manufacturer of dogfood can count. That is why in the days before the NHS, when a doctor wanted a reasonable living, he had to buy the practice of some existing doctor.

Advertising does at least get over this situation where the customer is reluctant to take the risk of trying a new supplier at all—and there is always a risk, the cost of trying a new doctor may be death. Advertising gives the new supplier the same opportunities as the old one to make his product known. It thus makes innovation both easier and quicker.

This does not mean that advertising in itself produces technical innovation, except to the extent that, by reducing the risks of innovation, it encourages people to chance the risks innovation involves. But precisely because advertising reduces the risks of innovation so much, innovation inevitably produces advertising.

If what the advertiser is telling the consumer is perfectly well known to her, then it is either not worth telling her at all or, at the most, a gentle reminder will be enough. If one has a product which has not changed for a very long time and which everybody knows about, there is no point in extensive advertising. The Ministry of Public Buildings and Works does not need to advertise the Tower of London to the people of London. A little occasional reminder by London Transport is enough to ensure that there is always a queue to see the crown jewels. But if one's product is new or improved, then the public cannot know about the newness or the improvement unless it is told; and it has to be told loudly enough to overcome the initial mild disbelief which seems to afflict everybody in the face of novelty. The shaver cannot know by some inner instinct that a stainless steel blade has now come on the market and that it is better than any carbon steel blade. He must be told. The housewife cannot know that there is now a margarine which is softer or tastes more like butter than any previous margarine. She has to be told. The amount of advertising which is necessary for an industry, therefore, is a function of the rate of technical innovation in that industry.

One of the reasons why the soap and detergent industry has been famous for its advertising for eighty years is that it is an industry where the rate of technical innovation has always been high and where the technical innovations which have been achieved are of great importance to the ordinary housewife. This not only means that the hard soap of today is better than the hard soap William Lever first advertised, but that the detergent of today is better than the detergent of ten years ago. Both these statements are true, but secondary. What is primary is that there has been a steady stream of totally new types of product. Once upon a time women washed clothes with hard soap, often badly made, sometimes filled with non-detergent cheapeners. That was very hard work indeed. Then they got a first-rate hard soap without filling, which was rather less work. Then they got a soap powder, which was better still. Then they got a non-soapy detergent which, for certain purposes, was even better. Now they can have detergents with fluorescents and enzyme soakers and controlled lathers. That the amount of technical change has been enormous any young woman who tried to do her washing with an 1870 filled soap, would very soon discover.

However, the new product can never be better than the old one in every way. Every improvement has its disadvantages. Detergents cost more than hard soap. Moreover, some housewives are very conservative. They like the old product, whatever its defects. Perhaps it is associated for them with days when they were younger and happier. It would be impossible, or at least unjust, to lay down a rule by which the new product is allowed to proclaim its virtues and the old product is not allowed to assert its counter virtues. Could we prohibit butter from advertising against margarine?

Because each innovation has thus to compete for its place in the consumer's shopping list, advertising must cost money, sometimes a lot of money. The assumption usually made is that the consumer bears all the cost. She gets a saving of time and a high level of innovation but she pays for it. There would be nothing unreasonable about this if it were so. One cannot expect very much for nothing. However, with advertising one is lucky. One quite often does get these advantages for nothing, at least in money. The real cost to the consumer is usually the surrender of some small part of her freedom of choice in order to provide the manufacturer with the economies of scale, economies not so much in manufacture, though these may well be considerable, as in marketing itself. These economies are often so considerable that they more than pay for the advertising.

This proposition is worth expanding upon. Everybody has slightly different tastes, as any mother who has to find a menu to please all the family every day knows to her cost. This is true even of a straightforward product like a detergent or a toilet soap. Everybody has one overriding demand of a detergent. It must wash white. With toilet soap there are already two overriding demands. It must get one's hands clean and it must be kind to the skin. In addition to these overriding demands, everybody also has a whole series of subsidiary demands. Some people like their detergent to smell of one perfume, some of another. Some people like it to be white, some people like it blue. Some people like it to come as a powder in a packet, others prefer a liquid in a bottle. Some people are prepared to buy a rather lower quality at a lower price, others are not. Some people like a lather which feels soapy, others do not mind. Some like a lot of lather, others have washing machines which are allergic to lather. There are fifty different qualities that people look for in their detergents and the possible combinations of these different qualities are almost infinite.

It is clear that no manufacturer can possibly tailor-make his detergents (or whatever it may be) to each housewife's requirement. To do so would be to make detergents more expensive than Paris model gowns. The factory would need an enormous number of production lines, the shops would be full of nothing but detergents, the warehouses would cover square miles and the sales forces would employ a considerable percentage of the total population.

The manufacturer, therefore, has to try and persuade the public to limit its demands, to concentrate on a few brands and only a few brands. The cheapest way of all, of course, would be if the public were willing to concentrate on one brand and one brand only. A total monopoly needs no advertising. The only advertising Water Boards ever do is to tell one when one cannot have the water one would like for one's garden or one's bath. No Water Board ever tries to increase its market by persuading people to bath every day or to improve their health by drinking water rather than alcohol. No soft water authority has been known to point out to its public the delightful taste of its product or to compare it with the really rather horrid taste of London's water.

A monopoly may be able to save on advertising. But it can only do so at the public's expense. The public loves variety. The businessman who has to travel regularly from London to Manchester values a choice of route. The child who gets tired of the taste of the Water Board's water buys lemon squash or ginger ale. No two women like to appear at a party in the same dress, or to find that they have decorated their drawing-rooms with the same wallpaper. As people get more educated and more affluent, this desire for variety, for individuality, strengthens. Motor cars come in more and more colours, packaged holidays are provided to more and more countries.

To have no choice of brand is intolerable for people who can pay for choice. But to have an infinite diversity of choice is in the end equally intolerable; it is too expensive. Few can afford regularly to give the special handmade chocolates of Marie of the Faubourg St Honoré to the children. Advertising is one of the main ways, perhaps the main way, by which the public is persuaded to limit its choice to its own economic advantage, to get the benefit of the fact that if enough people can be persuaded to choose Cadbury's Dairy Milk it will be a lot cheaper than Marie's specials.

Why is it so important for advertising to persuade the public to concentrate its choice on a limited number of varieties?

First, there are the obvious economies of production of which every economist talks. Raw materials can be bought more cheaply if they are bought in large quantities, the factory can be more automated if the production runs are longer—one may, for instance, be able to change over from hand to machine packing—the research costs the public less if it can be spread over a large number of units.

Secondly, there are the economies which come from the manufacturer's being able to choose a cheaper marketing mix. The manufacturer has many weapons in his armoury. He can use in varying proportions theme advertising, promotions, the sales force, retailers' margins, the regularity of his deliveries to shops, his product variety and so on. If he chooses a large advertising appropriation it means that the cost of the advertising is less than the extra cost he would incur on the other elements of the mix if he advertised on a smaller scale. If it does not mean that, the reason is normally nothing more sinister than that he has miscalculated. The reason why advertising enables him to make economies on the other ingredients of his mix is that advertising pushes the public into concentrating its buying on those products which provide the balance of qualities which is most satisfactory to the largest number. This will not be one product, even in margarine or breakfast foods or milk. The public's tastes are not standard enough for one product. But it may well be that the vast majority of the market can be persuaded to be content with half a dozen, where without advertising, they would have wanted fifty or a hundred. I have seen in Moscow eleven different brands of toilet soap in the same shop, all of them in the same price range. The main difference between them was the factory which produced them. The Russians have a different brand for each factory so as to keep a check on the factory manager's quality.

The savings which result from this concentration are impossible to calculate exactly. The costs of a situation which does not exist cannot be demonstrated. But there are many indications.

First, let us take the advertising itself. Half a dozen campaigns of £$\frac{1}{2}$ m. each would be a total of £3 m. This would be very large indeed, a sum only reached with a very few product groups in the United Kingdom. Yet, if there were a hundred products competing in the market (and nineteenth-century experience suggests that in a world without mass advertising, a hundred would be a very plausible number) this would allow them only £30,000 apiece. One cannot do very much in mass consumer advertising with £30,000. If they were advertising at all, some at least of the hundred would spend more.

Half a dozen brands may be produced by two or three companies. Fifty or one hundred brands could hardly be produced by less than ten or a dozen. There would be more factories, more small movements around the country, more warehouses, more stocks. If one is talking about a truly mass, frequently purchased consumer good like breakfast foods or margarine, the extra stocks alone might involve an investment running into millions. In addition, there would have to be more sales forces. A fully national sales force for a mass consumer good can hardly consist of less than a couple of hundred men and if one includes their allowances, their pensions, their motor cars and so on, they are not likely to cost much less than £3,000 each. At half a million or so each, these sales forces would be very expensive for the consumer.

It is not only the manufacturer who has to bear extra costs, it is also the shopkeeper. If he is displaying fifty brands instead of five, they take up much more space on his shelves; and space is money to him. If he does not display all the fifty, some of his customers may go elsewhere, others will have to buy a brand which is not the one they prefer; either way he loses goodwill. Moreover, the shopkeeper too has to have higher stocks. If one brand sells one-fifth as much as another it does not mean that the shopkeeper need only stock one-fifth as much. He will be fortunate to get away with stocks half as large.

Above all, where there are more brands and higher stocks each individual brand will sell more slowly. The shopkeeper will have his money tied up for longer, he will run more risk of being left with unsold stocks which he has to remember, he will have to spend more time advising his customers on their choice, he will have to buy in smaller quantities at lower discounts, he will find it more difficult to make effective displays and striking price-cuts, he will therefore have to charge higher margins. Thus in the UK, detergents which are heavily advertised are sold by the shopkeeper at an average margin of perhaps 15 per cent. Paper tissues, which are less heavily advertised, sell at an average margin of perhaps 35 per cent (one cannot be too pedantic about the figures as different shopkeepers charge different prices and take different margins in different weeks according to which products they are cutting). The difference is not entirely the result of advertising, paper tissues are bulkier, and they are naturally slower-moving. But a good deal of it is. Advertising pushes products through the shop. The shopkeeper can therefore take a lower margin. This difference in the shopkeeper's margin in its turn pays for a great deal of the advertising.

Probably nothing in advertising is more criticized than what is called wasteful competitive advertising. In other words, large advertising campaigns for products all of which the critic considers to be very similar.

Sometimes this criticism is merely misconceived. The products may be technologically similar, but they are not similar in other ways. As Henry Ford found out, a black motor car may have exactly the same engine as a car of some other colour and the consumer may still prefer a car of another colour even at a slightly higher price. The assumption is frequently made that the consumer minds only about those technical qualities of a product which are testable. This is not so. There are technical qualities which it is very difficult to test adequately; mildness to hands for instance. There are other qualities, smell for instance, which are a matter of subjective judgement and where it is extremely difficult, even by the most sophisticated market research, to get at the real reasons for people's preferences. If one is told that perfume A is 'nicer' than perfume B, it tells one very little about the way in which the composition of perfume B ought to be altered in order to make the customer prefer it to perfume A. Moreover, to make confusion worse confounded, the consumer is likely to say that she finds perfume A 'nicer' simply because she prefers the product in which perfume A is incorporated, to the product in which perfume B is incorporated. The true reason for her preference then has nothing to do with the perfume at all. The pleasant association created by the other qualities spills over to the perfume.

It is, therefore, very difficult, except by the test of what the consumer actually buys, to say that one product is or is not the same as another, or that one product is or is not the better buy. Those who say that an unwrapped peppermint cream which is sold more cheaply than the identical peppermint cream wrapped in a pretty box is a better buy are making a value judgement about whether people *ought* to like their peppermint creams wrapped, or perhaps a judgement on what they consider wrapping to be worth. They are no more making a straightforward comparison between two identical products than is somebody who says a semi-detached with four bedrooms is a better buy than a Georgian house with four bedrooms because its price is lower.

Nevertheless, there will be occasions when products which

really are substantially similar are heavily advertised on much the same platform. This is obviously a position the advertiser dreads. He is having to spend a lot of money for a purely defensive purpose. Moreover, if he is in a market where purchases are frequent, he knows that his goodwill, his brand loyalty, will erode fairly quickly as the public discovers that there is no great difference between his product and his competitor's. Furthermore, he knows that advertising is a cost, and sometimes quite a considerable cost. If he is paying to say nothing in particular, he is offering an opportunity to a new entrant to get into the market by offering a similar product at a cheaper price. If the manufacturer is paying for heavy advertising for a product with no real advantages, he is offering the Co-operatives and the multiples a superb opportunity to put on brands of their own and take his business away from him simply by cutting their price by the cost of his advertising. Or another manufacturer may do the same. There has recently been a case in Italy where a manufacturer of hard soap entered the detergent market by cutting his price and saying on his packet in a vivid way that he was cheaper because he was not advertising.

The position where the advertiser is not really telling the public anything is therefore inherently unstable. Either the advertiser gets under-cut by new competitors or he finds some improvement which gives him something genuine to say. These improvements, moreover, may be in the same product or may be in a new product.

Once again it can be argued that this is wasteful. The manufacturer should pick his winner and back it. Unfortunately, the manufacturer does not know which is his winner, particularly at the margin. Hard soaps have been losing ground to toilet soaps, powders and liquids for eighty years but they still sell in very considerable tonnages. It would be ridiculous either to drop them or to stop telling the public about their merits. Only a monopoly can decide on the public's behalf which of its products the public should buy. The electricity, gas and coal industries are all owned by the State in this country. They nevertheless advertise against each other, and quite rightly. Only the public knows exactly how it wants to balance the various merits of these various products against each other; and this balance will necessarily change from time to time as, for instance, more smokeless coal is made available or the price of gas changes relatively to that of electricity. If the Gas Council is not allowed to shout its wares the result may be that the public will go on using some other fuel long after gas has become the cheapest for some particular purpose, simply because people do not keep making price comparisons unless their minds are jogged, and do not always find them very easy to make even then.

The difficulty in making price comparisons is the main reason why manufacturers so often make their price cuts not by a simple price reduction, but in some way which gives them a bigger chance of catching the housewife's attention, in other words, by a promotion—3d. off, a daffodil on the packet and all that. The average housewife doubtless carries more prices in her head than the average professor or MP. She nevertheless cannot possibly remember all the prices of all the 4,000 articles in a supermarket and still less all the prices at the half dozen supermarkets in the High Street, plus those in her two or three local shops. She quite reasonably concentrates on remembering a few main prices, makes deliberate price comparisons for those goods which are expensive and infrequently purchased, and buys the rest at the shop she normally patronizes. This is an unreasonable way to behave only if one assumes that the housewife's time is of no value. Comparing prices from shop to shop takes time, and for a woman with a house and children to look after and possibly a job as well, time is very valuable.

The manufacturer has to accept that if he charges, let us say, 1s. 11d. against his competitor's 2s., the housewife may or may not be conscious that he is cheaper, though it is true that nowadays when products are displayed side by side on the supermarket shelf with the price marked beneath, the chance that she will realize it is much higher than it used to be. Nevertheless, in the detergent market, for instance, Surf, at a time when it gave 18 per cent more powder than its major competitors, never got more than 6 per cent of the market, and that mainly amongst the better off and the better educated.

The manufacturer therefore looks for some method of price

cutting which is more certain of getting attention than merely reducing his standard price. He turns to promotions. These are necessarily gimmicky. They would not attract attention if they were not, and attracting attention is the essence of the operation. The fact that they are gimmicky does not mean that they are poor value. On the contrary, for the great majority of the population they are admirable value. If they are not admirable value, they will fail. Not enough women will be persuaded to change from their regular brand, and a promotion which attracts nobody but one's regular customers, who would have bought without the promotion, is a straight waste of money. The essence of a promotion is that by buying plastic daffodils by the million in Hong Kong and tying them on to the packet, a manufacturer by spending 3*d.* can provide the women with something which would cost her 1*s.* or 1*s.* 3*d.* in the shop and by which most women will therefore be attracted.

It is fundamental that the promotion should be thus attractive to most women. The criticism which says that promotions annoy housewives is off the point. If they really annoyed housewives, housewives would not buy them and they would stop straight away. What really happens is that they annoy a minority of housewives, the better off and the better educated. If one is reasonably well off one does not normally buy plastic flowers, little rag dolls, cheap glasses and all the other articles that get used as promotions. If one is reasonably well educated, one may even feel that it is non-U to have plastic flowers in the house and that the glass is not only cheap but badly designed. The woman who feels in this way would naturally prefer a straight price cut; and she is not bothered by the fact that the cheap glass or the plastic daffodil is a much better bargain for her poorer sister. Since most of the people who make opinion, whether MP's, editors or professors, have wives who are either better off or better educated than the average (or possibly both), they get a distorted view of the general opinion of women about promotions. The shopkeeper is a better judge of what his customers like. It is always possible to persuade a Co-operative or multiple or good private grocer to provide a large display and often a price cut at his own expense too for a good promotion.

Promotions serve a further purpose. They are a cheap way of sampling. If one is confident that one's product is good, so good that its qualities speak for themselves, the best way of all of bringing it to people's notice is to provide the public with a free sample so that the housewife can see for herself. This is quite often done with such products as toilet soaps, but it has the disadvantage of being immensely expensive. A free sample for every house in the country very soon runs into many tens or even hundreds of thousands of pounds, and it does not always happen that the housewife rates one's product as highly as one does oneself. The risk of loss is considerable.

Naturally, the manufacturer tries to obtain the same effect at less cost. He therefore puts on a promotion. He offers 6d. off or a plastic bucket or a steak knife, anything which he thinks will appeal to enough millions of housewives to make sure that his product is extensively sampled. To do this, of course, he has to be reasonably confident of his product's qualities. A promotion may cost all of the profit on the product or more. Unless he gets a lot of new customers as a result, all he is doing is to cut his profits. He will, therefore, not go for this sort of promotion unless he thinks that once the housewife has tried his product at a cut price she will be prepared to buy it again at the regular price.

Relevant here is the famous story of how Parmentier introduced the potato into France. He ploughed up the Champs de Mars and put soldiers on to guard it but with instructions to make theft easy. Everybody came to sample and the potato was successfully launched.

Since advertising is thus on the whole, the cheapest and most effective way of ensuring the customer gets the goods, and particularly the innovations, she wants, it is odd that it is so much criticized. To read some of the critics, one would think the sellers of soap and chocolate and breakfast food were subverting society on the scale of Socrates or Calvin or Lenin. This is flattery.

The commercial advertiser is not trying to change anybody's system of beliefs in any important way. He is trying to persuade them to eat mints or try a new hair-spray, not to change their view of the universe, their concept of society or even their idea of what is proper between a boy and a girl. The only advertisers who do try to change us are the State and those clergymen who put posters calling us to salvation outside their churches; and they are not commercial.

There are good reasons why the advertiser accepts the main beliefs and standards of his society.

If the advertiser is a corporate body, as it normally is, the executives of that body would not normally feel it right to crusade against society for their personal ideals at their shareholders' expense; and they do not generally know for which ideals their shareholders would wish to crusade. They can reasonably make the assumption that their shareholders wish to persuade the public to buy the products of the company in which they have shares. They cannot reasonably make any assumption about their shareholders' beliefs on sex, status and good manners, except that it is most unlikely that these are subjects on which all their shareholders would be in agreement. It is, therefore, of the very nature of modern business that the normal commercial advertisement will not be directed at changing society but will accept the standards of society as they are.

This does not mean that advertisers have particularly low moral standards. There are very few firms whose executives would be prepared to advertise in a way which would, even by implication, argue for a breach of any of the Ten Commandments. I cannot remember ever having seen an advertisement which supported adultery, theft, murder, blasphemy or disrespect to one's parents. The one exception is perhaps the Tenth Commandment. Advertisements do sometimes encourage envy, but they only do so in order to suggest the way by which that envy may be assuaged. The sinful desire is hardly aroused before it is sated.

It would not pay any large advertiser to go against the general moral sense of the community. He is, after all, trying to persuade a large number of people to buy his products, and if he is a manufacturer of consumer goods he is trying to persuade them to buy these products again and again. Moreover, unless he is selling pop records, or male toiletries, or some such product, the great majority of his customers are respectable middle-aged women. There are few less effective ways of sell-

33

ing to respectable middle-aged married women than to praise immorality.

The whole point about the advertiser is that he does not set himself up as better than his customers. He is not, except where his own product is concerned, a teacher. Nor is it proper that he should be. To be a director or advertising executive of a large firm does not make one an archbishop or even Professor Raymond Williams. It gives one no right to impose one's own standards of aesthetics or good manners upon the rest of the population. The average business executive can lay no claim to being any better than his neighbours at distinguishing an elegant from an inelegant use of the English language, or an artistic from an inartistic film.

Even so, one can exaggerate the failure of advertising to achieve adequate artistic standards. The creative men and women in the advertising agencies usually are people of taste. Therefore, while it is rare for advertising to be *avant garde*, quite a lot of it is in line with the better standards of its period and some of it—the typography, for instance—is positively good.

The advertiser reflects rather than creates the standards of his society. It is nevertheless the favourite allegation of the critics that the advertiser lowers these standards by concentrating unduly on sex, status, the material things of this world and the vulgar interests of the common man.

To some extent this is plain nonsense. No television commercial would rate an 'X' certificate. Certainly no commercial would dare to glorify juvenile delinquency and teenage sex and disobedience to parents in the way *Romeo and Juliet* does; yet *Romeo and Juliet* is a GCE text, which ensures that it will be studied by tens of thousands of teenagers with an attention they never give to commercials. No television commercial would dare to present adultery in the favourable light in which it appears in *Anna Karenina* or as the regular and amusing fact of life which it is to Boccaccio. Yet Tolstoy and the Decameron are favoured sixth-form reading. All that the commercial ever does is to suggest that perhaps young women prefer a young man who does not smell when he sweats and perhaps young men prefer a young woman whose hair has been properly shampooed. It may be argued that compared with the communion of body, mind and soul on which true marriage rests, these are rather trivial considerations, but it can hardly be denied that it is a social fact that they matter at parties, and that it is not the advertising which has made them matter, but the fact that they matter which has made the advertiser talk about them.

Similarly, with status. No commercial is as frankly snobbish, as keen on the man who has £10,000 a year without working, as a Jane Austen novel. Yet I have never read a critic of advertising who suggests that teenagers should not be permitted to read *Pride and Prejudice*. No commercial stresses the importance of the right family background as does the *Iliad* or describes the delicate gradations of keeping up with the Joneses like a novel by Trollope. Yet these are recommended reading, a necessary part of our culture. Those who criticize commercials and praise the classics presumably credit the classics with extraordinarily little influence on the minds of their readers.

The criticism of advertising on the grounds that it encourages status seeking misunderstands the way status is achieved in our society. The advertiser does nothing to make worse any of the truly divisive aspects of our society. He is essentially egalitarian. He never suggests that one accent is better than another or that those who read poetry and dote on Rouault are in any way better than those who read women's magazines and like the *Monarch of the Glen*. It is not the advertiser who attaches status to the culture, scholarship and taste that most people can never possess. All he does is to suggest that one will be slightly better regarded by one's neighbours if one's clothes are clean, one's kitchen is modern and one's children are bonny. These are all objectives everybody can attain and it is not clear why they are in any way harmful objectives. Cleanliness is, after all, next to godliness; a modern kitchen means much less work for the housewife; and surely we would all like our children to be bonny. They are objectives, moreover, where one can test whether they have been achieved or not. The advertiser, therefore, is compelled to offer products which really will make shirts clean, kitchens modern and babies bonny.

The most that can be said against the morals of advertising

is that it emphasizes unduly the minor virtues. The advertiser likes hair kempt, girls attractive and young men who are getting on in the world. Most advertising places importance on material possessions, some emphasizes social success. The major virtues, the love of one's neighbour, the pursuit of holiness, are rarely mentioned.

If one takes the view of life of Mahatma Gandhi or St Anthony in the Desert, this is a final condemnation of advertising. Advertising does help to produce the attachment to this world deplored by the Bhagavad Gîtâ, it does distract from the contemplation of eternity which is the monk's ideal.

This would not, however, appear to be the main gravamen of the charges of its critics, most of whom lay no claim to personal austerity. In its attachment to material things, advertising only reflects the national ethos. If there is at the moment a single major national objective, it is the desire for the economy to grow more quickly than it has done in the past. Yet 4 per cent growth as against 2 per cent growth does not mean 4 per cent more self-sacrifice or 4 per cent more happiness in marriage or 4 per cent more loving our neighbour. It means 4 per cent more material goods and services, 4 per cent more of all the things the advertiser is trying to persuade us to buy. It is illogical to attack the advertiser and vote for a national plan; to attack the advertiser and accept investment incentives; to attack the advertiser and to look forward to a world where everybody will have a car and a washing machine of his own.

The allegation most frequently hurled at the advertiser is that of vulgarity. This is a difficult subject to discuss. One may be in favour of or against class distinction; in favour of or against culture; in favour of or against fornication. But at least these are all words whose content of meaning is fairly well defined. One knows what it is that one is in favour of or against. Vulgarity is merely another case of the old saying that my orthodoxy is your heresy. Vulgar behaviour is behaviour of which I or my group do not approve. Vulgar commercials are commercials which do not reach the cultural, aesthetic or moral standards of the critic. As a term of abuse, the word vulgar is of infinite value. As a definition, as a statement of exactly what it is of which one is disapproving, it is of no value at all. There are very few forms of action which are generally accepted by the population as a whole as vulgar. Spitting in the drawing room might nowadays be an example, but it is clearly not this sort of action of which the critic complains when he alleges that advertising vulgarizes our standards. Nobody in a commercial would ever be shown spitting in the drawing room or even eating peas with a knife. What the critic nearly always means is that the commercial, instead of uplifting its audience, accepts them as they are (or perhaps as they used to be) in exactly the same way as, say, Coronation Street does, or the more blood-thirsty Elizabethan tragedies did.

Nobody would allege that advertising is perfect. Some advertisers are vulgar, some of their customers are commonplace. Some advertisers spend a lot of money on bringing to the public's notice qualities in their product which they think important and nobody else does. Some advertisers cover up a paucity of ideas by a great deal of noise. Some promotions have more gimmickry than value.

None of this is surprising. Some political speeches are pernicious, some sermons preach doctrines that the congregation regard as immoral, some professors of literature and critics of art have tastes in books and painting that the public find very odd indeed. *Which?*'s best buys are not in fact absolutely and infallibly the best buys. Some vulgarity and some error are inherent in all human operations. Advertising is an admittedly imperfect way of telling the consumer about the qualities of one's products and why she should rate them as better than those of one's competitors. She is not very interested in listening, so the advertiser has to talk to her rather loudly and rather repetitively in exactly the same way as clergymen have to when they are talking about sin or politicians when they are talking about social reform. But if there were no advertising, innovation would be much slower because the innovator would find it so hard to get at the public; and prices would frequently be higher because the market would be so fragmented.

The alternatives to advertising are either the cheating and bargaining which go on in middle eastern bazaars (and went on in British grocers' shops and fairs in the days before advertising) or the accumulation of unwanted goods in the shops in Russia.

We need advertising, so we will have to put up with its imperfections. We can stiffen the standard of truth required as has been done in the recent Merchandising Marks Act or we can insist on a certain minimum of good taste as the Independent Television Authority tries to do. All such marginal improvements are useful, but nothing that anybody does will turn the average advertiser into someone with George Washington's passion for truth, Professor Hoggart's ear for words and Mr Berger's eye for visual effect. Such a paragon would not be in business at all. He would be the president of an Oxford College. The rest of us must be permitted an occasional exaggeration and an occasional lapse of taste.

3

The value of advertising in marketing

Kenneth Simmonds

The value of advertising can be looked at from the viewpoint of the firm using it as an element in its marketing mix, or from the viewpoint of the community as a whole. This chapter will confine attention to the value of advertising to the individual firm.

In Britain, by far the more fashionable concern is that for advertising's value to the community. Even when this is the sole interest, however, the value of advertising from the firm's viewpoint cannot be ignored. Advertising decisions by profit-motivated firms may be directly linked to value to the community through their effects on volume, cost, prices and range of products offered. If we do not go to the point at which the decision to advertise is made—if we stand off and examine from afar the implications of the decisions with little understanding of why and how they are made in the first place—then we will be limited in our conclusions as to the value to the community. Furthermore, without such insight there is a tendency to equate control of advertising, with limitation of advertising. The possibility that community value may be increased by stimulating or encouraging advertising is pushed to one side, and attention focused on such issues as the morality of appeal to hidden motivations, or the influence of advertising in shaping the news media.

The complexity of the value concept
No simple statement can be made that advertising is or is not valuable to a firm. Value from the use of advertising will vary from product to product and from time to time, because value

39

is not inherent in the advertising expenditure but rather in the situation in which it appears. And every situation has different participants, different purchasing power and different products.

Value of advertising is also affected by the amount of competitive advertising—and by the competitive reactions it calls forth. If an apparently 'successful' advertisement leads a competitor to alter his price and buy back business lost, then the ultimate value of the advertisement may even be negative.

Nor is the value of advertising independent of the firm's other marketing actions. Advertising in a well-run firm is not spent willy-nilly. It has an objective or a series of objectives concerned with imparting a message to influence demand—and to the professional marketer this advertising message is part of an integrated plan that relates all the elements in the marketing mix, including product design, distribution, selling, pricing and advertising. It may be that a brand has to be supported by a quality or reliability image, it may be that the customer has to be informed that salesmen will come and demonstrate, or it may be necessary to remove dissonance in customers who have already purchased, so that they do not pass on a negative reaction to potential future customers. Value is not something that can be easily separated for one variable in the marketing mix. The mix is what it implies—a mixture of interdependent variables. And the value of advertising exists only in relation to that mix.

It is also inadequate to think of advertising as simply a monetary figure. Value comes not from spending a sum of money but from spending on an advertising package, or mix, that is the outcome of a chain of decisions. Every advertising expenditure must incorporate decisions as to the copy and the layout, the media to be used, the placing of the advertisement within the media, the timing and the number and spacing of repetitions. To the marketer, advertising is itself a carefully determined mix of media, messages and timing consistent with the broader marketing mix. Any attempt to measure value for amounts to be spent on advertising must thus consider how these are to be spent.

Finally, value is not independent of the source. The acceptance of an advertising message has been shown to vary with the viewer's belief in the trustworthiness of the source of the advertisement. So strong is this image that a notation that the product is advertised in such places as *Life*, *Parents' Magazine* or *Good Housekeeping*, is sometimes used by advertisers to capture the 'believability image' for the benefit of their product.

The value of advertising in marketing, then, is not a simple concept, and for any meaningful measurement of value, advertising's role in the marketing plan must be clearly specified.

Measurement for marketing decisions
To the economist, a reasonable measure of the value of advertising might be the resulting cash inflow discounted to present value and related to the outflow. Moreover, the profit motivated firm of conventional economic theory would continue to increase expenditure on advertising until the last increment just equalled the resulting increment in net revenue. It would appear then that all that need be measured is the marginal revenue from advertising.

But such a measurement is more difficult than at first it seems. The measurement of marginal revenue assumes some time span for the effectiveness. Yet advertising may influence sales many years later. It may even *cause* repeat sales. Furthermore, it is next to impossible to separate the influence on any one sale of different advertising efforts and other elements of the marketing mix. The concept of marginal revenue may also hinge on the ability of the firm to produce goods that advertising 'sells'. To attempt to measure marginal value of advertising through examination of sales results thus presents major difficulties.

Despite these difficulties in measurement, management does have to assess value. Without some indication of the value from incremental advertising, or belief in such value, there can be no rational basis for deciding the amount to be spent on advertising. But the needs of the manager are not those of the theoretical economist. Management science has not yet developed to the extent that the manager can start with precise prediction of the marginal returns on all the marketing variables he might adjust, and then decide the combination mathematically. Instead, he usually works creatively to sketch in the outlines of an integrated marketing plan that specifies the role of advertising alongside that of product design, packaging, distribution channels and other promotional efforts. For the market oriented manager, this will usually be achieved by arguing from identification of characteristics, motivations and resistances of the consumer, and the extent of environmental constraints on achievement. And it will be achieved in most cases without any precise calculation of return on cost for each element in the marketing mix.

More precise prediction of advertising effectiveness is usually postponed until after the initial formation of the marketing plan. The measurements required will then have more specific focus—and more chance of a sensible answer. The manager will have an idea of the role to be played of advertising and now be faced with selecting the media and determining the messages and the number and frequency of advertisements.

Advertising—with more precision
This chapter cannot hope even to scrape the surface of the literature concerned with methods of more precise selection of advertising mixes. A few examples of some of the practical considerations, however, will illustrate what this literature contains.

Consideration of the effect of an advertisement in changing attitudes towards purchase is a good starting point. Purchase can be regarded as one stage in a process that starts with complete ignorance of a product and leads through initial awareness, understanding of its features, familiarity and actual consideration to the ultimate purchase and repeat purchases. Every consumer will have to progress through each stage and if advertising expenditure moves a potential consumer from ignorance of the product to awareness, it may be just as valuable to the firm as if it moved another consumer from consideration to actual purchase.

A range of methods have been developed for measurement of attention, awareness, comprehension, emotional response, imagery, association, recall and other measurable facets of 'attitude'. This class of measurement falls very much in the domain of psychology, with all the measuring experience of the psychologist available to the advertiser. A large 'box of tricks' has been appropriated from this source, including measurement of physiological responses, association techniques such as Rorschach and word associations, sentence completion techniques and so on.

While the measurement of attitudes to any aspect of an advertisement can have a value in guiding management in its composition of the advertising mix, measurements must ultimately be quantified for value and related to cost. Methods for doing this can vary from simple indices of customers reached per £ of advertising cost to careful assessment of the effect of the advertisement on potential consumers at each stage in the awareness scale. A most refined model would build into the value of moving consumers along the scale an assessment of the later costs of moving them right to the stage of actual purchase.

Indices of potential customers reached per £ of advertising cost are quite common. They are widely used in selecting between media, for example. But even these simple measures must be used very carefully. In selecting a combination of media, care must be taken to use indices that avoid double counting. The added audience and the added impact on the same audience must be separated for subsequent choices as soon as one medium has been chosen. The circulations of the *Sunday Times* and the Sunday *Observer*, for example, are roughly 1,400,000 and 900,000. Having included the *Sunday Times* in a planned advertising programme, however, less than 900,000 are added by also including the *Observer* in the programme. There is an estimated overlap of about 300,000 subscribers who would be exposed to the advertisement for the second time. Alternatively it is possible that the repetition of advertising in the same journal, newspaper, radio or television programme will increase coverage. Not every customer buys the same magazine each month or visits the same doctor's waiting room when the next month's issue is lying on the table.

The need for a measure of effectiveness of repeat advertising thus arises early in designing most advertising programmes. Is it the case that effectiveness falls off for all exposures after the first? It may not be so, particularly if a weight of impact through number of exposures must be reached within a limited time

43

period if a potential customer is to be moved along the awareness scale. For other circumstances, however, a series of short campaigns may maintain sales volume much better than major campaigns with intensive saturation at less frequent intervals.

The value of advertising in a particular medium must for many firms be taken further than relating cost to the number of viewers. Each medium appeals to a different combination of potential customers and the more their characteristics resemble those of the consumers against which the firm's marketing mix was designed, the more valuable advertising through that medium is likely to be. A whole range of methods is available for comparing a target customer profile against viewer profiles for alternative media in which an advertisement might be placed.

Media also have very individual images and the advertisement should be placed with these in mind. The more the message to be conveyed matches the image of the media, the more successful it is likely to be. If the purpose is to transfer information concerning outlets, then the back pages of the evening paper may be ideal. But one would hardly place an advertisement designed to stimulate basic demand for the product in the same place.

Practical limitations to measurement and prediction
The time required to vary advertisements and measure effectiveness is such that few firms can afford the experiments needed for detailed measures of advertising. Besides the cost of collection, there is the cost of less than optimal market performance during experimentation. Most firms adjust very rapidly when advertising improvement seems possible. Measurement can thus be made only for some products and some markets—and the results from these may not be transferable. Even then, it is a painstaking task to control the test so that it is the effect of advertising that is being measured and not the many other variables.

The possibility of variation in quality of advertising must also be separated if the advertising manager is to test the effect of quantity. Poor advertising could influence a test to show poor returns to incremental advertising expenditure, when a quality advertisement would have shown outstanding returns. While it is possible to devise tests which allow for differences in advertising material these can be very costly indeed, and it is more usual to rely on some sort of controlled panel measurement to provide an index of an advertisement's quality.

However extensive the data from past advertising expenditure and returns, or from experimental tests, it can never be extrapolated with certainty into a new situation. Value will be conditioned by the same advertising history that has produced the data and by the differences in consumers now at each stage in the awareness chain. Furthermore, each real situation has so many variables that it is never simply a matter of applying test results.

The greatest variation may well be the amount competitors spend on advertising. If the advertising is influencing customers to buy the advertiser's product in preference to a competitor's, rather than simply influencing customers against spending their money in some way other than on this class of product, then the more competitors spend, the less effect a given amount of advertising will have. Any attempt at precision of measurement or prediction must allow for competitors' advertising expenditures and their effect on customer demand. More and more refined decision models are being constructed to aid calculations of value in competitive situations, but the precision of the conclusions can be no better than the prediction of competitors' actions and those of potential customers viewing the advertising.

No matter how refined the tests and measurement of advertising value, then, decisions to spend on advertising will inevitably require a leap of faith. Some situations which are more stable require less of a leap in the dark than others, but how few there are, and how dull the advertising task can become in these few cases. Petroleum and detergent advertising are examples. Other situations require bold belief in value. Take, for example, the case described recently in the *Sunday Times* (Gwen Nuttall, 'Pin-men back the electric knife', 18 September 1966).

Whitecroft-Scovill, who had previously concentrated on pin manufacture, was described as about to launch five electric kitchen appliances in the Southern Television Area. The weight of the campaign was behind a 12-guinea electric knife intended to carry with it a blender, mixer, mixette and can-opener-cum-knife sharpener. Michael Jarrett, managing director of Whitecroft, had as evidence on which to base this major decision, two successes by other subsidiaries of Scovill Manufacturing Company, which was Whitecroft's parent corporation. In America the Hamilton Beach division of the parent had launched an electric knife late in 1964 in competition with forty existing brands. All advertising was concentrated on the knife and by the end of 1965 Hamilton Beach had a 30 per cent market share. Moreover, at the same time, sales of the blender which had been running at 150,000 per annum, shot up to a million—on the back of the knife advertising. The other success was in France where a Scovill appliances subsidiary increased sales from nothing to £3 million in just over a year, with the electric knife accounting for half. These indications of value are hardly precise measures for predicting what might happen in an entirely different British market. Not surprisingly, the *Sunday Times* article ends with a quotation from Jarrett, who has to take responsibility for the leap of faith—'I've stuck my neck out on this one and I won't be let off the hook.'

From the outside looking in
Up to this point, the focus has been the measurement of value of advertising for internal decision, and it has been argued that value differs from situation to situation and with the overall marketing plan adopted. Furthermore, even when specific conditions are known, measurement and prediction can be very difficult and perhaps never eliminate a great deal of uncertainty. It follows, then, that from outside the firm it is also wrong to expect a single answer to a question 'What is the value of advertising in marketing?' It is rather like the question 'How much is many?'

'How then', one may ask, 'can any decision be made concerning control of advertising?' And certainly this is a justifiable query in the light of the earlier claim that control should be based on an understanding of the value to the individual firm.

The concept of value relevant to the outsider concerned with decisions as to control of advertising, however, has differences. For this purpose, the value of advertising is really the incremental value that advertising brings over alternative variables in the marketing mix. In some situations, the firm would do almost as well with direct selling as with advertising. In others, there may be no practical substitute for advertising. The contribution of advertising to sales, however, could well be the same in both types of situation were advertising used and its contribution measured.

It is not difficult to find examples of situations in which there is no practical substitute for advertising. A firm needing a rapid build-up in sales in order to justify introducing a product with heavy capital requirements might be unable to justify introducing the product without access to television advertising. And there are few practical substitutes to advertising for combating after-purchase dissonance. It has been widely shown that purchasers are frequent readers of advertisements for products they have already purchased. This provides reinforcement for their decisions, reminding them of the features they valued highly at the time of purchase. Without continuing exposure to advertising more brand switching might be expected, and it would not be practical to use salesmen to contact past purchasers simply for this purpose.

Conversely, the removal of advertising as one of the features the marketer can adjust, might produce little change in sales for some firms. This might be true for some consumer goods, say detergents. If the heavy amounts spent on advertising here were channelled to price reduction—and all competitors were forced to eliminate advertising—sales might be little different. Advertising might have become simply a competitive weapon adding little to the total demand. But the effect of regulating advertising might not be to channel its cost into lower prices. It might well go into higher profits with no competitor able to influence his market share because to do so would require extensive advertising coverage—and this is prohibited.

If advertising is to be increasingly regulated in order to eliminate purely competitive padding, a great deal more thinking and research is needed about when and how to impose regulation. One important consideration, however, clearly emerges from any examination of the value of advertising in marketing. Advertising is not an homogeneous and separable element and to regulate it as such would be extremely ill-advised. Yet there is a widespread tendency to overlook this fact and to discuss the pros and cons of advertising from a community welfare viewpoint with little or no reference to the specific situation. A much more fruitful approach would be to discuss and classify the types of *situation* in which advertising should, or should not, be regulated.

Summary
In summary, there is no such thing as an absolute value of advertising either in its contribution to marketing achievement, or to community welfare. Whatever value exists is a function both of the particular situation and of the point of view from which it is judged. Those concerned with advertising and community welfare, therefore, would be well-advised to adopt the approach of the marketer and to concentrate on developing tools and methods for situational decisions—rather than pursuing regulation aimed at advertising as a generic class.

Part two

Advertising and public confidence

4

Where is it all leading us?*

Richard Hoggart

By turns hurt, defiant, apologetic and heavily self-justifying, advertising men seem particularly sensitive to criticism just now. Criticism has certainly been heavy in the last few years, perhaps because the number of reasonably well-informed people is somewhat greater than it used to be.

You need a fairly widespread critical public opinion to get the Consumers' Association, the Advertising Inquiry Council and similar organizations off the ground. Yet few people in advertising have taken the measure of this development. Some have seen its superficial aspects and made their advertising more self-conscious and sophisticated; but the widening of critical opinion has so far escaped almost all of them.

I will try to sum up as directly as I can, but without rancour, the case against advertising. Even so, I do not expect to have much, if any, effect. None of us like our profession to be attacked, and we fight back bitterly when it is. But usually someone somewhere in the profession steps out of line and says that he does see some justice in the criticisms, that some things in our particular house do need to be put in order.

This can be seen, for instance, in the quite fierce arguments about the function and the financing of universities today. But I have never heard any spokesman of the advertising (or public relations) industry admit to anything other than minor faults (that claims are sometimes a bit exaggerated, say, or not strictly truthful); I have never heard any spokesman of the industry

* This chapter has been substantially published as an article in *The Advertisers' Weekly* and we are grateful to the editor for permission to reprint it here.

take the measure of the major case against advertising, let alone answer it.

Why is this? Is it because a profession which lives by manipulating reality, by weaving attractive but deceptive verbal links between products and potential consumers, gets taken in by its own sleight-of-hand? And that, by-and-large, such a trade gets the servants it needs, who fit its demands and are suited by them?

For such men, when they find themselves criticized, the temptation to sell themselves a rationalization, like an outfitter clothing himself from stock, must be very strong. I do not say this to be rude, but to make it clear that, if the case against advertising is going to be seen (not necessarily accepted, but at least seen), then people in advertising have to make a harder effort than they have made so far. The time for easy rides, especially for the big public spokesman of advertising, is long past.

Let us try to get a few red herrings out of the way at one go. Yes: there can be some unexceptionable advertising (and it needn't be dull). No: it hasn't been proved that advertising in its present form (the kind of advertising that is being criticized) is essential to the economy, or that it reduces costs. Yes: the industry has done some self-police-ing; but only at an innocuous, true-or-false, level. No: no one in his senses is proposing a vast censorship; anyway, the important problems could not be touched by censorship.

The really serious questions raised by advertising are much wider than advertising itself. If critics spend a lot of time attacking advertising this is not because advertising is a peculiar kind of vice, but because it is representative, because it exhibits more plainly and more persistently than anything else the issues raised by mass persuasion. At bottom the case against advertising is the same as that against political propaganda, much religious proselytizing and any other form of emotional blackmail.

The case is this: that advertising tries to achieve its ends by emotionally abusing its audiences. Recognizing that we all have fears, hopes, anxieties, aspirations, insecurities, advertisers seek not to increase our understanding of these feelings and so perhaps

Richard Hoggart

our command of them, but to use their existence to increase the sales of whatever product they happen to have been paid to sell at any particular time. They exploit human inadequacy.

There is no point in illustrating, since illustrations are all around us, nor in elaborating on the occasional exceptions. The basic charge is indisputable, unless you adopt a purely predatory—every man for himself—attitude; in which case there is no basis for argument. But if you accept some moral responsibility in your conduct towards others then you are up to the neck in troubles which verbal manœuvres can only evade, not solve.

Some apologists of advertising seek to rebut all this by taking up the Stance of the Licensed Pantaloon. You are altogether too solemn, they say. No one really believes what we say. The ordinary chap is much more subtle than you give him credit for. He recognizes that we add to the amusement and colour of his life—and that's all there is to it.

Coming from anyone who has read the research literature this is downright disingenuous. The evidence shows, and a reasonably close acquaintance with 'ordinary people' will tell you anyway, that a surprisingly high proportion do literally believe what they read in the ads. Surprisingly high, when you think of the educational effort which goes into training in literacy. Still, that effort has been long delayed and is still small in proportion to the need.

Most men in advertising are, of course, more effectively trained, more articulate and mentally quicker than their audiences—which doesn't make the trick any pleasanter. It is true that a percentage of people are pretty sophisticated and not likely to be taken in by the cruder ploys. But this percentage is much smaller than most apologists purport to think.

What usually passes for sophisticated advertising (e.g. in the Sunday glossies) is at bottom as simple in its appeals as the stuff in the mass circulation papers; its stage-properties are different, that's all; its snobberies those of minor status differences. Outside that range there really is, I suppose, a small core of self-aware intellectuals who do enjoy, or claim to enjoy, advertisements as aesthetic objects, as sources of verbal, sociological or psychological fun.

Most talk of this kind strikes me as intellectually and imaginatively meretricious; but how grateful men in advertising are for it. It both confirms their status as harmless amusers and pays tribute to their verbal inventiveness. Since there is a poet or novelist manqué inside many a copywriter, this is a benison. And an outsider may feel that, though it is a sad little claim they are making, at least it isn't portentous.

It is easy to appreciate the excitement, even the mild glamour, which advertising can have. Playing with words, making them do tricks for you with narrowly prescribed rules (this product, this target audience, this number of words), is obviously fascinating and in some ways similar to working within the rules of a simple literary form. I once passed hours, on a sticky hot journey by troop-train from Italy, inventing copy (with a man who is now a very popular columnist) for 'Critch', a mythical powder which would eliminate the awful persistent itch in our crutches. Still, how long can that sort of fun satisfy a man? A long time, I suppose, if the rewards are good, and if you find something cathartic for your spare time. But it's a shabby business at best.

Which is why the least attractive people in the whole advertising business are the front men with the big public relations voices—the men who cheer up conferences with fighting keynote speeches about the public-service element in advertising and make prepared palliative statements on all other suitable occasions. Their routine is usually predictable. They assert that advertising is the lynch-pin or lubricant of a modern progressive economy. They take a few cheering-up-the-troops swipes at critics (this is a fairly recent development), and they offer the services of advertising to promote any good cause the community can name—citizenship, education, religion.

With people like that you are really up against it. They seem to have lost all sense of the difficulty of truth and of the need to respect other people's effort after it. How do you explain that if religion is to mean anything, it must be founded on a personal commitment, arrived at with all the help others can disinterestedly give, but in the end arrived at personally and in the fullest possible emotional clarity? Or how do you explain that illicit manoeuvres (associating religion with status or togetherness or smartness) cannot really convert anyone and only prepare the ground for equally illicit manœuvres with much more questionable ends. As 'professionals', Goebbels' ad men were very efficient indeed.

There is, of course, good persuasion as well as bad persuasion; and advertisers keep the debate murkier than it should be by sliding between the two types. In one sense, any good book is a form of persuasion. But the gap between that and the persuasion of advertisers is so large as to make virtually a difference of kind. Good persuasion, whether in dispassionate argument or in a powerfully moving novel, has two root qualities: respect for the reality of the subject, and respect for the listener's right to judge for himself his attitude to the subject. This definition does not rule out emotional engagement; any important commitment is a mixture of emotion and intellect. But it insists on emotional relevance—that the emotion, in both its nature and its intensity, shall fit the theme.

Naturally, the line between this and blatantly illicit emotional persuasion is a continuous one, and it is difficult to decide just where the watershed comes. But look at each end of the line and you see the distinction at once, and see its importance; and that makes it all the more important not to blur distinctions in the large middle area (which is where most of the battles about persuasion are fought), but to try to make them clearer.

It is important for outside critics not to use advertisers as scapegoats for bigger social problems; they reflect more than they affect in society. There are a lot of reasons why a society throws up so much persuasion like this, and so to many people in advertising theirs seems as respectable a trade as many others.

So much can be readily granted. But it is even more important not to make easy accommodations. The overriding fact is that much of the work of this profession, as it is at present practised, consists of exploiting human weakness through language. Anyone who thinks that it is better to try to understand one's weaknesses than to indulge them, anyone who thinks that language (the articulation of our thoughts and feelings in communicable form) can help in that better grasp, anyone with these two premises must regard most modern advertising as, at the best, a stupid waste of good human resources and at the worst, a wicked misuse of other people.

54

5

Restraint in advertising—is it necessary?

J M Wood

The advertising industry, with an annual turnover of more than £500 million, evokes powerful emotional responses both from its devotees and its critics.

At the conference of the Advertising Association in 1964, the chairman of the Rank Organization called the critics enemies, reactionaries whose spiritual home was in the feudal system; foolish, debunkers, detractors, denigrators and 'ignorant people who spare no effort to damage us, even though it be at the expense of our nation'. The advertising practitioners see themselves as the upholders of free competition, dedicated to raising the standard of living of the masses and increasing the satisfaction of consumers. They claim to play a leading role in the economy by stimulating demand and economic growth, and making possible the benefits of mass production.

In marked contrast, A. S. J. Baster asserts that the major part of 'informative advertising' is, and always has been, a campaign of exaggeration, half-truths, intended ambiguities, direct lies and general deception.[1] The critics see the 'ad men' as hidden persuaders, seducing the minds of consumers with false or non-existent values, undermining editorial freedom, enticing innocent housewives and even little children to spend more money on things they need less and less. Worse than this, they are now reaching down into the sub-conscious to manipulate consumers without their being aware of the fact.

The purpose of this chapter is not to examine the function of advertising in modern economic and social life and to inquire how well or ill it is performed, but to ask what justification there is for subjecting advertising to restraints other than those required by considerations of public morals and to conform with reasonable standards of business practice.

Advertising, in origin and intention, is a form of promotional activity, and probably a necessary part of the marketing process in a modern mass-production economy. According to the British Code of Advertising Practice, the function of advertising is the advocacy of the merits of particular products or services. If the persuasive aims of advertising determine the nature and the scope of the information it disseminates there will be a tendency for advertisers, in the absence of restraints, to subordinate the wider interests of the public to the primary object of selling goods.

The Molony Committee on Consumer Protection[2] found that a good deal of national advertising makes no attempt to present relevant and helpful product information, and is designed above all to impress a brand name upon the potential buyer. But if the presentation of 'relevant and helpful product information' was the best method of selling, would not this method be more widely adopted? One of the most successful advertising practitioners, David Ogilvy, has advocated just this. 'If advertisers would give up flatulent puffery and turn to factual informative advertising, not only would they increase their sales, but they would put themselves on the side of the angels.' Unfortunately, Mr Ogilvy has not yet succeeded in convincing his colleagues on either side of the Atlantic that this dictum is true.

It is difficult to see how advertisers can appeal successfully to the intellect by truthful, factual presentation of relevant information about products, if the brands from which the consumer is invited to choose are alike in all essential qualities. Are there really any significant differences between the competitive brands of whisky, beer, detergents, petrol, cigarettes, cake mixes and radio sets? Some manufacturers are known to produce similar goods under different brand names to meet the wishes of different distributors. If economic theory assumes that consumers act rationally, this is certainly not the experience of the advertisers.

There is a school of thought which teaches that advertising creates a difference between technically identical products. Martin Mayer,[3] for instance, suggests that people would think more clearly about the subject if they worked from the premise that advertising, in addition to the purely informative function, adds a new value to the existing values of the product. The fact that a value is fictitious as seen by the consumer does not mean, according to this theory, that it is unreal as enjoyed by him. Although it may be objected that advertising creates false values for a product, the answer seems to be that in an economic context it does not matter whether a use value enjoyed by a consumer is true or false. Mayer argues that outside standards of judgement cannot be applied to assess the reality of private gratifications, and that the truth or falsity of advertising values is a matter of individual opinion, not a subject for objective analysis.

There is an element of truth in these statements. The *Prescribers' Journal* for September 1961 contained an article on 'tonics'. It pointed out that many patients still expect a 'tonic' after an infectious illness or surgical operation. The tonics commonly prescribed under these circumstances usually contain glycero-phosphates, vitamins and strychnine. The article stated:

It must be appreciated that in the circumstances and doses in which they are given they have no appreciable pharmacological action. Their effect, if any, depends entirely on therapeutic suggestion. As infections and surgical operations lead to a considerable catabolism of lean tissue the money would be better spent on additional first class protein. Unfortunately some patients will not accept willingly this advice and insist on having a bottle of medicine with supposed tonic properties. . . .

The history of human vice shows that values most widely regarded as false always seem real enough to command a price on the market place, but civilized communities do not allow these vices to be freely advertised. Without restraints of this kind the social fabric would disintegrate. Even if some people believe they derive benefit from tonics which contain no true tonic properties, this is no reason for allowing advertisers to exploit this common human failing by making false claims for such products. The Food Standards Committee in a report published in 1966[4] stated that no controlled trials have demonstrated true tonic properties for any food, and as there is no scientific justification for any claims for tonic properties none should be permitted.

What kind of general criteria should be applied to the form

and content of advertisements? Lord Drumalbyn, Chairman of the Advertising Standards Authority, has said that the idea that people should have to tell the truth in advertising is absolutely unknown in this country, but that advertisers *should* tell the truth has long been recognized. This does not appear to take account of positive legislative requirements for certain products or classes of products. The Minister of State, Board of Trade, the Right Hon. George Darling, MP has recently insisted[5] that advertising must be honest and must not mislead the public in any way. Consequently, there must be a limit to the persuasive character of advertising. The problem, however, is where to draw the line. Mr Darling suggested that it is where persuasion takes on exaggerated, misleading and perhaps false descriptions of the publicized goods and services. By this standard there does not appear to be much room for the creation of false values of the kind described by Martin Mayer.

The general test applied by the British Code of Advertising Practice is that all advertising, whatever the medium used, should be legal, honest and truthful, and that no advertisement likely to bring advertising into contempt or to reduce public confidence in advertising should at any time be permitted. This is a counsel of perfection which may be acceptable in a voluntary code, but is difficult in its application. The Chairman of the Advertising Standards Authority has admitted that telling the truth is not all, and that truth can itself be so expressed as to mislead. The Retail Trading Standards Association has advised its members that it is a first principle of advertising that it must not mislead.

You should remember that it is quite possible to write an advertisement which is wholly truthful yet totally misleading. Don't do this. Make it a matter of personal pride that if called upon you can substantiate any claim that you make in an advertisement.[6]

The State-sponsored Consumer Council is not opposed to advertising, but believes that imaginative, accurate and informed advertisements play an important part in helping people to make an intelligent choice. The Council is however opposed to misleading advertisements,

the exaggerated spiels craftily designed to implant a false impression in the mind of a potential buyer, which are often presented in such a way that makes it impossible for anyone who has been 'had' to make out any case except for one that indicates that he must have been foolish to take the advertisement's claims seriously in the first place.[7]

The Reith Commission[8] saw a conflict of interest between consumer and advertiser. To the advertiser the transmission of information is a means of selling his product, and selling a means to private economic goals. On the other hand, the consumer is interested in receiving information not primarily for buying the product advertised, but for discovering its existence and assessing its usefulness or desirability in relation to possible alternatives. If the consumer were capable of making a rational choice between competitive products, or of judging for himself the accuracy of the claims made, there would be far less need for State intervention. Certain forms of legal protection for the consumer have, however, existed almost since commerce began. Cole and Diamond[9] trace their origin to the practice known to the Romans of milling the edges of gold and silver coins in order to prevent the sharper citizens from filing them to their own profit and the loss of the rest of the community.

The basic legal doctrine governing relations between buyer and seller, *caveat emptor*—let the buyer beware—developed during the Middle Ages when transactions were simple and usually took place directly between the parties. In the nineteenth century the growth of the towns brought about a need for measures to protect public health. In 1893 the common law relating to the sale of goods was codified in the Sale of Goods Act, which represented a considerable erosion of the principle of *caveat emptor*. This Act is still the basic law on the subject, although it came too soon to take account of the great development of industry and commerce in the twentieth century. As the Molony Committee pointed out: 'While the law has stood still, new selling methods have been introduced and an infinity of new types of complex goods have appeared on the market. The modern retail purchaser may find himself in his perplexity and ignorance at grave disadvantage.' The Committee recommended that the Sale of Goods Act should be brought up-to-date, and this was done in the Misrepresentation Act of 1967.

The housewife of even fifty years ago usually possessed a good deal of knowledge and experience which enabled her to recognize the composition of goods on sale, and to assess their quality and fitness for purpose. This is no longer so. The discoveries in the field of synthetic materials; the development of highly sophisticated electrical equipment; new additives to foodstuffs designed to improve their appearance, taste or keeping qualities and the new packaging methods, make it difficult for the ordinary consumer to compare values or to judge whether advertised claims for merchandise are truthful. Even the retail trader is now less able to perform his traditional function of giving expert advice to the consumer. This trend is seen in its most advanced form in self-service or self-selection in retailing. The conclusion of the Molony Committee was that in such a maze the consumer finds it beyond his power to make a wise and informed choice and is vulnerable to exploitation and deception.

The consumer has certain rights under both statute and common law, and if they are infringed he may take action in the civil courts in order to obtain damages from the advertiser or seller. It is, however, unreasonable to expect consumers to fend for themselves in this way. The need to protect the public as a whole, rather than as individual consumers, must be met by an appropriate public body, such as a local authority or a government department. The criminal law has therefore been steadily extended to enforce minimum standards in trade. The object of a criminal case is not compensation for the injured party, but punishment for the offender, so that the community as a whole is protected.

The intervention of the State and other public authorities to protect the consumer has also been of benefit to all honest traders. A kind of Gresham's law operates in commercial transactions so that poor merchandise and deceptive advertising tend to drive out the better. This partly explains why traders and advertisers have associated to establish voluntary codes of various kinds in order to raise the general level of business standards. In writing on the new Weights and Measures Act,[10] Mr W. Roger Breed, Chief Inspector for the County of Dorset, has pointed out that although it may be the natural tendency of mankind to depart from the fixed standard, with the seller wanting to give a little less and the buyer to get a little more than had been bargained for, in this modern age it has been subordinated to the common sense of a highly commercialized community. But even so, comments Mr Breed, 'if the public were left with the sole safeguard of *caveat emptor* and inspectors ceased to safeguard their susceptibilities one can image a rapid reversal of the general feeling of confidence which we believe at present pervades the act of buying'.

There is abundant evidence that advertisers dare not trust each other for fear of losing a competitive advantage. When in 1894 there were protests about advertisements for Beecham's Pills appearing on bathing huts at Scarborough, Thomas Beecham said he would remove them on condition that no other firm was allowed to advertise there, and added: 'While they are open to be used in this way the decoration may as well be "Beecham's Pills" as any other.' There is recent evidence that competition between two giant rivals has the effect of putting each in a position in which it cannot reduce its expenditure on advertising and sales promotions without losing its market share. Attempts to reduce expenditure by agreement have failed, partly due to the relative ineffectiveness of any alternative such as price reduction, and partly to the difficulty of preventing evasion.

Is there a case to be made out for restraints of an economic character on advertising? The Minister of State, Board of Trade, has outlined a number of conditions to which advertising should conform, one of which was that it should be economic. By this he meant that the expenditure on advertising should be related to a proper study of markets and should not be so great that it substantially increased costs and prices in circumstances which did not permit any really substantial increase in sales of the advertised products. This matter has recently been brought into public discussion by the Report of the Monopolies Commission on Detergents.[11]

The Commission found that two firms dominate the detergent market, and that the policies pursued on advertising and promotion and their price policies were things done by them for the purpose of preserving their 'monopoly' positions which operate against the public interest. The main criticisms of the two leading suppliers were:

1. that their advertising matter is more concerned with emphasizing unprovable qualities and building up a 'brand image' than with informing the public about the practical attributes of the product and how the best use can be made of it;
2. that their promotional activities encourage the consumer to buy particular products for the sake of benefits (gifts, prizes) which have nothing to do with the products themselves;
3. that the effect of emphasizing the brand image is particularly uneconomic when it leads a manufacturer to market two very similar products under different brand names;
4. that this emphasis also leads the manufacturers to undertake wasteful expenditure on launching new products or changing the formulation of existing products for the sake of 'improvements' which are of little or no intrinsic value to the user;
5. that because competition between the two companies is concentrated on advertising and promotion, the expenditure of both of them in this field is unduly high;
6. that as a result, not only does the public have to pay for costs from which it obtains no benefit but also, at least as regards powders, newcomers to the industry are deterred by the high cost of entry.

Broadly speaking, criticisms 1 to 4 may be said to concentrate on the character of the manufacturers' advertising and promotion, while criticisms 5 and 6 relate to the level of their expenditure.

The Monopolies Commission stated that in spite of the fact that the two companies had to earn their profits in competition with each other, the return on capital earned by both of them on household detergents was high, and in one case it was very high. This situation arose because the competition between them was concentrated in the field of advertising and promotion, which not only results in wasteful expenditure, but also deters potential competitors who might, otherwise, provide a safeguard against excessive profits. The opinion was expressed that if competition could be diverted from excessive advertising and promotion to prices, the result would be not only a saving in cost but also a more effective check upon profits than in the past.

The Monopolies Commission discussed with the companies and carefully considered possible objections to restraints on advertising and promotion, whether voluntary or imposed by the Government, and finally recommended that the Board of Trade should encourage them to agree that at least a 40 per cent reduction in selling expenses should be made, to accompany substantial reductions in wholesale selling prices. It was also recommended that the Board of Trade should consider the possibility of introducing some form of automatic sanction that would discourage excessive selling expenditure in the field of household detergents, such as, for example, the disallowance as an expense for tax purposes of selling expenses in excess of an approved percentage of net wholesale turnover.

The National Board for Prices and Incomes in its report on the prices of household and toilet soaps, soap powders and soap flakes and soapless detergents[12] was also highly critical of the advertising and promotions of the two market leaders, which was stated to be around 18 per cent of their total net selling price. A significant part of each company's expenditure was found to be designed to ensure that the other company did not steal an advantage, and that their marketing costs were in part retaliatory rather than informative. The Board expected that, in the light of its conclusions about the need for stable prices, the companies would exercise restraint over the whole of their expenditure on advertising and promotion.

Quite apart from the possible waste of resources in competitive advertising, where is the logic in allowing manufacturers to urge consumers to spend more when the government is deliberately restricting consumption by various devices, including taxation, credit controls and export incentives? There is at least a *prima facie* case for considering the restriction of advertising expenditure in conformity with national economic policies.

The government has already taken an important step in the direction of taxing advertising expenditure. The independent television programme contractors paid £21 million in the levy on advertising receipts in the year 1965–6. This sum and a balance of £1·4 million from the previous period were paid to the Treasury by the ITA under the Television Act, 1964.

These are not matters on which superficial judgements should be made. What is needed is a careful study of the economic effects of advertising. It should not be overlooked that advertising not only provides a free alternative television service in this country (the whole of the television licence fee goes to the BBC), but subsidizes the press to a very substantial extent. It may, however, be argued that consumers of these services pay for the advertising in the prices of the goods which they buy.

There is a field in which advertising is almost entirely banned —that is the professions. The reason for this policy is to be found in such statements as the British Optical Association's Code of Professional Conduct (1963):

Advertising is prohibited in all older professions because the whole basis of professional practice building is by recommendations from satisfied patients or colleagues. If I do my work properly my patient will recommend me to someone else and I shall get more work accordingly. That is the basis upon which professional practices are built. To state or imply by advertisement 'Consult me, I'm good', or even 'consult me', does not convey an impression of professionalism. In a profession all men, theoretically, have equal chances of success. If one man can afford to advertise and does, while another cannot, this equality is disturbed. The Optical profession will never attain its true dignity and be recognised as a profession universally until advertising by individuals is abolished.

Advertising is now controlled by rules prescribed by the General Optical Council. The profession did not obtain Statutory powers until 1958, and the rules were made in 1964.

Critics of advertising may be inclined to approve the policy of the professions, but many members of the public will regard the above explanation as naïve. Professor D. S. Lees (Professor of Applied Economics, University College, Swansea) has grave doubts about the economic consequences of professions who rigidly adhere to strict professional codes of conduct which among other things do not allow advertising. In commenting on the Code of the BOA he states:

Now all this may be clear enough to a medieval historian but to an economist schooled in the theory of competitive markets it seems at first blush suspiciously like mumbo jumbo. Of course the professions 'sell' their services, just as do dry cleaners and British Railways.[13]

He goes on to argue that if there is no substantive distinction between 'professions' and 'trades' then it is muddled and unfair to bring the whole weight of public opinion and policy against restrictive practices in the latter and to approve and quietly extend restrictive practices in the former.

There is reason to believe that the abolition of advertising in some of the professions may deny to the public relevant and helpful information. For example, it is difficult to see how the public interest is served by forbidding opticians to attach prices to the frames displayed in their windows.

There are a number of other examples of total or partial bans on certain types of advertising. The television advertising of cigarettes and cigarette tobacco ended on 31 July 1965, by direction of the Postmaster-General under Section 7 (5) of the Television Act, 1964. This step was taken in the interests of public health. The Pharmacy and Medicines Act, 1941, prohibits advertisements to the public relating to abortion and certain diseases (Bright's disease, cataract, diabetes, epilepsy, glaucoma, locomotor ataxy, paralysis and tuberculosis). Similarly the Venereal Disease Act, 1917, and the Cancer Act, 1939, prohibit the general advertisement of remedies for treatment of these diseases.

Vance Packard has drawn a somewhat horrific picture of the use of subliminal advertising in the U.S.A.[14] The Pilkington Committee on Broadcasting[15] described subliminal advertisements as visual or aural sensations so faint that the viewer is not conscious of them. It had not been put to the Committee that they had been used in Great Britain, and it was understood that their use was regarded by all concerned with advertising as abhorrent. Nevertheless the Committee thought it might be tempting on some occasion to use them for an end which was good in itself. So that no one would yield to the temptation, the Committee recommended that they be specifically prohibited. The White Paper on Broadcasting published by the Government in July 1962 pointed out that the Television Act, by implication, did not permit subliminal advertisements, but it was agreed that the ban should be made explicit in new legislation.

65

Accordingly, Section 3(3) of the Television Act, 1964, states that no advertisement may include any technical device which, by using images of very brief duration or by any other means, exploits the possibility of conveying a message to, or otherwise influencing the minds of, members of an audience without their being aware, or fully aware, of what has been done.

Advertisements inviting deposits from the public are covered by the Protection of Depositors Act, 1963. This Act was passed to protect people who in response to an advertisement deposited their savings with a company about which they might know little. It stipulates, *inter alia*, that no company may advertise for deposits unless it has filed with the Registrar of Companies prescribed accounts. It makes it an offence to solicit for deposits, if the inducement is fraudulent or reckless. The advertising of betting and lotteries is controlled by the Betting Act, 1874, the Betting, Gaming and Lotteries Act, 1963, and the Pool Betting Act, 1954. Aerial advertising and propaganda are prohibited under Section 7 of the Civil Aviation (Licensing) Act, 1960.

There is a substantial body of legislation concerned with various aspects of public health. The Food and Drugs Act, 1955, in England and Wales, and similar enactments covering Scotland (1956) cover the composition, labelling and advertising of food and drugs, as well as questions of fitness of food for human consumption and hygiene in the food trades. These Acts forbid the sale of any food or drug, which differs in substance, nature and quality from that demanded by the purchaser, and make it an offence to use false or misleading descriptions either on labels attached to goods or in advertisements. The Labelling of Food Order, 1953, requires prepacked foods to carry the manufacturers' name and address, the common name of the food, and in some cases a statement of the ingredients in the order in which they predominate. Ministers are advised by the Food Standards Committee on the need for such regulations to control the composition, description, labelling or advertising of foods. Under the Food and Drugs Act, 1955, any advertisement which falsely describes any food or drug, or is calculated to mislead as to the nature, substance or quality of any food or drug, is an offence. The Bread and Flour Regulations, 1963, make it an offence for any person to publish any advertisement for any such food which is calculated to indicate directly or by ambiguity, omission or inference that the said food is an aid to slimming, unless the advertisement bears or includes a clear, legible and conspicuous statement to the effect that it cannot aid slimming unless it forms part of a diet in which the total intake of calories is controlled.

The Report of the Food Standards Committee on Claims and Misleading Descriptions[4] laid down three guiding principles which should apply both to the labelling of food and to advertisements, as follows:

(a) regulations must be designed to protect consumers and honest traders;
(b) if consumer and trade interests conflict, then the interests of consumers must take precedence;
(c) all labelling should be as clear and informative as possible.

The Committee pointed out that the acceptance of these principles must inevitably mean some restraint on the freedom of advertisers and labellers. The Ministry of Agriculture, Fisheries and Food is at present preparing new food labelling regulations based on this report.

The main restraints upon the advertising of non-foodstuffs are contained in the Merchandise Marks Act, the purpose of which is to ensure that trade marks and trade descriptions applied to goods for sale are both honest and accurate, and that there are no misleading claims to most of the ascertainable characteristics of goods. The first Merchandise Marks Act, passed in 1862, was called 'an Act to amend the law relating to the fraudulent marking of merchandise'. The Act of 1887 which is still in force, superseded the Act of 1862. It not only extended the definitions of trade descriptions and added to the list of actions deemed to be offences but, when such an action was proved, threw on the defence the onus of proving that there was no fraudulent intent.

Several extensions were made to the parent act in 1926 and 1938. In 1953 the Acts were considerably strengthened and their scope greatly increased by an amending Act which widened the definitions of trade description and false trade description, and also made it an offence to use a misleading, not only a false, trade description. Such a description included references to the standard of quality of any goods according to a classification commonly used or recognized in the trade, or as to fitness for purpose, strength, performance or behaviour of any goods. One result of the strengthening of this legislation was an increase in the number of prosecutions brought by the Board of Trade.

The Molony Committee made a close study of the Merchandise Marks Acts and made a number of recommendations designed to extend the protection which they can afford to consumers. Early in 1966 the Government published the Protection of Consumers (Trade Descriptions) Bill, which was designed to replace and extend the existing legislation relating to merchandise marks. The Bill restated the existing offences of applying a false trade description to goods and selling goods to which a false trade description is applied, but extended them to cover a wider field than hitherto. One clause dealt specifically with statements made in advertisements. The Bill was intended to give the Board of Trade power to make orders defining terms when used as part of a trade description of goods. A new principle was introduced in the Bill to enable the Board of Trade to make Orders requiring certain information or instruction to be given in advertisements. False indications concerning the price of goods were also prohibited. The Bill applied to services as well as to goods. The Bill fell when Parliament was dissolved, but was reintroduced towards the end of 1967 as the Consumers Protection Bill.

A positive requirement to supply information is laid upon advertisers by the Advertisements (Hire-Purchase) Act, 1957. If a trader offers goods for sale with an indication that credit terms are available, he is obliged to give specified details of the terms in all advertisements so that a prospective customer may see what he will be required to pay for credit compared with the cash terms.

The Report of the Pilkington Committee on Broadcasting, in its conclusions on advertising on independent television stated:

> On the content of advertisements there has been much disquiet, and we believe it to be generally justified. There is, in our view, a need for

much more effective restraint, and we have made recommendations designed to secure this.

Section 8(1) of the Television Act, 1964, states that it shall be the duty of the Independent Television Authority—

(a) to draw up, and from time to time review, a code governing standards and practice in advertising and prescribing the advertisements and methods of advertising to be prohibited, or prohibited in particular circumstances; and
(b) to secure that the provisions of the code are complied with as regards the advertisements included in the programmes broadcast by the Authority.

Under other sections of the Act the Authority must consult the Postmaster-General about the classes and descriptions of advertisements which must not be broadcast, and the methods of advertising which must not be employed, and is obliged to carry out any directions he may give them in this respect.

The general principle which governs all television advertising is that it should be legal, clean, honest and truthful. This principle is not peculiar to television, but because of its greater intimacy within the home television gives rise to problems which do not necessarily occur in other media, and it is essential to maintain a high quality of television advertising. In relation to medicines and treatments, the Authority has adopted the basic requirements laid down in the British Code of Advertising Practice.

Codes of practice, and even legislation, must be policed if they are to fulfil their purpose. During the year 1965–6 the ITA's Advertising Control Office examined a total of 7,700 pre-production scripts for television advertising. About 8 per cent of those concerned with general consumer goods and services had to be amended before acceptance. The others were concerned with 250 different products of a medical or semi-medical nature, of which up to 30 per cent had to be amended. When the finished films were examined about 1 per cent needed editing before final approval could be given. Even so, the Consumer Council found a number of advertisements which it believed were in breach of the code. This is an indication of what the public might expect if television advertisers were left to their own devices.

The right to display outdoor advertisements is controlled by Regulations made under the Town and Country Planning Acts. The history of poster advertising makes fascinating reading, and E. S. Turner has described the long campaign for statutory powers to protect the public against the destruction of amenities by advertisers.[16] The general rule is that express consent must be obtained from the Local Planning Committee before an advertisement may be displayed, otherwise than on premises where the goods or services are sold. All illuminated outdoor advertisements require express consent. Some advertisements may be displayed by deemed consent, including business names, and advertisements relating to goods or services supplied on the premises, provided they are not more than 15 feet from the ground. A Local Planning Authority has the right to challenge such advertisements, that is, to require an application to be made for express consent, if they are thought to be detrimental to amenity or public safety. In 1965 there were 43,467 advertisement applications, of which 9,333 were refused consent. The fact that the Regulations do not apply to advertisements in shop windows, with the result that many high streets are covered by a rash of garish displays, has been strongly criticized.

Another objectionable feature of outdoor advertising which has not been dealt with by legislation is the 'clutter' of posters, too crowded and badly arranged, which are to be seen on small newsagents', grocers', tobacconists' and confectioners' shops. In an effort to get rid of 'clutter' and to avoid any extension of the Regulations, no fewer than twenty organizations have agreed upon a voluntary Code of Standards for Advertising on Business Premises, which was first published in 1960. General oversight of the Code is exercised by a Consultative Committee, but the specific task of clearing clutter has been undertaken by an Advertisers' Working Committee. Much dissatisfaction has been expressed about this arrangement, but the Minister of Housing and Local Government has agreed to give it a fair trial.

There are other measures of self-discipline imposed by the advertising industry on itself from mixed motives. The Advertising Association and the Institute of Practitioners in Advertising, together with other advertising organizations have drawn up the British Code of Advertising Practice which establishes rules for the guidance of all connected with the industry. The Code was first published in 1962, revised in 1964 and 1967. It lays down the general principle that all advertising shall be legal, clean, honest and truthful. The British Code of Standards relating to the advertising of medicines and treatments, which was published in 1948, is now a part of the wider Code, and lays down minimum standards relating to the advertising of medicines. It does not apply to products advertised only to doctors, dentists, nurses or pharmacists in media addressed particularly to them. The Code of Advertising Practice Committee is responsible for the administration of the Code in its amalgamated form. Specific abuses in advertising are investigated by such organizations as the Advertising Association and the Newspaper Society and remedial action is taken. Other abuses, such as subliminal advertising, have been condemned by these bodies.

In July 1962, the advertising industry set up the Advertising Standards Authority, an independent and autonomous body, to act as a watchdog to assure compliance with both codes. The joint Censorship Committee of the British Poster Advertising Association and other associations also maintains a code, which seeks to prevent the exhibition of posters which might offend public sentiment.

These efforts at self-discipline in the industry have not been without critics. In 1964, after examining the machinery that existed for the control of advertising, the Consumer Council called for statutory control. Subsequently, in the light of surveys of both television and press advertising and a number of discussions with the Advertising Standards Authority, the Council issued another statement explaining why its views about the desirability of statutory control had not changed. This said that the Council's surveys of press and television advertising and the response of the appropriate bodies to the findings of those surveys had exposed two main weaknesses in the present advertising control systems:

1. Although the Independent Television Authority has statutory powers over television advertising, the exercise of those

powers is not its main function and it does not necessarily judge advertisements in the light of their impact on ordinary viewers.

2. The Advertising Standards Authority, in the view of the Council, is not in a position to make objective judgements of the effects of some types of advertising on the general public. In addition, its coverage of press and direct mail advertising is not comprehensive and its policing machinery is inadequate.

As with all powerful forces in a pluralistic society, modern advertising is now faced with what Galbraith has called counter-vailing force. Sceptical consumers have organized themselves nationally and locally into groups, sometimes with the help of the State.

The Consumer Council was set up in March 1963 in accordance with the recommendation of the Molony Committee. It is an independent body consisting of twelve members appointed by the President of the Board of Trade, and is financed by a grant-in-aid of £190,000. The terms of reference of the Council are wide enough to enable it to study the effect of advertising upon consumers, and it has made a number of pronouncements on this matter.

The work of the British Standards Institution on consumer protection and guidance has several aspects, the most important of which, as far as advertising is concerned, is the promulgation of glossaries of terms used in trade, which have been accepted by the courts as the correct descriptions in cases concerning misrepresentation. The BSI is also concerned with the labelling of goods, for example, woollen fabrics, the size coding of clothing and with a code for informative labelling of carpets. Manufacturers whose goods come up to the prescribed standard are encouraged to use the 'Kite' mark, which is protected by law against misuse.

The Consumers' Association was formed in 1957 as a non-profit-making company limited by guarantee. Associate membership is open to any member of the public, or any organization, and at the end of 1967 there were 450,000 subscribing members. The aim of the association is to provide members with the results of independent comparative tests of named brands of consumer goods, and of consumer services. The publications of CA frequently expose misleading advertising.

The Retail Trading Standards Association was set up in 1935 by a number of retail stores and textile manufacturers. Its function is to establish satisfactory standards of advertising and general trading practice, especially in relation to trade descriptions. The membership is now widely representative of the distributive trades and there are links with many trade associations. The RTSA keeps a close watch on advertisements and takes action, through the courts if necessary, in cases in which goods appear to have been falsely or misleadingly described. It has also played an important part in securing amendments to Merchandise Marks and other protective legislation. The RTSA publishes codes for the guidance of retailers, recommending not only glossaries for various classes of goods, but also correct practice in relation to sale offers, identification of seconds and the like.

In a memorandum to the Reith Commission in 1963,[17] the National Union of Teachers expressed concern over certain tendencies of methods of advertising in common use, because it believes that they are socially bad and hinder the attempts of education to improve standards. Although the Union did not feel that it was part of its duty to propose specific remedies, it suggested that if the voluntary acceptance of standards proved unattainable, then support would be given to control by regulation, exercised if possible from within, but if that was not possible, from outside the advertising profession. In the Spring of 1965 the educational magazine *The Use of English* introduced a new quarterly series of exercise sheets under the title 'Looking at Advertising'.[18] It was submitted that a secondary school education that did not bring the experience of advertising into scope would be failing as dramatically as a junior school that excluded the Highway Code. The object of these exercises is to help pupils to judge for themselves whether a particular advertisement is good or bad (as opposed to effective), and to educate them in objective discrimination. There is a need for much more work of this kind in schools.

With such a substantial volume of legislation to control advertising, voluntary codes drawn up and policed by sections of this industry, and the various supervisory bodies that now keep a critical watch on advertising in the interest of consumers, it might be supposed that little more remained to be done. On the contrary, there is still much dissatisfaction with the administration of the existing controls, both statutory and voluntary, and a number of proposals have been made for strengthening them.

The Consumer Council has suggested three forms of control:

(a) a statutory code based on the existing CAP and ITA Codes;
(b) machinery for maintaining a comprehensive scrutiny of all forms of advertising, something on the lines of the Federal Trade Commission in the USA;
(c) a judicial system, perhaps through a special court, for dealing with disputed cases and for imposing statutory penalties.

The Retail Trading Standards Association believes that the Advertising Standards Authority has failed to grapple with the hard core of deceptive advertisements which may represent only a small proportion of the total but which are bringing advertising increasingly into ridicule and contempt. In its evidence to the Molony Committee the RTSA argued that the conflict of interests within the advertising industry appeared to negative any form of voluntary control, and came to the conclusion that the only possible solution is the appointment of a permanent independent committee along the lines of the Federal Trade Commission, with powers to issue 'cease and desist' orders with regard to misleading or otherwise harmful advertisements. In this way, an advertisement subject to such an order should neither be handled by an advertising agency nor carried in any media until the required amendments had been made to the satisfaction of the independent committee.

The Reith Commission held that the persuasive intent of advertising is incompatible with the impartiality and abundance of objective comparative data that would be looked for in a fully adequate source of consumer information—which, after all, advertising does not set out to be. The Commission conceded that criticism on this count would be misplaced, but recognized that advertising cannot be an adequate substitute from the consumer's point of view. In the belief that the public is entitled to receive more unbiased information about products and services than is at present available to them, a number of proposals were made for meeting this need. Firstly, the valuable work of such bodies as the Consumer Council has laid a basis which now needs to be consolidated and expanded, so that consumer interests may carry the weight due to them in a democratic society. Secondly, the fundamental solution to the problems created by advertising itself must lie in measures designed to educate consumers, not merely to protect them from misleading advertising. An adequate supply of consumer information is not only desirable in itself, but would be both a corrective to misleading advertising and an incentive for advertisers to use rational methods of persuasion. Thirdly, the foundation of a consumer service is the gathering of information by research and testing, and the appropriate dissemination of the knowledge thus gained. The Commission proposed, therefore, that an independent body of public corporation status should be established. This body could either absorb or be a development of the Consumer Council, and could be known as the National Consumer Board. Its membership should adequately represent both consumers and the medical profession. The Board's work should be financed by a percentage levy on the domestic advertising expenditure of firms.

A Board which would steadily accumulate factual information about products and services would be in a position to advise or act knowledgeably about any undesirable advertising. Accordingly, the Reith Commission recommended that the NCB should keep a close watch on all forms of advertising and on the progress of the voluntary control system under the ASA and the CAPC recommending changes and improvements in the light of its experience; and should be empowered to prosecute offending advertisers, as the result of individual complaints or of its own investigations, if found necessary. Nevertheless, the Commission saw the value of the voluntary control system as the most effective way of dealing with the vast quantity of advertising material, and it hoped that further growth in the advertising industry's sense of responsibility would continue, and that the ASA and the CAPC would redouble their efforts. The Commission believed that a code of advertising practice, based on the existing codes, should be made statutory, and that where voluntary supervision and negotiation failed to achieve adequate control, the NCB should be able to intervene and prosecute. It was suggested that the Board should be able to operate rather as does the Federal Trade Commission in the USA by issuing challenges and initiating prosecutions. The weight of proof of all claims should lie with advertisers, and an advertiser challenged to substantiate his claims should be required to produce such proof within a given short period. If the Board found the proofs submitted inadequate to justify the claims made, then the advertiser should have either to withdraw his claims or risk prosecution, either directly by the NCB or by the Board of Trade.

The principle has been firmly established that there should be restraints upon advertising, and there is now a substantial body of legislation for the protection of consumers. Moreover, the advertisers have themselves acknowledged the need for self-discipline. But neither legislation nor voluntary codes are likely to be effective unless they are policed, and sanctions are available in the event of non-compliance by a minority. There is evidence that legislation has lagged behind developments in advertising, and that voluntary codes have been flagrantly disregarded. These matters should continue to receive attention from consumer organizations and government departments.

Although it may not be the responsibility of advertisers to educate and inform the consumer, they have a duty not to exploit human weaknesses or deliberately mislead the unenlightened. However carefully legislation or voluntary codes are drafted, they cannot deal effectively with every advertisement in this highly sophisticated industrial society, and there will remain room for honest disagreement, and on occasion irreconcilable differences of opinion. As the Molony Committee commented, in matters of morality and taste, their assessment depends on opinion, not on fact, and any attempt at either exploitation or at control is circumscribed by the limits imposed by the composite of public opinion. Advertising is no more than a single factor in any decline of public morality and taste, and the practitioners should not be blamed for abuses which are not rightly their responsibility. If, for example, people choose to smoke the cigarettes which the manufacturers provide, and the Treasury benefits to the tune of £1,000 million per annum, it is hypocritical to blame the advertisers for not heeding the muted warnings of the Ministry of Health about the danger of lung cancer. It is right and proper, therefore, that advertising, instead of being treated as a separate subject for legislative and other restraints, should be regarded as one aspect of the much wider problem of consumer protection, education and enlightenment.

References
1 Baster, A. S. J. *Advertising Reconsidered*. P. S. King, 1935.
2 *Final Report of the Committee on Consumer Protection*. HMSO, 1962.
3 Mayer, M. *Madison Avenue, U.S.A.* Penguin, 1961.
4 Food Standards Committee Report on *Claims and Misleading Descriptions*. HMSO, 1966.
5 *Board of Trade Journal*, 7 October 1966.
6 RTSA, Trade Information Service, December 1965.
7 The Consumer Council. *Focus*. December 1966.
8 *Report of a Commission of Inquiry into Advertising*. Labour Party, 1966.
9 Cole, H. R. and Diamond, A. L. *The Consumer and the Law*. Co-operative Union, 1960.
10 Breed, W. R. *The Weights and Measures Act 1963*. Charles Knight.
11 The Monopolies Commission. Report on the *Supply of Household Detergents*. HMSO, August 1966.
12 National Board for Prices and Incomes. Report No. 4, *Prices of Household and Toilet Soaps, Soap Powders and Soap Flakes, and Soapless Detergents*. HMSO, October 1965.
13 Lees, D. S. *Economic Consequences of the Professions*. Institute of Economic Affairs, 1966.
14 Packard, V. *The Hidden Persuaders*. Penguin, 1960.
15 *Report of the Committee on Broadcasting*. HMSO, 1962.
16 Turner, E. S. *The Shocking History of Advertising*. Penguin, 1965.
17 National Union of Teachers. *The Teacher Looks at Advertising*. 1963.
18 Marland, M. 'Looking at Advertising.' Introduction to *The Use of English*, Chatto and Windus, Spring, 1965.

6

Do we worry too much?

James P O'Connor

What can this title have to do with advertising? Who is the 'we' in the title? Is it the 'we' in the advertising business? Is it the 'we' who are the consumers? Or is it the 'we' who are the governors and legislators? Presumably the meaning includes all three of these, so I will take them in turn.

But first of all I must start by asking 'What is advertising?' And, of course, advertising is nothing by itself. It has no kind of independent or separate existence at all. It exists only as part of the selling process of a manufacturer. It is a tool—one of the tools—within the marketing kit, and one with no independent existence.

Advertising tends to mean different things to different people. Very often advertising is thought of simply as ads in national newspapers and television. But that isn't the half of it.

Advertising is today's *Daily Express*, today's *Guardian*, to-morrow's *Sunday Times* and the *News of the World*. It is to-night's commercial television, and the ads in the cinema down the road. It's the ads on the Manchester United's football sheet this afternoon, and around the fences that divide the watchers from the players. Advertising is also a card in a stationer's window from someone wanting a gardener. It is the back end of a bus and all those shop window displays. It's the bell on an ice-cream van, and the voucher that comes through your letter box for 2*d*. off a new toothpaste. It is an appeal for charity by direct mail. It is the 'Ideal Home' exhibition, a British week in Brussels and a cereal packet competition. It is an artist finishing a piece of artwork for an ad; a process engraver and a printer at work. It is the recruitment ads in the local newspaper alongside

the ads for a local timber merchant. It is an electronics company's ads in an electronics journal. It is all these and much
more. On and on we could go.

If, therefore, anyone has to worry about advertising, then he
has first of all to understand the length and breadth of it. And
all things and services and people that are involved.

And so to understand it all better, take up a newspaper.
Forget all your preconceived ideas about advertising and the
things half-remembered from the past. Look carefully at each
ad in that paper. See what each one says and what product it
advertises. See how the ads vary in their content and their
approach. See what different products there are on offer and
the information or persuasion conveyed.

It is surprising how little some people know about advertisements. Their impressions can be so often wrong. A question
was recently asked in Parliament by an MP. 'How much has
been spent in the last two years on that campaign "Someone,
somewhere, wants a letter from you"?' The Minister very
rightly replied: 'Nothing. The campaign finished before two
years ago.'

How many people talk about and criticize ads which have
been dead and buried for many, many years. 'Whiter than
white'—how many years is it since that ad stopped? And yet
how frequently there are references to it. Perhaps some ads
should never have been created in the first place. But advertising is what is now. Not what is past.

Now we come to 'worry'. What is 'worry'? The dictionary
talks about 'letting the mind dwell on trouble'. It talks about
'to fret'. It also talks about 'uneasiness'—which is perhaps the
thing that we are more concerned with in the present context.
So let us consider our three kinds of possible worriers.

First, there is the consumer. Does the consumer worry? If so,
what about? If there is an advertising worry, is it about advertising or about the advertisements? Because these two are different. Actually the consumer has a very high inbuilt discount
rate—if we can call it that—for advertisements. And also something called indifference. Something like 85 per cent of all consumers seem to be indifferent to all advertisements. I don't
know whether this is a good thing or a bad thing for the

consumer. But out of this statistic, at least, we can surely draw the preliminary conclusion that maybe the consumer—as a consumer—doesn't worry very much about the ads.

Remember what an advertisement is. It is information and it is persuasion. No advertisement, to my knowledge, was ever created that could be one without the other. Yet some people behave a little oddly about this word 'persuasion'. In an advertisement, information is all right, quite acceptable. But persuasion, well that's different.

Now there is political persuasion, religious persuasion, philosophical persuasion, financial persuasion. All these appear to be acceptable, honest, moral. But persuasion in selling is found, somehow, to have an immoral flavour to it. This puzzles me.

Advertising is persuasion, is advocacy. Indeed it has been described as 'truth in its most favourable light'. I hope you will not laugh too cynically at this description. Truth is a very easy word to use, and it is easy to say that some statement is untruthful. But, in fact, truth is very elusive. It is a very complex thing. If you have ever sat round the industry's table, as I have, and seen the endless pains taken to ensure that this approximation of truth is discovered, you will see my point.

How do we find the truth in our own business, or even in our lives? Is it really such a simple thing? Although I grant you that it is easier to talk about truth in advertising than about truth in one's own personal life. The 'blacks' are easy and so are the 'whites'. Most of the worries fall into the very large in-between area—the 'grey area'.

Take, for example, the word 'free'. Supposing you are going to send a packet top and get something absolutely free in return. But, paying the postage—is that 'free'? You cannot get it 'free' unless you pay the postage, but the object received is free. Or, how does one decide what is the average price for an object in the shops throughout the country, when someone is selling the same thing at a lower price and saying so? What about that famous phrase 'cannot be repeated'. Is it true? Could it be true one minute and false the next, in any case? What about 'come to sunny Spain'. Supposing it is raining the day you arrive? Truth is very difficult, often, to decide—even in all honesty.

The educationalists tell us we are leading the consumers

astray. Especially, in their case, we can understand they feel even more strongly that we are leading their children astray. There are, however, some simple remedies but teachers tend not to use them. What is more simple, for example, than to explain the general problem of an economy where manufacturers are needed, and then have to sell their goods. Advertising is soon mentioned and one can point out to the children what they should learn. If the advertisement says 'Guinness is good for you', the teacher can explain that Guinness say 'Guinness is good for you'. While Kodak say 'Save £10 on the Instamatic camera', and Lloyds Bank say 'Let Lloyds help you to plan'. This puts the whole thing in a nutshell and in perspective.

In the world today there are millions of people with added discretion in spending power. We call it an increased standard of living. They work to earn their money. They spend their money on their choices of things—things that, these days, go well beyond just the level of necessities. No longer do they just want a cave, a tiger skin, a little fuel and food. Now there are extras and new utilities—and even sheer luxuries.

To all these people, advertising is purely a service of suggestions, a highly desirable service to them. This parade of possibilities is an indispensable service today, when people have real choices to make. It is the prospect of what their money can buy that makes them work. They want satisfaction in goods and services for their efforts. This keeps them working in the community, keeps them striving and aspiring.

These are the ordinary people of a country. Don't mix them up, please, with the people who feel superior to all this, who already have a better standard, who are the intellectuals. These people may not need the ordinary satisfactions of life, and this parade of products. They know where to go, and what they want to get, and what they want to do. But remember the other 95 per cent. I do not believe that it would be good to regulate that 95 per cent of the community out of their satisfactions into some higher 'satisfactions', chosen for them by people 'who know better'.

Are these 95 per cent of consumers worrying that advertising, in the process of giving this service to the public, propagates, for example, spurious values? Or that advertising is creating a candy-floss society? Or that advertising discredits objective controls of the price mechanism? I think not.

The mass of the consumers do not appear to worry. They complain, of course, about poor quality—if the goods are shoddy—or if the purchase doesn't deliver what the advertiser or the shopkeeper said it would. And rightly so.

What about the legislators? Do they worry? It would appear that they do worry. Perhaps too much. It has been said that it was in the 1930's that economists knocked advertising. In the 40's it was the novelists. In the 50's, the sociologists. Now, in the 60's it is the legislators.

There are, of course, a lot of laws governing advertising. Consumers are safeguarded by these laws, which are far-reaching in their scope, and appear to be very comprehensive. But legislators, by and large, want more laws—that is the business they are in.

The economic necessity of advertising in an economy like ours—and in our present discussion we are not concerned with questioning *that*—is readily acknowledged by the legislators. Nevertheless they worry about:

—the price of advertising, as reflected in the product
—the effectiveness of advertising—does it work?
—the role of advertising—mirror to society or trendsetter?—its intrusiveness, even impertinence
—the honesty of advertising
—any unfairness of advertising techniques, especially those playing on emotions.

The public, of course, pays for the advertising in the price. The public also pays for the labour, the machinery, the raw materials, the managing director, the telephone calls, the canteen, the transport costs of distribution, the retailers' margins, i.e. everything by way of cost, plus profit.

But if there were, say, less (or no) advertising, what happens to the price? It isn't just reduced. Retail margins may take more, or less efficient sales methods may take more and so on.

What about the effectiveness of advertising? This is always more difficult to appreciate for those who have never marketed, or sold, or advertised. Those in business do not doubt its effectiveness in all the right circumstances, but they tend to keep quiet about it for competitive business reasons. Talk to a business man and ask him. Or even Government Ministers. They do not doubt the value of the advertising their departments carry out either. They cheerfully answer questions about it in Parliament. They defend it, say it does a good job in their case, and want more of it. (Incidentally, how many people know that more civil servants were *added* to government service in 1965-6 than are employed in the whole of the advertising agency business in this country?)

Is advertising a mirror to society? Obviously yes. It is really no good talking to a mass audience in the language of just the top few people or just the bottom few people. It has to be the mass average. Hence, incidentally, the abrasiveness of advertisements, their intrusiveness and their repetition, or even, some would say, their impertinence. But this abrasiveness is usually only felt by intellectuals—to whom the ad may not even be addressed.

Is advertising a trendsetter? It might initially appear so, but here the answer is really 'No'. How much more important as trendsetters must be the influence of magazines, television, cinemas, plays, books and music. But we are all painfully aware that advertising reflects the problems of our society on to a gigantic screen daily.

Is advertising honest enough? We have probably the most honest advertisements in the world. Yet we have improved considerably in the last five to ten years. We have further to go, and the advertising industry is still not satisfied. Most of the improvement has been due to the great work of the Advertising Standards Authority and the Code of Advertising Practice Committee of the whole industry. The Board of Trade think that we are doing a good job. Mr Wood, however, has suggested that there is evidence that the voluntary codes have been flagrantly disregarded. Such evidence, if it exists, cannot have been easy to find. The Advertising Standards Authority had only about 200 complaints of any kind in the last year—out of millions of press advertisements alone. Where is this evidence? All my evidence points to the good behaviour of the vast majority.

Finally, what about the advertising business itself? Are we worried? Yes—and probably more than all the others put together. But we worry about rather different things.

We are a very specialized industry. It is hardly a useless task to specialize, in our view—most industries do it. And like so many others, we are a necessary specialization. We help to keep the goods flowing from factory to home, here and overseas. We help keep up employment, and make profits for the manufacturers (and ourselves). From these profits come funds for government, for education and social welfare among others.

We, being specialized, worry about things like:

—understanding the consumer better. Probably the consumer is so complex that she (or he) will never be properly understood. It is a difficult prospect to try to stand in the very shoes of the people who are our markets
—understanding markets better
—making advertisements more efficient—even 'better'
—refining our mass media knowledge and approaches, so that the 'scattergun' of mass media approaches with its wasteful overspill is not used so much. We need to get more cheaply at the narrower segments of the people forming the product's potential market
—getting proper measurements of difference between, say, use of television and press
—making the advertiser's pound go just as far as possible
—watching out for undesirable trends developing—such as 'knocking copy' wars that confuse and don't help the consumer
—policing our own affairs voluntarily and efficiently.

These are some of the things we are constantly worrying about. And just as sometimes people say to us that it is futile to spend a whole day, week or even month, on some small aspect of selling a cereal or a toothpaste, so we say that some of the leaders of opinion might often be better employed than trying to pick theoretical holes in a business they so woefully misunderstand. They might concentrate instead on looking carefully at some of the more important issues of life, like the balance of trade, inflation, economic growth, employment, crime, education and so on.

We know that we are filling our world with the sights and sounds of advertising—the words and pictures, the jingles and jangles, the crying and the crowing. Are we doing a good thing for the world we live in? Amongst the ranks of the advertising people, there are few doubters. For what could take the place of advertising?

For those who have never had to sell anything, I should like them to consider what action they would take if they woke up on a Monday morning to find they owned a bicycle factory— making twenty bicycles a week and employing four people. The only way of paying those employees on Friday would be by selling the twenty bicycles. Perhaps as a result of going through this exercise mentally, one can expect a better understanding of the manufacturer's selling problem. It is too easy to feel one-self on the side of the angels—but is this because one is living in the clouds?

The heart of the 'Should we worry?' issue really lies in the economic and social context. In economic terms it is basically a choice between the competition and dynamics of our free though imperfect market at work, and the academic's easychair-theorizing of what John Hobson has called 'a world dancing to some lifeless quadrille of perfect supply and demand, perfect price mechanism, perfect competition'. With all its short-comings the present system is working to the people's benefit. The alternatives are theories, unproved and perhaps unprovable.

In social terms, the question becomes 'Is the interest of the community safer under a system in which industry responds to the tastes, attitudes and wants of people as they are? Or should the whole flow of mass communications be so controlled that a tiny intellectual minority can impose its pattern on society?'

Our legislators are right to worry about all this—but not too much—for there are many other equally important social problems awaiting solution. As for the consumers, they do not need to worry very much. They are well safeguarded by the laws. There are money-back guarantees and other guarantees to safe-guard them when they are in trouble or have complaints.

Perhaps the only people who really need to worry are the advertising people themselves. They have essential standards to keep, and to improve. This is easier to expect than to achieve.

Part three

Forms of control

7

Copy control in television advertising

Archie Graham

Knowledge of the situation which exists as regards control of television advertising in the public interest is not very widespread. So I shall try to set down as many of the facts of the situation as I can, starting off with a fairly short and somewhat historical section about the introduction of Independent Television and the development of the standards that exist today.

It is now a matter of minor social history that the Television Act of 1954 had a very rough and stormy passage through Parliament. *The Times* said in 1954, that the initial proposal to set up ITV was attended by 'a scene of noise and confusion seldom seen in the House'. The original Act gave ITV a life of ten years, so there had to be a new Act in 1964 if the service was to continue. This Act was presented to extend the life of ITV for another twelve years, and it went through without opposition. The uproar was over. A unique experiment had been seen to work. It was unique that a public board should be set up to provide a *public service* of broadcasting, but get its programmes from private enterprises under contract to it; and that the whole of the revenue should come from the sale of 'time' to advertisers. In the same way as advertisers bought space in the newspapers they would buy time on the television, and would have nothing to do with the programmes or with any programming decisions.

The 1964 Act strengthened the Authority's powers but left the fundamentals undisturbed. A good deal of the early uproar was about advertising and it was not all from one side of the House. It came from all quarters, because a lot of people were sincerely worried about the prospect of opening such a powerful medium to advertising. We had no experience of it in this country, of course, but we heard a lot of what was supposed to go on in the United States. We had heard of some horrible things going on in commercial radio before the war, and it was understandable that in 1954 people should have been upset. The biscuit probably went to one Member of Parliament amongst all the foretellers of doom. He asked the House to visualize a television programme tour of the Royal Yacht, and he said, 'What will happen—the carpets and the furniture will be described over the air for the benefit of the advertisers. And this will lead to the spread of Communism up and down this land.' He might have been joking, but if he was joking, he was the only one, because tempers were running high on all sides in 1954.

But there was a calmness about advertising in the House in 1964. There was a calm acceptance of the average of six minutes an hour that the Authority allows, and the three breaks an hour, which is how its distribution works out. Everybody seemed to have come to the conclusion that here was a reasonable way of paying for a service, instead of charging a bigger licence fee. It's as simple as that to Parliament, to the Independent Television Authority and to the people of this country. To the advertiser, it is a channel of communication to his potential customers. It is accepted. There is no argument about it now. It is part of the fabric of our lives.

I do not think I am being contentious when I say that in the sphere of advertising standards, the advent of Independent Television, which looked as though it might be a social disaster, has turned out to be a social asset. Because of it the standard of advertising in this country has improved noticeably. There can be no doubt at all about that. Advertising standards have improved because of the interaction of three main forces: the force of public opinion, the force of the Independent Television Authority under the Television Act and, a very important third force, the force of the self-control of the advertising industry itself.

Everybody in 1954 knew that television advertising would have an unusually powerful impact and that its power would have to be used with responsibility. But it's odd, very odd to recall that, in 1954, Parliament was satisfied that in the press of this country the advertisers had already achieved an admirable standard. From *Hansard* it can be clearly seen that it was felt by Parliament that the television advertiser should aspire to, or should be forced to reach, a comparable standard. Mr George Darling, now an important Minister, and the late Sir Leslie Plummer, made very interesting speeches along these lines. But Parliament was mistaken. These admirable standards were not to be enough.

The surprising factor, which sprang directly from the sharp and inescapable impact of the medium, was the way in which the public gave thought, not only to what the advertiser was saying or trying to say, but to the way in which he was trying to say it. People took television more literally than they had ever taken print advertisements. A simple example will show the difference. 'Persil washes whiter and it shows' had been on the hoardings and in all the newspapers for years. There were a little boy and a little girl in cartoon. One had all the shadows taken out and the other had the shadows over-greyed a bit. Nobody thought anything about it. Now do that on the television in live action and, bingo, 'misleading advertising' is the immediate cry. A lot of the conventional exaggerations and age-old advertising clichés, which seemed good enough in print, turned out to be ridiculous and indefensible when they were translated into sound and motion, and were being looked at and listened to by a newly-attentive audience. A new situation developed in this country as soon as advertising began to walk and talk.

There was, moreover, another crucial difference in the conditions attached to the new medium. It was run by a public board. Ministers could be questioned in Parliament about the performance of the Independent Television Authority and members could criticize the techniques and the claims made in individual advertisements. Thus the question of advertising standards was thrown into the political arena as well as becoming a public issue. A lot of fast re-thinking had to be done. The advertisers reappraised their own techniques and the centralized controls within Independent Television became firmer and more complex, to the limit of the powers to be found in the old Act of 1954. Within a very short time these arrangements began to develop efficiently and smoothly. In 1964, Parliament was so impressed by them that they were written into the Act of 1964 in considerable detail.

One has to smile when one hears advertising men point out in all seriousness that advertising is not free to do what it might like. It is strange that the public should occasionally need to be reminded of this. In fact there are over thirty Acts of Parliament which restrict, control or otherwise affect advertisements. These range from the Accommodation Agencies Act of 1953 back to the Venereal Diseases Act of 1917. But, in a sense, the most generally powerful of all these Acts is the Television Act.

This Act gives to a public board, the Independent Television Authority, the duty and the power to exclude from television any advertisement that could be said to be misleading. Secondly, the Act requires the Authority to decide, in consultation with the Postmaster-General, the classes and descriptions of advertisements and methods of advertising that are not to be acceptable for broadcasting. Thirdly, the Act requires the Authority to draw up and impose a code of standards and practice for the regulation of all television advertising. So it is reasonable to say that the Independent Television Authority is, by statute, one of the country's instruments of consumer protection in the field of advertising. So much for the basic conditions under which the Authority operates. Now we can look at the present situation.

There are 22,500 new television advertisements a year. They do not simply 'offer for sale'. They use salesmanship; they do their utmost to persuade viewers to buy and to keep on buying this or that product or service in preference to others. There are a great many approaches to the job of selling thousands of different products or services, and obviously it cannot be a very simple task to ensure that not one of these thousands of advertisements is likely to mislead, or that all of them are acceptable in a multitude of other respects. It will be obvious from the 'Independent Television Code of Advertising Standards and Practice' that there is a lot to take into account in relation to 22,500 advertisements a year. How is this done?

In the first place it is sensible to bear in mind that the firms which use television for their advertising are reputable people who want to stay in business. They subscribe to voluntary codes of practice designed to raise standards of advertising through self-discipline in all media. They accept that the use of such a powerfully persuasive medium as television presents special problems and calls for a great deal of responsibility. They are, and always have been, prepared to co-operate with the statutory powers-that-be in working out, and sticking to, sound principles. If you look at the thing from the point of view of the reputable advertiser's self-interest, he has got nothing at all to lose and a great deal to gain from powerful safeguards, because they heighten the quality of the medium and keep out the spivish minority that hangs about on the fringes of marketing, just as it does around other areas of human affairs. So, for that reason alone, the advertising industry, tensed up though it may be at times about our attitudes, is generally speaking in favour of high standards in television.

The Authority fulfils its obligations at two levels. First it is concerned with general principles, and draws up a code in consultation with an advertising advisory committee, a medical advisory panel and the Postmaster-General. Then, in co-operation with the programme companies, the Authority's advertising control staff examine the advertisements in relation to the rules, before they are accepted for broadcasting.

The advertising advisory committee is appointed by the Authority in accordance with a constitution laid down in the Act. It has an independent chairman and twelve members. Four of the members are broadly representative of the public as consumers. Four are concerned with medical advertising— from the Ministry of Health, the BMA, the British Dental Association and the Pharmaceutical Society. The other four are from the advertising world. The committee is concerned mainly with broad principles. It plays a very important part in the preparation and periodic review of the code of standards and practice. With its balanced membership, it provides a first-class forum for the exchange of views on general standards between advertising experts and those outside the industry.

A Medical Advisory Panel is also appointed by the Authority under the terms of the Act, in consultation with the main twelve or thirteen bodies of organized medicine, such as the BMA, the Royal College of Physicians, the Royal College of

Obstetricians and Gynaecologists and the British Dental Association. The panel of nine or ten distinguished doctors, dentists and specialists in various branches of medicine are consulted in the drafting of the code but their main function is to advise the Authority on medical advertisements in the broadest sense. No advertisement for a proprietary medicine, a toothpaste or for any one of a wide range of quasi-medical products, is accepted unless it has been approved by the Medical Advisory Panel.

The code, to which I should now like to refer, is a very comprehensive document (see below—Appendix A). It has a general section and two important appendices: one of them an Appendix on advertising and children, and the other on the advertising of medicines and treatments. You will find a very important provision in rule 2. Almost all of the statutes, which at present deal with consumer protection, were written before commercial television. In the case of some Acts, notably the Merchandise Marks Acts, rules applicable to other forms of advertising may not, on a strict interpretation, cover television advertising. Television advertisements must, however, comply in all respects with the spirit of these Acts. The code rules out subliminal advertising. There never has been such a thing in this country and just in case anybody is stupid enough to wish to use it, the code will prevent them. There can be no advertising of religion and politics—you cannot buy time to propagate views or to sell ideas, only to sell goods and services. The unacceptable products or services include those of money lenders, matrimonial agencies, fortune tellers, undertakers, unlicensed employment services, betting (including Pools), cigarettes and cigarette tobacco.

The detailed rules on advertising and children exclude from advertisements which large numbers of children are likely to see, anything that might result in harm to them physically, mentally or morally, or which would take advantage of their natural credulity or sense of loyalty. For instance, children must not be encouraged to enter strange places or speak to strangers in an effort to collect coupons. Free gifts must be shown either in a child's hand or against something which reveals the true size of the gift. Children should not be seen to be unattended in street scenes unless they are obviously old enough to be out on their own. And an open fire in a sitting room with children must have a fire guard in front of it.

It is easy to run away with the idea that you can write any set of platitudes, wave them about, and everything in the garden will be lovely. But these rules are strictly applied. For instance, an advertisement has had to be re-shot before it was accepted for broadcasting because the 'mum' went off and left a bottle of medicine at the bedside of a child 'invalid'—obviously a very silly practice. You might be inclined to wonder whether we go too far, but you cannot accuse us of falling far behind our necessary function.

Let us consider the medical code. The highly detailed Appendix on medical advertising stresses the need for great care to avoid the harm that may result from exaggerated, misleading or unwarranted claims. In addition to ruling out the advertising of a great many classes of product or treatment, it excludes the use of phrases like 'loss of virility', 'not to be used in cases of pregnancy' (which, in the old days, was an invitation to buy the stuff in a case of pregnancy), or 'miracle ingredient'. Such phrases cannot be used on TV, nor in the press, either, these days.

The medical code rules out testimonials by people well known in public life, sport, entertainment, etc. It disallows any reference to a hospital test of a medicine unless the medical committee of the hospital is prepared to vouch for its validity. It prohibits the presentation of doctors and others who might seem to be giving direct professional advice to viewers. The result of these stringent controls is, I suggest, to be seen quite clearly on the screen. The television advertising of proprietary medicines is concerned almost entirely with conventionally formulated products for the relief of common ailments: headaches and minor aches and pains; colds and influenza; digestive troubles; minor skin ailments, and so on, for which self-medication is generally held to be reasonably safe. Not only are there no claims to cure cancer or consumption—which are banned by law in any case—there are no 'iodine lockets' which were advertised in prewar days for curing rheumatism, no copper bracelets, no hair restorers. This is hardly surprising for

the first step in the consideration of the advertisements is to
check the medical facts. Whether it is a brand of aspirin, a
cough medicine, an indigestion tablet or what-have-you, the
medical claims must be acceptable to the independent con-
sultants of ITV.

The next step is to consider the method of presentation, the
words and phrases and pictures to be used. This involves purely
subjective judgements. Nearly everything in the area in which
I work is bound to be a matter of opinion, and at this point it is
as well to remember the fact of life that an advertiser is trying
to communicate with as many as he can of 13 or 14 million
families in their own homes, and *in their terms*. What are these
terms? It must be relevant that seventeen or eighteen copies of
the *Mirror* or the *Express* go into the homes of this country for
every copy of *The Times*. In television, 'Coronation Street' and
'Compact' reach through to more people than 'Tempo' and
'Monitor'. The advertiser of mass produced goods is not, I
submit, in the uplift business. He is in business to sell things
and it seems to me to be a fair assumption that if he tries to do
this with a *Times* or 'Tempo' style stamp on his advertising, he
is fast on his way to the bankruptcy court. So he figures out how
to communicate, and his method of communication might not
be one that would appeal to some of us! You may think it
sentimental, not intellectual enough, or full of mumbo-jumbo.
Well, fair enough, some of the stuff makes my own stomach
turn. So what? You have to have better reasons than these
before you start interfering in a free society with another's right
to communicate—a right granted to him by law.

The basic thinking around some of the questions of presentation can be illustrated if we consider the application of two of
the rules. In rule 4 in Appendix 2A of the code there is provision
against impressions of professional advice. It is designed to
make sure that no doctors, nurses, dentists, chemists, etc., or
actors playing their parts, can appear on the television screen to
advise viewers about the merits of a proprietory medicine. Also,
as I have already mentioned, we do not allow public figures, like
football players or stage stars to appear in medical advertisements to give personal testimonies. In other words, we are ruling
out the delivery of personal testimony by professional medical

people or 'big shots' whose personal power could have some effect on the viewers. We are saying 'Sell your medicine as a salesman and not as a doctor or a Gilbert Harding'. That is why, in front of a distinguished looking chap who sometimes looks more like a doctor than any doctor I know, you will find a desk plaque or some other sign which labels him very clearly as a 'market research' man or a 'sales director' or some other worthy, but very unmedical person. There have been arguments from time to time about gentlemen in white coats. You will see one occasionally fiddling about with a test tube or a pencil or carrying out some experiment. He is not allowed to talk to viewers to give them the benefit of his professional advice. But the Authority and its advisers don't think that viewers will come to much harm from the mere sight of a white coat, which seems to us to establish that a laboratory plays some part or other in the manufacture of a medicine. But the wearer must not talk. There is not a complete ban on all references to doctors. These must be reasonable in their context and must state established facts. Take, for example, an advertisement for Disprin. It says that Disprins are soluble aspirin and that soluble aspirin is the kind doctors prefer. Since the ITV medical advisory panel have confirmed that doctors do have that preference, it seems reasonable enough to allow the public to be so informed. The code does not rule out such truthful statements.

Rule 1 of section 1 of appendix 2B is also important. It prohibits the offer of cures. It does not, and it was never intended to rule out offers to relieve symptoms or to make you feel a bit better while you have got the 'flu by relieving your headache or bringing down your temperature. Given the strictness with which the medical facts are checked, it has not been thought reasonable to go so far as to prevent an advertiser from truthfully offering to alleviate a symptom—to get rid of your headache. We know that this is possible and the doctors say it is not only our imagination. So the advertiser is allowed to say so. But the first part of this rule is a little ambiguous. It says that advertisements should not contain 'a claim to cure any ailment or symptoms of ill health'. We adopted this rule from the British Code and I think it was written around the time, many years ago, when people were definitely claiming to *cure* symptoms, by which I mean get rid of them for all time. Get rid of a headache and never again get a headache—that was the sort of thing. We are in no doubt as to what the rule means; the advertising industry is in no doubt as to what it means; and the way in which we interpret it causes no harm to anybody else as far as we can discover.

Of the 22,500 new television advertisements a year, 15,000 are, fortunately, from small local advertisers. They are mostly the 5- and 7-second slides with very simple messages in sound and vision, to publicize local stores, restaurants, transport services and so on. They take up only 6 per cent of the total advertising time, and, because of their extreme simplicity, they can safely be cleared for acceptance locally.

The other 7,500, however, are those you would think of when you think of television advertising—the advertisements that occupy 94 per cent of the time. They have to be submitted for clearance to a central clearance point in Independent Television —the point at which my office co-operates with the Independent Television Companies Association which has a special secretariat for the purpose. The advertiser, before he films his advertisement, submits the script to this central advertising control point. The scripts, including the proposed visual treatment, are examined in every relation to the Authority's rules. Advertisements for medicines, toothpastes, medicated shampoos—in fact anything that has to do with health or fitness—go to the Medical Advisory Panel. In a year there are about a thousand scripts for advertisements of that sort dealing with about 250 different products. The general inquiries involve not only the checking of all claims, but also checking the validity of testimonials, and the identity of people who are to be introduced by name to deliver these testimonials, and discussion of the total impression that might be given in an advertisement whatever its line by line purport might seem to be. After all these inquiries, about 90 per cent of the scripts are found to be acceptable as they have been submitted by the advertising agencies. The other 10 per cent are amended by the advertisers to meet the Authority's requirements. Of the purely medical cases about a third are amended before acceptance. Finally the finished films based on these approved scripts are seen by the staffs of the Authority and the Programme Companies in daily closed-circuit sessions to make sure that they are in keeping with the scripts and that nothing unforeseen has developed during the film production process. About 2 per cent of the films need some minor editing before final acceptance for broadcasting.

Those of us directly involved in the control of television advertising and those of you involved in the production of television advertisements may perhaps be forgiven if we take a little comfort from tributes paid to the medium at the end of the first ten years. The Prime Minister has talked about the beneficial advances in standards and practice of television advertising, '. . . not least the reforms made in medical advertisements'. In an editorial contribution to *Contrast*, the television quarterly, the writer, having commented on the ten years' developments in television programming, went on to comment on a most creditable record in the area of advertising where the whole system had seemed to its critics to be likely to be most suspect. Then there was a *Guardian* piece on 22 December 1965 —of which I would not want to make too much. It asked the BBC Board of Governors to have a close look at the Authority's Annual Report and to look in particular into ITA's arrangements for the control of television advertising to see whether some similar arrangements might be introduced to improve the BBC's control of its programmes!

8

Advertising and the Press: an editor's outlook

Michael Finley

It is as well in discussing the relationship between advertising
and the Press to have one important fact stated quite clearly and
incontrovertibly: without advertising there would be no
Press.

The high cost of newspaper production means that the
financing of any publication by circulation revenue alone is
virtually impossible. At any rate in the case of daily newspapers
there are strong grounds for believing that the reader is simply
not prepared to face the price involved, which would be somewhere in the region of 1s. or 1s. 6d. per copy depending upon
the size of the paper. Nor can one look to the admitted savings
which may be made possible by the introduction of new techniques to bring about any significant alteration in this basic
situation. The high capital costs involved particularly where one
is thinking in terms of circulations in excess of, say, 100,000 still
demand a higher revenue return than would be available from
sales alone.

The extent to which the Press is dependent upon advertising
revenue for its continued profitability varies enormously. In
broad terms it is probably true that the proportion of income
derived from advertising varies inversely with the sale. Thus
the accounts of Beaverbrook Newspapers Ltd published in
June 1965 show that 52·3 per cent of income came from circulation and 46·1 per cent from advertisers. When one deducts,
however, the discounts to newsagents from sales revenue and
the commission to advertising agents from advertising revenue,
those percentages are almost exactly reversed. In the case of my
own company publishing a morning paper with a circulation of

70,000 and an evening paper of 200,000, the percentages are nearer 25 per cent circulation, 75 per cent advertising.

This is, of course, the background to the misgivings so frequently expressed by those who see something sinister in this financial dependence of the Press on advertising, and, therefore, on advertisers. But surely the alternative would only place the Press in a position of even more dependence directly upon circulation. One could well imagine that any newspaper or other publication which allowed itself to be debased by advertising considerations would be even more prone to debasement by circulation considerations. In any case as we shall see later in the end the two amount to the same thing.

Let us admit then without equivocation that the Press is financially dependent to a very great degree upon advertising for its continued existence. Superficially this would appear to place advertisers in a strong position of influence *vis-à-vis* the editorial content and direction of the publications which they use. Is their position in fact as powerful as it would appear, and is that power, to whatever degree it exists, exercised?

As a journalist, I am surprised by the degree of apprehension manifested by apparently reasonable intelligent people about the influence of advertising on the Press. Let it be said that I am equally astonished at the repeated protestations of those newspapermen who would have you believe that advertising has no influence at all. Perhaps to be charitable they even believe it themselves. If so, their thinking is remarkably shallow.

Perhaps what they mean is that there is no influence in the traditional 'bogyman' sense which most often inspires the question in the first place. This would find its crudest expression, say, in the case of a local newspaper where some prominent businessman in the town with a comparatively large advertising account attempted to have details of a scandalous divorce action, driving offence, or some such, suppressed as a consideration for his continued 'support'. Let me say at once that in fifteen years I have never known such a case or even heard of one.

Such approaches may have been made, but I challenge anyone to produce evidence that they have ever been successful.

It would be extremely naïve, however, if one were to say that because advertising does not 'influence' the Press in this sense that, therefore, it has no influence. The tremendous financial dependence of newspapers upon advertising revenue means that the influence is of a much more basic, albeit indirect nature. The real effect of advertising has been upon the basic patterns of the Press.

At this point it will be useful to consider very briefly how newspapers have evolved since the repeal of the Stamp Act in 1855 opened up the prospect of a vast new readership. The introduction of the penny newspaper combined with the rapid advances made in the education field gave rise to the mass circulation paper. It is probably true to say that the main concern of such papers was with their readers; the advertising revenue must have been a secondary consideration and indeed probably not a consideration at all. This basic preoccupation with the direct appeal to readers in the mass continued in more recent times and indeed was the motivating force of the circulation battles of the 20's and 30's. Here it is probably worth acknowledging that the success which newspapers gained in those battles was probably more a reflection of promotional ingenuity than of editorial merit. Francis Williams has claimed that the fact that the *Daily Herald* became the first paper to top the 2 million mark was to a large degree the root cause of its later troubles when the unreal inflation of circulation by promotional activities was withdrawn.

The war period and its aftermath with the rationing of newsprint and the restriction of circulation created an artificial climate in which all newspapers prospered without a great deal of effort and there was always far more advertising than space available.

When newsprint rationing ended, the newspaper industry had hardly had time to settle down to resuming its own civil war when another belligerent appeared on the scene—commercial television. The immediate effect was greatly to exaggerate the competitive forces at work, and, of course, a great many newspapers found it impossible to survive in such rigid conditions.

The results of this were seen immediately in both the national and provincial paper field. In the national field the number of papers became smaller, and the differences between the successful and unsuccessful more marked. The success itself became ever more harshly defined so that even a paper selling $1\frac{1}{2}$ million copies found life difficult. The situation in fact appears to be that the bottom marker will always find life difficult no matter what sales figure can be shown. Thus if one were ever to arrive at a situation where there were only three popular daily papers left, let us say the *Daily Mirror*, the *Daily Express* and the *Daily Mail*, life would still be exceedingly difficult for the *Daily Mail* from an advertising point of view. The reason for this is that no matter how great the bottom marker's sale, it is almost certain that it will represent for the most part a duplication of the sales of one or other of the two above. The only solution is for such a paper to carve out a quite separate market.

This, of course, explains the strength of papers like *The Daily Telegraph* and the *Financial Times* who have survived and indeed greatly prospered with relatively small circulations because of their appeal to special advertisers. The development of this situation has brought about within the newspaper industry in recent years a recognition that circulation expressed in sum numbers is not everything, and that for many papers the road to salvation will lie in the development of a special kind of readership whose appeal is not so much in its sheer size but in its dominance in some particular social or economic strata. In general this leads to the simple division between popular and quality papers, and to the different kind of advertising which each attracts.

A similar result is to be seen in the provinces where the post-war years brought about a considerable reduction in the number of papers, and in particular has brought about a situation where the majority of evening papers now enjoy a monopoly and the numbers of morning papers has been greatly reduced. The provincial morning paper almost without exception has come to see that economically its future can lie only in the cultivation of a special type of readership which will give it access to advertising revenue for which it does not find itself competing with the bigger-selling evening. This process is, of course, accelerated because the evening paper, where it exists, is owned by the same company.

Some of this may seem to be a statement of the obvious but

it should be borne in mind that although the trend may be discernible over a long period, the positive recognition of the situation by newspaper publishers is of fairly recent origin and direct action upon that recognition probably even more recent. In the case of my own company, for instance, it was as late as September 1965 that the final steps were taken to complete a process begun some eighteen months earlier to change the appeal of the morning paper and to recognize that its role should be quite different from that of its sister evening rather than directly competitive with it.

Although it would be an over-simplification to suggest that this change owes its origins entirely to the requirement to seek a different source of advertising revenue from the evening paper, nevertheless this must be seen as at the very least a catalytic agent and probably, in reality, by far the greatest influencing factor.

This then represents the greatest impact which advertising has made upon the Press. It has directed in a very fundamental way the editorial policy in so far as that relates to general content and appeal of newspapers, or at least has consolidated newspapers into certain recognizable groups.

A further illustration of this is to be found in the tremendous growth of classified advertising over the past five or ten years. In so far as the national press is concerned, this is almost wholly concentrated in the quality press. Surely any proprietor who decided to launch a new national newspaper today would have uppermost in his mind the notion that the paper that he produced must be of such a kind as to secure the readership profile which would attract this great volume of advertising?

Of course advertising also affects the content of newspapers in a more direct and down-to-earth fashion. The most obvious example of this, recognizable surely to all, is the advertising feature, whose justification is not its possible reader interest but its potential as a bait to advertisers.

The advertising feature was, I believe, an invention of the provincial Press, but today no newspaper scorns its use although admittedly some are capable of presenting their advertising features in a more sophisticated way than others, and the reader interest varies very greatly. Nevertheless, the dominating factor which decides whether a newspaper prints such a feature or not is acceptability not to its readers but to potential advertisers.

This kind of influence is to be seen in perhaps a less obvious and more insidious way in the manner in which certain sections of newspapers have developed over the years. The City and business pages have grown larger, have become even whole sections on their own. Motoring notes are carried at length and the merits—and perhaps even on occasion the demerits—of each new model discussed at length. Even *The Times* has its women's page.

Now I am not seeking to suggest that the expansion of these sections is due solely to the influence of advertisers, their eagerness to advertise or the eagerness of the newspapers to persuade them to advertise. It is beyond question that to a degree they represent a growth of interest among readers in these subjects and the very proper concern of newspapers to meet that growth. Nevertheless, the advertising consideration is a large and often dominant factor in deciding how much space the newspaper will allocate. A readership interest with no advertising potential will not, I am afraid, commend itself very highly to a publisher unless, of course, it has a massive readership appeal like sport.

British popular newspapers are frequently criticized for their lack of attention to foreign news. It is interesting to speculate what their attitude would be if embassies suddenly started going in for half-page advertisements. Indeed one need not speculate. One has only to think of the many times when the virtues of various parts of the Commonwealth are extolled at length in space surrounded by advertisements usually connected with emigration or investment.

Still having said all this and having pointed out the way in which the content of a newspaper and the distribution of its space is influenced by advertising considerations both directly and indirectly, nevertheless one must come back to this cardinal fact: the newspaper still has to find a buyer. The buyer is the reader, and the reader has to find a newspaper acceptable. The advertiser is not after all indulging in an academic exercise. He is selling either goods or services. If a newspaper were to fill its entire columns with business news interspersed with a few notes on fashion and motor cars, it would be unlikely to find any readership at all and, therefore, even the most gullible financial, motoring or fashion advertiser would fail to find it an attractive proposition as a medium for his advertising.

You cannot produce a newspaper designed principally for advertisers. You have to appeal to readers so that ultimately it is the influence of the reader which counts in any newspaper.

Of course the presence of advertising and the need to secure it brings its problems to the editorial department. Perhaps the biggest bone of contention between the two sides has been the production of the advertising features referred to earlier, and their preparation by journalists.

Journalists have for a long time resented what they felt to be an encroachment upon their right to present the news as they saw it. Now the journalist has come to recognize that his interests are best served by ensuring that the journalistic standards applied to these features are no lower than those applied to the rest of the paper.

There is also the problem of the crooked advertiser. I am not referring here to the question of the validity of claims made in advertisements. This field is adequately covered by the machinery which the advertising industry has itself set up. I am drawing upon personal experience and referring to advertisements placed on behalf of organizations or individuals which are discovered to be basically illegitimate in intent.

In our own case, early in 1965, I was made aware that a number of people, operating as estate agents in Sheffield and advertising in our papers, were operating something less than fully honest businesses. The difficulty for newspapers in a monopoly position faced with this kind of suggestion is, of course, that of proof. If we refuse advertising from such a company, we virtually kill their business. Certainly we have a duty to protect our readers and indeed our own reputation but equally, surely, we have a duty to allow anyone the right to conduct a business until and unless they are shown to be dishonest? Applying the spirit of our law to this situation, one may say that suspicion is not enough, proof is necessary. However, editorial activity in due course unmasked a number of these people and resulted in court cases and convictions.

There was also the case of a company operating in motor insurance whose proprietor was a man with a criminal record. Here again this simple fact was surely not enough to justify the refusal of a monopoly organization to accept the advertising? We had no proof at all that the insurance operation was other than honest. Eventually in this particular case the proprietor was convicted of receiving stolen property, but to this day the rectitude of his insurance operation, although its administration in some particular instances has been criticized occasionally in the courts, has never seriously been questioned. (Under the new requirements relating to the capitalization of insurance companies it is now defunct.) Nevertheless, our newspapers have not carried his advertising for some time.

One of the best demonstrations that I can think of of the way in which the editorial department will function freely in spite of apparent advertising interest is in the recent case of the BMC cars which were suspected of a basic design defect. You will all recall that this story was given the fullest possible cover in all our newspapers, irrespective of the fact that every single one of them stood to lose a considerable amount of advertising from British Motor Corporation—had that company chosen to exercise its power in this way. It is to the credit I think of both the Press and the company that this factor did not prevent the matter from being fully ventilated. Indeed the Minister of Transport at the time even went so far as to criticize the Press, in my opinion quite unfairly and unjustly, for the way they had taken the matter up. This would indicate to me that Government is far more likely to be swayed by material considerations than are newspapers.

How far in fact should a newspaper be responsible for the advertising it carries? In law, of course, the editor bears full legal responsibility for everything that appears in his paper and no distinction is made between editorial and advertising columns in this respect. But what we are really concerned with here is not niceties of the law but simple consumer protection.

It was once suggested to me by a member of the present Government that a newspaper should be totally responsible for all the claims made by the people advertising in its columns. I suggest that this is an absolutely impossible requirement.

Suppose that an advertiser buys a small space in your paper and advertises, say, 20,000 pairs of binoculars. Are you to examine every pair of those binoculars? Are you even to make sure that there are in fact 20,000 pairs available? Surely all that can be required of a newspaper is that its advertising in general shall conform to certain standards and that in so far as individual advertisers are concerned it must give them the benefit of the doubt until such time as complaints received would indicate that they are no longer worthy of the benefit. In such cases I feel newspapers should be quite determined in their refusal to accept advertising from clients who are in the least respect doubtful.

I still think that there is room for greater control over certain types of advertising, but nevertheless I feel that newspaper advertising is as reliable a medium as you will find and one which on the whole conforms to a very high standard.

Any discussion of advertising and newspapers would be incomplete without a reference to the tremendous growth of classified advertising in the past few years. Today this is so much a commonplace that it is startling perhaps to recall that as little as five years ago there was very little classified advertising in the majority of national newspapers, and that a great many provincial newspapers have multiplied their classified advertising many times.

Without a doubt it is the impact of Lord Thomson's North American experience which has inspired this great advance, and again without doubt it must have been the salvation of many provincial newspapers, certainly my own.

Speaking from a provincial standpoint, the great quality of classified advertising is that it is local in character and, therefore, lies perhaps much more within the control of a local newspaper organization. It affords a protection, if protection is needed, from the impact of the mass advertiser and again particularly in the provincial newspaper field provides a cushion against the worst effects of any display advertising being syphoned off by rival media, such as local radio and television stations.

There has been some discussion here of the responsibilities of the advertiser to the Press. There has been a suggestion that the large institutional advertisers have a duty to preserve the diversity of the Press.

No, no and no again!

Advertisers have only one duty other than the simple one of honesty in their advertising; their economic duty to their share-holders, which is another way of saying that their duty is to preserve the economic stability of their companies. They must place their advertising to their own best advantage. In so far as the freedom of the Press depends upon its economic ability to survive, it is a freedom which cannot be conferred. This is a bitter lesson that a great many of our would-be Press preservers and reformers must learn. The only freedom which the Press can properly enjoy is the freedom which it earns by making itself financially secure and independent of any single interest.

Postscript

Since this paper was delivered, the question of newspaper economics has been highlighted by the problems of *The Times*, the *Guardian* and the *Daily Mail*, and has been very much discussed and debated. There have been the usual calls for yet another Royal Commission, suggestions for Government subsidy and sponsorship, all of which I must reject out of hand as impinging too greatly upon any real freedom.

I ask those who suggest that a newspaper could be run along similar lines to the BBC to consider how free the BBC really is, and to ask themselves what they would think of a newspaper which was unable to state an editorial opinion?

The only suggestion worthy of any consideration that has come out so far has come from Mr Tom Baistow, Assistant Editor of the *New Statesman*, who has proposed that legislation might be introduced to restrict the extent to which any newspaper could depend upon adver-tising revenue.

This proposition is a recognition of the fact that the selling price of newspaper is totally uneconomic and that the newspapers which enjoy smaller advertising revenues are, therefore, placed in the position very often that the more newspapers they sell the bigger loss they are likely to make. Newspapers in a strong financial position can be seen to have a vested interest in keeping selling prices down. Experience shows that any newspaper which attempts to increase its selling price unilaterally is going to suffer in terms of circulation anyway, and so the vicious circle goes on. In any case the gap between the actual selling price and a realistic one is so large that no newspaper could attempt to bridge it single handed.

No newspaper today so far as I am aware draws less than 55 per cent of its total revenue from advertising sources. Most draw considerably more than this. If one were to make a limit of say 50 per cent, any newspaper drawing more than 50 per cent of its revenue from advertising would be faced with the choice of either reducing its advertising revenue, which is hardly likely, or, much more likely, increasing its circulation revenue, which can only be done realistically by increasing the selling price. The bigger papers would thus be made more amenable to an increase in selling price, and although so far as they are concerned this would only have the effect of increasing their profits, it would enable other newspapers to draw upon a greater revenue directly from their readers.

As things stand at present, it is perfectly possible for a newspaper such as for instance the *Daily Mail*, to go on increasing its circulation and simply driving itself further and further into trouble because the gap between its circulation and its more successful competitors is so great that even an increase measured in hundreds of thousands is likely to have little, if any, impact upon its attraction as an advertising medium.

9

Problems of the advertisement director

W McMillan

It is likely that historians and sociologists of the future will ponder over the problem as to why in the 50's and 60's of this century so many apparently intelligent and often sophisticated people allowed advertising to worry them so much. One would have thought that apart from international problems, the continuing domestic problems of slums, poor educational standards, the loneliness of the aged, housing for the poor, etc., would have used up their marginal emotional energies.

In a BBC talk, Miss Laski is reported to have said, 'I hate all advertising'. This of course couldn't be true. For example, does she hate political party advertising, theatre and lecture advertising, book publishers' advertising——? Certainly not, as she is an author! What she probably meant was that she hates advertisements which are used to encourage the demand for consumer durables such as washing machines, and advertisements which encourage housewives to try out new frozen foods, new chocolate bars, new brands of flour; and, lest I be accused of cowardice, new detergents. Of course, when Miss Laski reads *her* morning paper it is unlikely to be one which enjoys a good coverage of what is called the mass market. Probably her views of advertising have been influenced by ITV commercials. If I am correct in this assumption, then surely she should view BBC 1 or BBC 2 and retain her hate for something of real importance.

I remember well the story of Ernest Bevin (there is some doubt as to whether he was only repeating the story). The remark was made about 1947 when he was in America, and he was going round among the homes of what we used to call

working-class people. He was amazed at the number and
variety of washing machines and refrigerators, etc., which he
saw. 'In Britain,' he said, 'there is poverty of desire!' He was
speaking, of course, of material desire.

Those who are old enough will remember that in the early
30's many people were involved emotionally with the problem
of want in the midst of plenty. Of course, again, we were thinking of material want. There are many things still wrong in our
society and many people are distressed about them. It could
well be that *the* evil is the old one, though it sounds pompous
to say it, of the hearts of men. If it be so, then surely it is a
problem for the churches, the humanists or the politicians.
People should stop thinking that, but for the market place, all
would be well with our society. Selling, with marketing skills,
which include advertising, is certainly on the market place.

May I say a few words on detergents. In 1947 or 1948, I
heard Sir John Boyd Orr, as he then was, address an audience in
New York City. He was very worried about the continuing
shortage of animal and vegetable fats and, as everyone knows,
old-fashioned soap is largely made from animal and vegetable
fats. He obviously had little knowledge of the immense effort
then being made by the soap manufacturers to produce a new
man-made detergent. Of course, there is still hunger in the
world but at least the often strident marketing of the new man-
made detergents reduces the demand for fats, which can be
better used as cooking oils or margarine. Perhaps the detergent
people spend too much on advertising, I cannot say. All I
know is that the 'Levers' and the 'Procter & Gambles' of this
world are not amateurs.

As my title suggests, I am responsible for the advertisements
which appear in the *Guardian*. Some two-thirds of our revenue
comes from advertisements and one-third comes from the
readers who buy the paper each morning. The other so-called
serious newspapers are in a similar position but the popular
press, selling millions of copies daily, is much less dependent on
advertisement revenue. It might be possible to publish a paper
like the *Mirror* or *The People* and, keeping the pages down to
six or eight, sell it at 7*d.* and still make a small profit. It would
be an odd-looking newspaper, but people might get used to it.

Until the introduction of commercial television, the press, which takes in magazines as well as newspapers, had really no competition as far as national advertising was concerned. Even with the competition of ITV the press still gets approximately 55 per cent of the money spent on advertising. In 1963 the total amount spent on advertising was estimated to represent approximately 2·6 per cent of consumer expenditure, as compared with 2·2 per cent in 1938.

In spite of what one might think, responsible publishers do try hard to ensure that advertisers keep to the rules laid down by the various watchdog organizations. On occasions an undesirable one slips into a paper or magazine, but in most cases it is the human element that has failed. After all, the Law Society tries hard to enforce its rules of conduct on its members, but on occasions, even in that profession, the sharp one gets away with it.

When Mr Graham was speaking of the rules of ITA he made a remark about marriage bureaux. Well, of course, it's very easy for anyone in ITA to say, 'Let's not accept marriage bureaux advertising!' This is, in fact, the policy with most national newspapers. But because of articles which have appeared in the serious newspapers in the last five years, it was obvious that a change had taken place in the public attitude towards marriage bureaux, and I thought that, as an advertisement director, I had to recognize this. Loneliness is a terrible thing. In the old days, people met at church organizations or even on a cruise in the Mediterranean. Now a properly-run marriage bureau can offer some social services. The problem is that some marriage bureaux are not properly run. Should one therefore take up this ITA solution—no marriage bureaux advertising? I did not think it should be as easy as that. I decided rightly or wrongly that if I could satisfy myself that a marriage bureau was properly run, then morally I had no argument against taking it into the *Guardian*. This has brought endless problems, and from a practical point of view, I wish I had never even started it. Who am I to decide what a properly-run marriage bureau is? I even encouraged an Association of Marriage Bureaux to be started. This has a very pompous set of rules but it has not been very successful because it has only three or four members. Nevertheless I think that the point is quite a good one; publishers have got to take up a fairly radical, liberal outlook as regards what they will accept and what they will not accept. I can assure you that on the *Guardian* we do this with a reasonable sense of social conscience!

One service we give is to look after the readers' complaints. Now I do not know what other papers do. I can only tell you what we do in the *Guardian*. We investigate each complaint and this is a time-consuming job, because some of our readers expect too much. One thing they do expect is that the advertiser can read with 100 per cent accuracy their names and addresses, which are often written in a most illegible way. The typical complaint concerns servicing facilities for consumer durables. Now, having answered them all, I know this problem inside out. If you get someone who buys a dish-washing machine and he or she has a home in the West of England, there may be one mechanic on the ground who is going to service the machines in that region. If he is ill, or if, by mistake, he takes a wrong spare part what happens is not because of any evil policy on the part of the manufacturer. It is simply because in this affluent society it is difficult to get mechanics, and, having got them, it is difficult to keep them. But I do not want to exaggerate the number of complaints we get. There is not one outstanding on the file—all have been sorted out.

It is quite clear that it is very much easier for the people in commercial television to set rules. It is a monopoly, and the people who have taken part in it have made a lot of money. To a certain extent, their problem is very simple, compared with ours. When it comes to the press, with its newspapers, and its hundreds, if not thousands, of magazines, the problem is much more acute. One thing you must remember is that publishers are not all members of the same association, and anyone who wants to do so, and has the money, can begin a publication tomorrow.

10

Problems of the professional
in a highly vulnerable field

Murray Leask

A major problem for those involved in the advertising business is to decide just how much attention to pay to criticism of our industry. The record indicates quite clearly that its members have not been unheeding of sound and pertinent criticism, and have elaborated for themselves a code of practice, which should do credit to any profession. Yet one cannot help feeling somewhat impatient from time to time with much of the criticism, which shows little insight into the realities of modern business, and the complex of pressures which are constantly affecting the operations of those engaged in this highly specialized and competitive sector of marketing.

The arguments of those who are antipathetic towards advertising so often centre round a belief that the consumer will be bamboozled and persuaded into buying goods and services which were not really wanted. Some of these people obviously believe in a different sort of society, from the one in which most of us earn a living. Basically they regard advertising as a symbol of the free competitive society, which they appear to abhor. The most vocal critics of advertising tend to be socialist planners, who believe that advertising, if permitted to exist at all, should not be permitted to shape the pattern of consumer demand, nor to operate in the interests of the producers. They usually seem quite unaware of recent trends in advertising in the Soviet Union and the other socialist planned countries of Eastern Europe. They believe firmly that advertising in the United Kingdom is excessive, and that the cost is borne by the consumer. It has little effect on them to point out that as a percentage of the net national income, which already accounted for

2 per cent some thirty years ago, total expenditure on advertising accounts for only 2·1 per cent today.

Some of these critics, I grant you, would accept advertising, and even regard it highly, if it were designed to educate the consumer, and to develop his taste. But it is rather doubtful whether this is a healthy attitude. For 'taste' would appear to be defined as being that of the critic, the arbiter of all good things, the imposer of 'desirable standards'.

We do not live, however, in that sort of society, and I do not think that many of us would wish to do so. We live in a highly competitive world where, both at home and abroad, our standard of living depends upon ever-increasing productivity. This in turn depends on our ability to sell more and better goods at profitable levels.

In the middle of this business of selling, is the advertising agency. Within an agency, whether large or small, are brought together people with special skills whose primary function is to help clients sell their products, whether these be industrial products, detergents, chocolates, motor cars, commodities like milk, or services like banking, insurance or the Post Office. These products and services they will endeavour to sell in the most economic and most effective way at their disposal.

The agency, however, can only be as successful as its clients' products. Both the voluntary controls set out in the Code of Advertising Practice and those administered by the Advertising Standards Authority together with the Merchandise Marks Act make it highly unlikely that dishonest and misleading advertisements will appear on television or in newspapers and magazines. Client and agency are both motivated towards the truth because they are well aware that from day to day the consumer is becoming increasingly discriminating. And in a highly competitive world it is natural that it should be difficult to successfully introduce a new product to the market place. The advertising agency exists to advise its clients how best to do so. Nor is it really surprising that as the economy grows and as people have, as a consequence, more and more money to spend, advertising should become more conspicuous. Advertising is inevitably the most conspicuous part of selling, and it should not be too difficult to understand that if advertising were not conspicuous, it would hardly be effective.

If we are to maintain any pretensions to commercial realism, we have simply got to acknowledge that advertising has become an essential element in any modern industrial strategy. The great majority of successful manufacturers survive by the periodic introduction of new or improved products. These products are not foisted on to an unwilling public, but rather result from an increasingly sophisticated public demanding the latest and the best.

The marketing activities of big advertisers have been attacked by a number of politicians and academics, perhaps most notably by Professor J. K. Galbraith. He has been arguing that in advanced societies the consumer has been dethroned as a result of the marketing operations of the great technocratic producing corporations which decide what people should want and what people are going to get. This thesis may have some truth in it, but it is too contemptuous of the support which consumers have given to some of the products offered to them by the big companies and too disregarding of the refusal of consumers to support other ad-backed corporation choices.

It is plainly unrealistic and even shallow to suggest that motor cars, washing machines, refrigerators, television sets, cosmetics, drip-dry shirts, detergents and all the rest are merely ad-created wants; and to be sceptical about the benefits which these have brought to the great majority of consumers. All these products have needed initially the impetus which advertising could give them. All have needed continuing advertising support to keep particular brands viable and profitable from the point of view of the producer firms. Some may need advertising to help even out seasonal fluctuations in demand, or alleviate over-stocked situations. Others may need advertising to keep retailers persuaded to stock them.

In such instances the advertiser can be helpful in breaking down obstacles to change, and even promoting more rational patterns of living. Perhaps the most comforting trend in British living standards at present is the growing adoption of central heating. Ten years ago there was hardly any demand for this. It was left to the advertising industry by an enterprising advertiser who put over the idea that central heating could be cheap, clean, modern, could eliminate fuel delivery problems and cut down housework; that it offered warmth, comfort and space to modern minded families. All of which is obvious and sensible enough after these attitudes have begun to replace the old traditional one attached to roasting hearths, draughty rooms and smoky chimneys. All this might have come in time by other forms of education and persuasion, but there can be little doubt that advertising helped to produce good social results in a remarkably short time.

Over the question of cost, too, there hangs an air of unreality. The Whitehall belief that only Whitehall is cost-conscious must amuse the Procter & Gambles, Unilevers, Cadburys and ICIs of this world, just as it must amuse the small manufacturer, conscious of his bank overdraft limit. Whether large or small, manufacturers work with their agencies to choose the most economical rather than the most wasteful means of reaching the public. Success for the manufacturer depends on selling in the most economical way when introducing a new or improved product to the market. Ensuring this is a major problem for those specializing in advertising. No manufacturer is going to throw his money away on special offers, price cuts or television advertising, without what appears to him to be good reason. With his agency he will have worked out the most economical way of persuading the consumer to select his product as opposed to his competitors' products. And, of course, the more he makes and markets successfully, the cheaper his product will tend to become, and the less the consumer will have to pay across the counter for the goods. If the agency is not effective in this respect, its chances of retaining accounts is slight.

The agency's viewpoint about advertising and its relationships to clients and public is simple and straightforward. Since we are in the business of selling, our task is to design advertising which will be as persuasive as possible. Since we know that the public increasingly tends to dislike and even resent poor taste, our task is to ensure that our clients' advertisements are in good taste. Of course, there are people who believe that girls in bikinis are poor taste, while there are others who believe it to be immoral to advertise tobacco or alcohol. These people are entitled to their views, just as are those who believe that you should not walk more than three miles from home on the Sabbath. The final arbiters of what is good or bad taste in a free society, however, are the public, and no manufacturer will willingly take the risk of offending his customers. No one would want to deny that it is possible to corrupt, but critics tend to find difficulty in pointing to any single advertisement which, wittingly or unwittingly, seems likely to do so. Some of the most vocal critics constantly fall back on purely subjective or minority beliefs in their discernment of the corrupting influence of advertising. In their attacks, they see advertising somehow as the main force in developing tastes for alcohol, or tobacco or speed which have existed in normal people for centuries, and which are quite acceptable to the great majority of the community.

Some of the more serious problems which the advertising professional has to face in his relationship with his clients can perhaps best be seen in terms of involvement, access, experimentation and persuasion. Ideally the part which the agency can play with the manufacturer in bringing advertising campaigns to successful fruition has been succinctly assessed by Lee Iacocca, of the Ford Motor Company.

According to Iacocca, the agency's role depends on four freedoms in its relationship with its clients. These he lists as:

1. Freedom of involvement. Agency personnel should be involved in the development of products, and encouraged to use their knowledge and research to ensure that the product, new or old, is what people want.

2. Freedom of access. Freedom for the agency staff to talk to everybody in the client's organisation, from executives to people on the factory floor, who know the facts.

3. Freedom of experiment. An agency requires money to make experimental commercials, or develop unusual promotional ideas, in order to ensure that their advertising sells in the most effective possible way.

4. Freedom to persuade. Not so much the freedom to persuade the public to buy the product, but the freedom to persuade the client that the agency thinks he is wrong, or that he should change his product, or improve it, or scrap it. The agency is paid for its ideas and reactions, so it must remain free to criticise.

In saying all this, I am less concerned with defending advertising, than to make clear the role of the agency, and to state my own belief that advertising plays an essential part in improving our standard of living. By inspiring a constant desire for better and better products and services, which help to satisfy human aspirations and material needs. Advertising agencies often detect a marketing opportunity well in advance of their clients. The agency can help its clients to test markets and to find out what people really want. Advertising cannot, of course, compensate for bad product planning or faulty manufacture. You may fool the housewife once, but that is all. Fortunately, every organization and association concerned with advertising, whether in the centre or on the fringes, willingly accepts the limitations voluntarily and legally imposed on them to ensure that the public is neither deceived nor corrupted. But advertising is an essential ingredient in a free society. For a free society means the opportunity to choose and select. Those who believe in a free society are also convinced of that society's right to choose to remain free.

11

Voluntary control within the profession

J C Braun

At the outset, I want to make clear my interpretation of community. I take this to mean two things, the community at large, or the people of this country, and the business community. The difference between these two conceptions is the difference between the area in which consumer protection is a motivating factor in the question of control and that in which fair trade is the source. This difference is of interest because it was from the latter activity rather than the former that the concept of control in advertising sprung. However, in the present context, we are concerned with public confidence and with the people as a whole, as consumers.

It is not my function to justify advertising—the need for it is evident enough—but I should like to pass on two quotations:

Let me begin with a basic proposition that must be accepted by everybody—apart from a few frugal and ascetic hermits—that advertising of goods and services is an essential feature of a modern, competitive trading economy. Indeed advertising in its widest sense has an essential role in a free society. (Mr George Darling, MP, Minister of State, Board of Trade, at the Guildhall, 1 December 1964)

In spite of its occasional excesses, advertising is a major source of consumer information. Without it, consumers must produce their own information and, in consequence, markets are more imperfect and choices are poorer. (Professor D. S. Lees, in *The Times*, 24 January 1966).

My task, however, is to consider voluntary controls within the profession, and I have decided that the subject can be better

119

dealt with if it is re-titled. So I have amended it to read, 'Self-regulation within the industry'. My reasons for the change are these. The words 'voluntary control' may give the impression that the system is something you can opt out of. On the contrary, those in advertising have taken great pains to set up a system of control which they pledge themselves to support. The use of the word 'profession' is wrong, because the interests of advertising are much wider. Advertising is like a three-sided pyramid, one side being the advertiser, another the media through which advertisements reach the public, and the third the advertising agencies which plan, prepare and place the advertisements. The pyramid may be referred to as the advertising industry, and the agencies, while not being a profession, may be said to be the professional side.

Nor is advertising in any sense a separate industry such as steel, oil, drugs and the like. It is not even a separate business, except for those persons employed in advertising agencies. Rather, it is a tool or instrument used by many different types of business men in many widely different fields and industries for their own highly specialized purposes in their own highly specialized ways.

When we talk, then, about the regulation of advertising, we must be careful to remember that we are not talking about the regulation of an industry, but of a multi-faceted diversity.

Statute law
There is a tendency to look upon self-regulation as an alternative to, or substitute for, the controls imposed by law and government. They are not mutually exclusive but complement each other. And lest anyone may think that advertising is lightly controlled by law let me quickly disabuse him. For it may come as something of a surprise to those people who call for more legislative control over advertising to learn that there are already nearly sixty Acts of Parliament which do this in one way or another.

One could say that there is more law affecting advertising than can be traced. When the Town and Country Planning Act 1947, was passed, the planners wanted to provide a complete code of legislation affecting outdoor advertising and the poster business. This was never done because it was found that there were so many local Acts containing some measure of control of advertising that it was not possible to trace them all. They got as far as something like 400 and then gave up.

These Acts that we do know about vary in range from the Larceny Act 1861, which made it an offence to publish an advertisement saying that 'no questions will be asked' if a thief would return stolen property, to the Television Acts of 1954 and 1964 which set up detailed procedures for controlling the 'commercials' appearing on Independent Television. Some statutes, such as the Advertisements (Hire-Purchase) Act 1967, set out specific rules for advertisements. There are others, such as the Cancer Act 1939, and the Pharmacy and Medicines Act 1941, which prohibit advertising to the general public of treatments for a number of serious diseases and complaints; and the Noise Abatement Act 1960, which restricts advertising by loudspeaker and bell-ringing. One Act, at least, the Civil Aviation Act 1960, abolished one medium altogether when it banned sky writing and sky shouting.

The reproduction in an advertisement of coins, banknotes and stamps is governed by the Coinage Offences Act 1936, the Forgery Act 1913, and the Post Office Act 1953, respectively. The Betting, Gaming and Lotteries Act 1963, affects competitions and 'give-away' schemes, while statutes such as the Indecent Advertisements Act 1889, and Obscene Publications Acts of 1959 and 1964, speak for themselves.

Advertising is also subject to general Acts such as the Sale of Goods Act 1893, which contains principles of contract, and the Copyright Act 1956, which governs the law on this complicated subject. Packaging is covered by the Weights and Measures Act 1963, and Sections 1 and 6 of the Food and Drugs Act 1955, affect advertising.

Statutory instruments
The many regulations which have been made under the Town and Country Planning Acts rigorously control posters everywhere and forbid them altogether in high amenity districts known as 'areas of special control' such as beauty spots.

In the field of food, the Labelling of Food Order, 1953, as

amended, places important restrictions on the labelling side of advertising. This Order is being replaced by new regulations as a result of the first report of the Food Standards Committee whose second report contains recommendations concerning wider aspects of advertising.

Other regulations have been made under the Hire-Purchase Acts and other statutes.

Self-regulation

Beneath this weight of legislation spreads out a network of self-regulation. Self-regulation is, of course, voluntary. In its purest form, it is entered into without compulsion or threat of penalties. More significantly it operates in three specific areas which are not dealt with by government regulation:

1. It encourages the development of individual, company and industry standards which are higher than those imposed by law.
2. It deals with matters of public taste, welfare and interest which are beyond the proper scope of legislation.
3. It promotes obedience to the law itself.

The merits of self-regulation have been aired by various members of the Federal Trade Commission of the United States, itself a governmental body. Their attitude will be seen from the following quotations:

Law enforcement agencies such as the FTC were created to root out the weeds, but there is danger in harming the carefully cultivated plants by the misapplication of weed killer. Care must be exercised in combating the evils found in some advertising, lest in the process, all advertising be harmed. This would be a catastrophe, not only to advertising but to our entire economic system.

Pressures for increased governmental control of advertising have been building in recent years. The best defence against such pressures is a demonstration that individuals and groups within the advertising industry can meet their responsibilities on a voluntary basis.

I believe in self-regulation. A free man can and will accept responsibility as well as privilege ... Individual integrity is the mortar cementing the foundations of our system of government. If the mortar cracks and crumbles in spots, it can be repaired. But the house will not stand without mortar.

It may be interesting to note also the following extracts from the Statute Law Revision Committee Report upon False and Misleading Advertising of the State of Victoria, Australia:

There are in existence already Associations of both advertising agencies and national advertisers, which each subscribe to a code of ethics said to be based upon the best information that can be obtained from personal observation and inquiry on the British Code. The code would appear to be effective in overcoming most of the evils aimed at. (Para. 95)

Generally, the Committee believes in the principle of the less restrictive legislation the better, and considers that the recent efforts towards more thoughtful voluntary control over misleading advertising should be given a reasonable period to develop and be tested.

The Committee formed the view that the misleading aspect in advertising is the area where voluntary restraints are most likely to be effective, and advocates that they be given a fair chance. (Para. 127)

The Consumer Protection Bill was introduced in 1966 to repeal the old hotchpotch of Merchandise Marks Acts, and implement, and in some places to go beyond, the recommendations of the Molony Committee. I will not digress on the detailed imperfections of this Bill, but state simply that a poorly enforced statute merely brings the law into disrepute and fails to serve its purpose (e.g. the Litter Act). In any case, as the Minister of State said on 19 February 1965, the very large element of voluntary control must continue to make its vitally important contribution. Advertising standards are not merely standards of law observance but also standards of conduct which statutory regulations can probably never be drawn fine enough to cover fully or be flexible or sensitive enough to guide. Nor, of course, can the processes of law move as quickly as the self-discipline system.

The field of advertising

It is as well to reflect for a moment on the immense area to be covered. Over 1 million display advertisements appear in newspapers and magazines each year, about 7,000 new television commercials are made each year, and many more thousands 'spots' are filled. The number of small 'classified' advertisements which appear in national daily newspapers alone reaches a total of over 17,000 *per week*, and if the 1,400 local newspapers are included as well, the total reaches something like 25 million classified advertisements each year. Many of these come from members of the public and are handed in on scraps of paper, or telephoned, at the last minute.

This figure does not include the vast number of advertisements that appear in our rich variety of periodicals of every kind, covering trades, hobbies, sports, specialized studies and general interest. Nor does it include hoardings, bus sides, escalators, handbills, communications by post and a mass of material at the point of sale, in shop windows, on counters and in-store displays. The very magnitude and range of advertising outlets demolish all suggestion of a pre-publication checking system by any outside body.

The control system
Building up from the bottom, the structure falls into five sections:

1. Self-regulation by individual advertisers, companies and corporations.
2. Self regulation by individual industries and industry groups.
3. Copy committees of media and disciplinary bodies within the various associations in advertising.
4. Code of Advertising Practice Committee.
5. The Advertising Standards Authority.

1 *Self-regulation by individual advertisers*
This, where it is operated under strict internal procedures is, perhaps, the most meaningful of all. It involves the adoption and enforcement, by an individual company, of its own specific rules or code of advertising standards and ethics. This is additional to the British Code of Advertising Practice to which I shall refer shortly. The Code puts the onus of proof on the advertiser to substantiate his claims. Responsibility for ensuring that no misleading advertisement appears rests, and must rest, primarily upon the advertiser and his advertising agency. Most of the very large advertisers in this country have their strict rules. Some have legal departments which have to check every piece of advertising copy and material before publication to ensure that it complies with the law, the code and the house rules.

2 *Self-regulation by individual industries*

This is operated through trade associations or consultative bodies within a product or service field, setting up standard codes of ethics and practices. There is usually some form of disciplinary committee to ensure that members stick to the rules. Examples of these are the Association of British Correspondence Colleges, the Association of Unit Trust Managers, and the General Optical Council.

British Code of Advertising Practice

The remaining sections are all concerned with the operation of the British Code of Advertising Practice and it is to this that we shall now turn. This has the support of seventeen organizations representing every aspect of the advertising industry. It was first issued in 1962, revised in March 1964, and a third edition was published in 1967. The Code incorporates the British Code of Standards relating to the Advertising of Medicines and Treatments which was drawn up in 1946. This Code has been set up for the guidance of all advertisers, advertising agencies, those controlling advertising media and suppliers of various advertising services. The Code requires that all advertising should be legal, clear, honest and truthful; and defines practices agreed to be undesirable by the organisations which have subscribed to it. As the function of advertising is advocacy, it is acknowledged that within the provisions of the Code, advertisers should be free to put forward the best case for the acceptance of their products by consumers.

The Code is in two parts, the first dealing with general principles such as presentation, appeals to fear and descriptions and claims. These relate to the control of scientific terms and statistics, testimonials, price claims, guarantees, disparagement and imitation. Special categories of advertising requiring careful scrutiny are instructional courses for so-called 'degrees', mail order advertising and direct sale advertising (which came under scrutiny when 'switch-selling' was rampant; this was the form of trading in which salesmen call in response to an advertisement for a cheap model and then try to persuade the purchaser to switch to a more expensive model).

Part B of the Code relates specifically to the advertising of medicines and treatments and has twenty headings under which specific references are banned. Thus, no advertisement may claim to *cure* any ailment, to diagnose by correspondence, to offer medicine or treatment for serious diseases or conditions which should receive the attention of a registered practitioner, or use the words 'College', 'Clinic', 'Laboratory' or such terms, unless there is in fact such an institution. Strict rules govern advertising of products or treatments for slimming, weight reduction or figure control, 'natural' remedies and haemorrhoids.

To understand how the Code works we must return to the structure of the control system and the three remaining sections.

3 Copy committee of media and the disciplinary bodies

There are no fewer than sixteen of these bodies, including the Joint Copy Committee of the NPA and Newspaper Society; the Copy Committee of the PPA; the television controls which have been fully explained already by Mr Graham; separate committees covering posters, cinema and 'clutter' on business premises; the separate code for proprietary medicines exercisable over all members of PAGB, whose Copy Committee handled over 1,300 pieces of copy last year; the Professional Purposes Committee and special panel of referees, both operated by IPA, and the Copy Claims Advisory Committee of ISBA.

Worthy of special mention, because of its scope and responsibilities, is the Advertising Investigation Department of the Advertising Association. The AID is not only looking *out* for infringements; it also looks *into* those it finds or which are referred to it; and it reports back the results. Secondly, it discusses with the advertiser or agency any copy which contravenes the rules and helps them to bring it into line with the Code. Thirdly, it functions not only as an investigation department but as an advice bureau; for it receives and deals with many inquiries for guidance on copy, on the correct interpretation of the rules and many other advertising matters. It retains the services of medical, financial, legal and other experts to advise in every field of advertising. It issues a periodic Confidential Bulletin to members of the Advertising Association and also supplies information in particular cases. The department also issues guidance leaflets upon certain categories of advertising, but these are not of a confidential nature and are available to the whole industry, and to the public (see above p. viii for abbreviations).

4 *CAP Committee*
In the past, difficulties inevitably arose because the various committees have given occasionally what seemed to be conflicting opinions. To prevent differences of interpretation of the Code and to ensure that all concerned work to the same high standards, their sponsoring bodies, now seventeen in number, have established the British Code of Advertising Practice Committee (CAP Committee), on which they are all represented.

Through this committee, the individual organizations exchange information about matters discussed in their own Committees and notify each other not only of their decisions, but also of the questions which they still have under discussion. They also put to the full CAP Committee any questions about which there might be conflict of opinion between the constituent members.

The CAP Committee's decisions are communicated to the sponsoring bodies which in turn communicate them to their members. The advertiser and the agency concerned are also informed by the CAP Committee or by their own organization. The most drastic decision is a recommendation of complete non-acceptance—drastic, because it means that no reputable medium will accept the advertising and that the agency, if it persists, may put its recognition, and hence its own business, in peril.

The Committee gives advice to the Advertising Standards Authority upon matters relating to the operation of the Code and ensures that policy laid down by the Authority is carried out.

5 *The Advertising Standards Authority*
This was set up in 1962 with the object of 'the promotion and enforcement through the United Kingdom of the highest standards of advertising in all media so as to ensure in cooperation with all concerned that no advertising contravenes or

offends against these standards, having regard inter alia to the British Code of Advertising Practice'.

The independent chairman is appointed by the Advertising Association for a term of three years and the members are appointed by the chairman on his personal invitation. They serve as individual members and not as representatives of any particular interest or organization. The Advertising Association has accepted responsibility for financing the Authority and this is done by an annual grant of money for the Authority to use as it may think fit.

The one thing about which all the members of the Authority are most emphatic is its independence. It must not be biased in favour either of consumers or of manufacturers, or of retailers, or of any other section of the community. True, it is financed by the Advertising Association. But a moment's reflection by the Authority's detractors, or at least the reasonable ones, would show them that the Advertising Association can have little possible interest in spending money on a body which is not independent. Oddly enough many of its detractors come from the academic world. Nine-tenths, nearly, of the income of universities in Britain comes from grants in one form or another, yet members of the university staffs would be horrified if it were suggested that this financial dependence made them stooges of the Government.

The sole justification for the existence of the Authority is its independence. The first chairman was an eminent professor of economics, and he has been succeeded by Lord Drumalbyn, a former Minister of Pensions and National Insurance and Parliamentary Secretary, Board of Trade. Of the other ten members of the Authority, one half is entirely free from advertising interests and one half has experience of advertising—two from among advertisers, one each from advertising agencies, the press and television. The five with advertising experience have proved, in fact, not one whit less independent in their outlook than the 'independents' and are, of course, indispensable in enabling the Advertising Standards Authority to make judgements and proposals that are practical as well as independent.

The Authority deals with any matter relating to advertising. No particular rules were laid down in the first place, except that it would be normal practice to deal with the industry through the Code of Advertising Practice Committee. It was intended that the Authority should impose its will on the industry by this means. Although the CAP Committee is responsible for the Code, the Authority has a duty also to see that changes or additions are made when the public interest demands it. The Authority is also the public body to which any individual or corporate body can make representation upon any matter relating to advertising. If the Authority feels that, in spite of the instructions which it has issued, its wishes are not being met, either by an individual or by the industry as a whole, then it has a duty to say so publicly.

As to complaints, some come from the general public, consumers and traders, some come from competitors. In the USA, with its background of 'fair trading' legislation, complaints tend to come largely from competitors. In this country we seem to prefer to get on with the game rather than appeal to the referee. Nevertheless, competitors do not hesitate to complain when occasion arises. Consumer complaints about advertisements come in to all parts of the control system. Some are passed on to the Authority by outside bodies such as the Board of Trade, the Consumer Council and Citizens Advice Bureaux.

The Authority does not have its own monitoring staff, though complaints also originate from observations of the members of the Authority. The AID acts as a common service for the Authority, for the CAP Committee and for the Advertising Association. There would be little point in the Authority duplicating that work and also having staff to look for breaches of the Code. The scope and regularity of monitoring obviously depends on the money available for staff. This has recently been increased, and is likely to be further increased in the near future.

But the system of self-regulation should not have to rely on centralized monitoring alone. Last year the Advertising Association made a drive to strengthen the network of publicity clubs throughout this country. There are now thirty-seven, falling into five regional groups. Each has appointed its own vigilance officer, who is able to detect infringements locally and, if necessary, report them to AID.

Statistics

I could produce figures of the cases dealt with by the Authority, the CAP Committee and all the other regulatory bodies, but these figures would mean little unless accompanied by a detailed analysis of their breakdown. Suffice it to say that the breaches of the Code which are brought to light are a tiny fraction of that huge number of advertisements created annually, to which I have already referred. Here it may be appropriate to quote from the 1964 Report of the Federal Trade Commission.

After mentioning its appropriation of $12,214,000 and its staff of 1,144 the FTC went on to say:

Statistics are so often misunderstood. Superficially, the more complaints and the more orders the commission issues, the more efficiently does it serve its purpose; yet, such statistics are misleading. The ideal statistic for the FTC to report would be that it had taken no actions at all because none were necessary. The goal is . . . to prevent violations of law rather than to achieve a statistical record for stopping them.

Changing the rules

An important aspect of the control system is its readiness and ability at all times to change its rules whenever it appears that there is an urgent need to do so. Furthermore it is always looking at sections of the Code to see what improvements can be made. From the Authority's point of view, new rules were needed in 1963 to deal with advertisements presented in editorial style, and with advertisements inviting inquiries which would lead to calls by representatives at the home of the person inquiring, and possibly to switch selling. New rules were also made in 1964 to deal with guarantees, appeal to fear and disparagement of competing products. In 1965 we continued to study guarantees in the light of the previous change, and have just issued a new ruling. Rulings regarding treatments for slimming and baldness, and for advertisements involving 'inertia selling', have also been made.

Sanctions

Some people say that the system is defective because there are no sanctions. They are labouring under a misunderstanding. Would you rather be fined £10 or £100 or have all your advertising stopped?

The sanctions could hardly be more powerful. Where an advertiser fails to satisfy any section of the control system, his advertising is immediately stopped and he is denied access to the columns of the press or the television screen until he can justify his product or the claims he makes for it. This powerful sanction is never applied lightly or arbitrarily, and the advertiser and his agency are given every opportunity to make their case. They are told in detail the nature of the objections and through AID they can be assisted with copy.

Uninformed critics have referred to the committees as 'Star Chambers', and consider that all this complicated and specialized work should be done in public. To make such comments is to fail completely to understand the basic principle of self-discipline. Statutes have to be administered through public courts because liberty may be at stake (if penalties include imprisonment) and sanctions are compulsory. The advertising control system is based on consent and discussion. The public at large are not really interested in the niceties of amending copy.

Sanctions, of course, when they have to be applied, are always applied rationally and by people with a sense of responsibility. It would be very easy to allow personal prejudices to interpose. It was Lowell Mason, a former member of the FTC, who wrote in his splendid book *The Language of Dissent*; 'If everybody's pet aversions against advertising were adopted as criteria for what should be banned, there would be no sales promotion.'

Publicity
It is often asked why the Authority has not named offenders against the Code. I should like to answer this by quoting from its First Annual Report:

The Authority is happy to report that it has not been necessary during this period to resort to publicity as a disciplinary measure to pillory, as it were, a chronic and persistent offender against the minimum standards required by the advertising codes. As the Chairman explained at the Advertising Association Conference in May 1963 'The Authority will always wish to wield this instrument with deliberation, with due regard to the needs and circumstances of the particular case.' We have no intention of brandishing publicity as a fetish, or a tomahawk, notching up scores of success. We are not scalp-hunting. In investigating complaints the Authority's first aim is to see that inadvertent lapses are fully adjusted, that improved checks against recurrence are instituted, and that complete satisfaction is obtained. No doubt the public statement will be used as occasion seems to require.

Is the System Comprehensive?

Another criticism, and one in which there is some merit, is that there will always be a small fringe who will not belong to any of the organizations which are pledged to uphold the control system. Nevertheless non-members understand as well as members the advantage to themselves of complying with the rules and the need to do so if statutory control is not to be imposed. Happily, when infringements are drawn to the notice of non-members they almost all agree to take the appropriate action. Personal contact, with explanation of the system, works extremely well.

Self-regulation or legislation?

That wise American judge, Justice Earl Warren, has stated:

In civilised life, law floats in a sea of ethics. Each is indispensable to civilisation. Without law, we should be at the mercy of the least scrupulous; without ethics law could not exist.

And, going back twenty-five centuries, Confucius said:

Guide the people with governmental measures, or regulate them by the threat of punishment, and they will try to keep out of jail, but will have no sense of honour. Guide them by morals and principles of social responsibility, and they will have a sense of honour and respect.

Looking to the future, I can do no better than to borrow the summing up in the Report of the Advertising Advisory Committee to the US Secretary of Commerce:

1. Self-regulation must be approached realistically. It is not, and never can be, a cure-all for all advertising problems, any more than government regulation is a panacea for all social evils. A realistic objective is steady and measurable improvement, not the attainment of some absolute and impossible goal.
2. Self-regulation, by definition, must be approached as the expression of free men in a free society, rather than as an instrument for imposing the tastes, will, wishes, ideas or bias of any outside element on any business group. Any attempt by an outsider to dictate the terms and

conditions of voluntary action denies the very nature of the process itself.

3. The key to genuine self-regulation is the individual; and any effective programme for building self-regulation must be directed to him—and must stem from him. Our approach must always be to men, not to methods.

Neither our economy nor our society is static. Public values, tastes, and standards are subject to change. New media evolve. New products and services are developed. Concepts, tastes or codes applicable to one decade may not reflect, or be adequate in the next.

Every individual in the business community is called upon to re-appraise and reassess his practices constantly, in the light of the conditions at the time. All those engaged in the advertising control system will encourage such a continuing reappraisal and seek to spotlight the new areas and opportunities for effective self-regulation which meet the needs of the times.

To all this I agree wholeheartedly, and would only wish to add that these principles and attitudes seem just as appropriate to the British community as to the American community.

12

Can legislation play a useful role in promoting better advertising?

Harry Street

I am speaking as a lawyer, and although, in a sense, I might seem to be striking a critical note, I accept the case for advertising. It suits me very well altogether, especially when I listen to Mr Finley. I am one of these people who, I think, can read through newspapers without noticing any advertisements at all, and it suits me very well that I do not have to pay two shillings for my *Guardian* or whatever it may be.

What I would like to do is to talk about the present state of the Law and then take a brief look at the new Bill, which the Government sprung on us the day before the Hull by-election, and on which I certainly do not regard myself as an expert.

I see the legal problem as something like this. That the main function of the Law ought to be to ensure that the consumer is not deceived about the product which he is being invited to purchase. There are other smaller issues with which the Law should also concern itself, I suppose. It should be concerned to see that one manufacturer does not steal an unfair march on another by virtue of false advertising, and there are such matters as the question of amenity with respect to outdoor advertising, problems of safety, morality and so on, but I would have, thought that its main aims are to protect the consumer, and, secondly, to ensure fair business competition.

One has first of all to ask the question, how effective is the Law at the moment in securing these ends? There is not any section of the Law which has as its object the attainment of these ends. There is no law which has been designed to protect the consumer against advertising. It is a case of asking the question to what extent has the set of existing legal principles been found capable of being applied to problems affecting advertising?

The first way in which the Law could look at the problem is illustrated in more or less the first case on the law of Contract that any law student is ever told about. This is a case towards the end of last century where a firm called the Carbolic Smoke-ball Company made something called a Carbolic Smokeball. They advertised in the *Pall Mall Gazette* a reward of one hundred pounds to anyone who contracted influenza, or a cold, after having used their product as directed. They said they deposited a thousand pounds in a named bank to show their sincerity. A Mrs Careill read the advertisement; bought the product and contracted influenza. She thereupon sued the manufacturer in breach of contract, and succeeded. But the whole gist of the case from the point of view of the lawyers was that because they had deposited this thousand pounds in a named bank, this in the court's view showed that this represented a serious intention to enter into contractual relations and distinguished it from a mere puff. But no doubt all advertising agencies are familiar with Careill. At least I assume so because no advertisements of this sort, to my knowledge, ever appear today, and it is perfectly clear that merely to guarantee the efficiency of the product, to say that it will do what it says it will do and so on, will never afford an action of the sort that Mrs Careill had. You must have something to reinforce the intention to enter a legal contract such as was evidenced by this deposit of a sum of money in the bank.

The next branch of the Law which could be relevant is the Law of Deceit which, in effect, says that if a person makes a false statement knowing that it is fraudulent, with the intention that someone else shall act on it, and that if that someone else does act on it and acts on it to his detriment, then he can recover damages from the person who makes the false statement. This, in practice, is a terribly difficult action to win. The courts have rather been taken in by this word 'fraud'. They have confused, I think, the consequences of saying, that a man committed fraud if he was being prosecuted in some criminal proceedings where the outcome could be imprisonment, and the consequences in the sort of action I am talking about, where all that is at stake is whether or not the defendant has to pay cash compensation to the person who suffered loss.

At any rate, what they have said is that they require a greater burden of proof on the part of the litigant in these actions than in any other kind of civil action. So, you have got to be able to prove that the statement is untrue, that it was a statement of fact, that it was a material statement, that the ordinary reasonable citizen and not merely the gullible would have been taken in by it, and that this man was, in fact, taken in by it, and that he suffered a cash loss in consequence. It proves to be so difficult to get over all those hurdles that the law of deceit is not an effective weapon for the protection of the consumer.

I will not deal with this next point in detail, but you might ask the question 'Would there be any remedy for making a careless statement?' While it is true that the ordinary idea of law is that if a person is careless and he causes loss by his carelessness, e.g. when driving a car, he has to pay damages to the victim, and despite a certain change of direction on the part of the courts in the last year or two, I think it safe to say that an advertisement which carelessly makes an inaccurate statement about a product will not subject either the medium of the advertisement, or those responsible for it, to any action in damages for negligence. The law of negligence has not gone that far, and if I were taking upon myself the role of prophet, I would be pretty confident that it is not likely to do so.

Then another way in which the law might have been helpful is through what we call warranties arising out of contract. If you sell a product and you make some warranty about its fitness for a particular purpose, then you may find yourself liable because the product does not live up to the warranty. But the position here is that you can only rely on a warranty where you and the person who made the warranty, if you like, are in a contractual relationship with one another. It is perfectly clear that if the advertisement is put out by the manufacturer and you rely on it and go to the retailer to buy the product and it does not live up to what you were told in the advertisement, that you cannot rely on the warranty contained in the advertisement because it wasn't a warranty linked with the person with whom you had the contract, namely, the retailer.

On the other issue of unfair competition between rival manu-facturers of competing products, there is another branch of the law. All these branches of the law I am talking about are, in-cidentally, nothing to do with Parliament but are branches of the common law developed by the courts themselves. There is another branch of law which says that if you maliciously make a false statement which is calculated to harm another person in his business, that also is something which gives rise to an action for damages. Curiously enough, one of the earliest cases in this branch of law also related to advertising although I do not recall another in the advertising context. This was a case where there were competing children's foods and perhaps it is not the sort of thing that would often happen today. The one product was being sold over the counter and a rival manufacturer had entered into an arrangement with the retailers that whenever they sold the product that they would wrap it in an advertising wrapper which said how much better the competing product was. This was in the 1890's or certainly over fifty years ago. You can probably tell me whether this is common practice today. The case went to the House of Lords. The aggrieved manufacturer's action was based on the branch of the law I have just mentioned —injurious falsehood—and the House of Lords rejected the claim. Their main ground was an issue of principle. They said that they were not prepared to become the forum for the decid-ing of the rival claims of advertisements made by manufacturers. That if they allowed this action, the inevitable consequence was that they would be inundated with litigation by manufacturers seeking a free advertisement out of the law lords with all the kudos that would be associated with that medium and they were stopping it right away.

It is interesting that, although the American law is basically derived from ours in these aspects, on almost every one of the points on which I have touched it is more comprehensive—and affords a wider remedy—than ours does. With regard to deceit their law of deceit does not call for that same rigorous standard of proof of fraud. Their law on unfair competition is couched in general terms, and they do not regard themselves as unable to allow advertisers to settle their differences in the courts. Warranties made by a manufacturer can be linked with the retailer so that the man who buys the product can sue the manufacturer for this warranty in many states although he is in no contractual relationship. I say many states because this branch of the law is not a federal matter in the United States. It is a state matter and, therefore, one can only speak of what particular states have done.

Now, I do not want to give the impression that Parliament has done absolutely nothing about the law of advertising. It has, but almost solely in the criminal area. There is a miscellaneous rag-bag of statutes which prohibit advertisements about certain matters like cures for cancer; hire-purchase advertisements are controlled; money lenders cannot say certain things in advertising and so on. In every one of these cases the result is a criminal penalty. It is not legislation designed to protect the consumer by giving him an action in damages. In almost every one of these statutes one can see the social connection between the statute and the background of the time. There is no cohesion in this branch of the law at all; much of it results from private members' bills as a matter of fact.

There is only one statute with any claim to generality and that is the Merchandise Marks Acts. They were a series of statutes going back towards the end of last century, the purpose of which was primarily to protect traders against the consequence of other traders making false descriptions of their goods. The sort of thing they covered was statements about the weight or the quality of the goods, and so on. Their sanction, too, was almost exclusively criminal. In a very marginal set of circumstances, there would be a possible chance of the consumer getting damages, but so out of line with the general functioning of the act that I don't think the intricacies are worth mentioning. There was no, and is no, arrangement for consistent policing of traders in connection with Merchandise Marks. The enforcement is left with the Board of Trade, and the Act is riddled with provisions calculated to make it as unlikely as possible that the Board of Trade will ever prosecute. If you want the Board of Trade to prosecute, you have to get all the evidence yourself; you have got to give the Board of Trade security against any costs that may be incurred in the prosecution, and so on. And the consequences are shown by the fact that prosecutions over a period of twenty-five years, by the Board of Trade, average less than two a year. Maybe it is going too far to say the Merchandise Marks Acts are a dead letter, because one never knows how many circumstances have arisen where manufacturers have pursued a certain course of conduct for fear that they would be prosecuted, if they did not observe these Acts. But the rate of prosecution is surprisingly low. The Acts make scarcely any impact on advertising. It is because the retailer won't be caught by a manufacturer's advertisement and is only in trouble over his own advertisement if the prosecutor-consumer can show that it was the false quality in the advertisement which motivated him in buying the product This is not a very easy onus to discharge in practice.

We can see how spotty the legislation controlling advertisements is from one casual illustration I have picked up from last year's *Hansard* when there was trouble about the Universal Health Studios Limited when, under the influence of the organizations with which Mr Braun is connected, the newspapers ceased to publish their advertisements because they did not conform to the standards which the ASA exacted. Then the Health Studios resorted to sending this advertising material through the post, and it emerged that nothing could be done to stop this, that under the Post Office Acts—again in contrast to the position in the United States—no offence was committed by sending allegedly false advertising material through the post, and there was nothing the Post Office could do to stop it. That is briefly the state of the law as of this moment.

Now to the question of reform which will be partly a look at the new Bill, partly a consideration of what I think it is worthwhile considering doing. There are three problems. The first is the adequacy of the definition of false or misleading advertising, the second is the effectiveness of the penalties and remedies prescribed and the third is the efficiency of the methods of administering the law.

I am going to make a series of rather dogmatic statements here about the adequacy of the definition. Protection is much less than adequate if it is confined to fraudulent advertising. I do not think that one could reasonably expect the consumers, or whatever public prosecuting agency is involved, themselves to prove that the advertiser knew the statement was false, and knowing it, went on and published it. This is such a heavy onus to discharge that you are going to make the legislation ineffective if you impose so rigorous a standard. The new Bill, I think, takes on this particular issue a fairly reasonable position. It does not require the prosecutor to show that the conduct was fraudulent, and yet at the same time, it does afford him a defence in certain circumstances. Roughly the position is this, that first of all the medium itself or the agency, if the agency is only a conduit pipe, are pretty fully protected by a clause which says that it shall be a defence to prove that the defendant is a person whose business it is to publish or arrange for the publication of advertisements and that he received the advertisement for publication in the ordinary course of business. That will cover the medium and with regard to the person responsible for the advertising, it is a defence for him to show that the commission of the offence was due to a mistake, an accident, or to some other cause beyond his control, and that he took all reasonable precautions and exercised all due diligence to avoid the commission of such an offence by himself or any person under his control. So in effect, what the Bill is saying is that if the person responsible for the advertisement can show that he took due care to avoid making a false statement, he is not going to be guilty of an offence under the Bill. I would have thought that this is about the right position to take in respect of offences under the Bill connected with the false description of goods.

The provision with regard to statements in connection with services is rather different. It would cover statements about accommodation, facilities, examination of services, location or amenities; forms of travel advertisement; estate agents and so forth. The state of mind required is rather different. You have got to show that the person who made the statement either knew it was false or made it recklessly. The difference is that recklessness is a much more restricted standard than carelessness and moreover, the burden of proving the fraud or the recklessness is on the prosecutor. Whereas in the case of goods, the burden of proving that due care was taken is on the defendant. So a very different position is taken with regard to services in the Bill that taken with regard to false statements about goods.

With regard to false statements about goods, the Bill makes it a criminal offence to make a false or misleading trade description about such matters as quantity, size, composition, fitness for the purpose, physical characteristics etc. This amounts to a pretty comprehensive list of factors material to goods. But the Bill only covers the particular items set out in it. It does not have any general condition that misleading statements result in a criminal offence being committed. It does not require any reliance by the consumer; it does not require that the statement be material; it does not bring in any questions about the effect on the reasonable man. None of these matters is written into the Bill, nor is it the most clearly drafted of Bills.

I would take the view, moreover, that it is simply not enough, if one is concerned with protecting the consumer, to restrict coverage to statements of fact, and that exaggerated claims, ambiguous assertions and half-truths and that kind of thing, are also something against which the consumer merits some form of protection.

The Bill does nothing to meet the sort of situation Mr Graham was talking about in his discussion on what happens in Independent Television advertising. He said that in the medical area an advertisement is not accepted unless the truth of the assertion is established to the satisfaction of medical experts before the advertisement is put in. There is nothing like this in this Bill. There is nothing to prevent an advertiser from going ahead and then putting on the prosecutor the burden of establishing the falsity of the material in the advertisement. There is no arrangement at all for requiring that the truth of an advertisement be established in advance. As for the services provision, I doubt whether it is wide enough, even though it covers travel advertisements. I do not think it is wide enough to do anything about all the ladies in bikinis in those places where they have a rainfall of twenty inches every August.

Any discussion of this Bill is, of course, dependent on one's view of how rigorously the Board of Trade is going to carry out its powers under the Bill. Is it fair to make assumptions about this from the way in which the Board of Trade has failed to do anything about the Merchandise Marks Act? I have no idea whether this is a case of a serious-minded determination to carry out everything in the Bill, or whether it is the distressingly frequent situation of passing legislation which looks good to the voter, but without any bona fide intention of implementing it. This remains to be seen. If you think, as I do, that it is important not only to prevent false advertising but also to ensure (and here it should be the function of the law to help) that the consumer is given the kind of precise information about a product that he needs in order to make a wise choice, then your assessment of the utility of the Bill must very much depend on how the Board of Trade carries it out.

There is a provision in the Bill that, where it appears to the Board of Trade necessary or expedient in the interest of persons to whom any goods are supplied that advertisements should contain or refer to any information, the Board of Trade may make an order that the specific product shall, when advertised, deal with certain facts. But how widely they will do that is the key question.

With regard to the effectiveness of penalties and remedies, the Bill is exclusively criminal in application, and says nothing about compensation at all. Everything that I said in the first part of my talk about the inadequacies of the law's remedies for compensation still stands and the big question when you are dealing solely with criminal remedies, is whether courts regard it much more seriously to say that a person has committed a criminal offence. If they do they are going to impose much higher standards of proof because of the fact that these matters are exclusively criminal.

Then there is the third major problem, which is concerned with the efficiency or methods of administration. What is being done here is to put the responsibility for enforcing this legislation on those Local Authorities which are responsible for enforcing the present Weights and Measures legislation. But can we expect that local authorities will effectively enforce this legislation? I doubt it. An example may help to indicate the difficulty. One of the jobs that I am involved with in the northwestern area is the Furnished Houses Rent Tribunal. Time and time again we find cases of landlords who just ignore the fact that we have fixed the ceiling for rents for their flats and just go on charging double the fixed rent. The power to prosecute is in the hands of the local authorities. Now there is one local authority to which we systematically report that so-and-so is overcharging—a criminal offence. They and they alone can prosecute. But they just refuse to prosecute and there is no power for the aggrieved citizen himself to do so. The landlords and landladies keep charging double the rent, and the Rent Tribunal can't do anything about it.

That sort of experience makes me wonder whether one can really expect local authorities to carry out enforcement with any degree of ruthlessness. By 'enforcement' I do not mean merely when a member of the public comes to the local authority to complain, but also whether they will seek out offences for themselves. One would expect, that very often when a member of the public complains, he will not have come with a cut and dried case, and that unless the local authority is prepared to do a lot of work on its own to reinforce what the citizen says, the question of enforcement is going to be, in practice, very doubtful. It is true that the Board of Trade has a supervisory power. It has got authority under the Bill to set up an official inquiry into the way in which a particular local authority is carrying out its enforcement. But I still have doubts about whether this means of enforcement will be efficient. What has happened here is undoubtedly that the approach of the Molony Committee has been followed by a general feeling that all the Law need do is to reinforce the Merchandise Marks Acts and the local authorities' enforcement powers, and beyond that to leave it to the voluntary mechanisms which Mr Braun has described.

My criticisms of this approach of leaving the matter at the voluntary level, beyond the possibility of exclusively criminal remedies which I have already discussed, are these. Are the Advertising Standards Authority and similar bodies, sufficiently independent of the industry? Do they show willingness to name those who offend against their rules? Can a voluntary system work effectively without pre-publication checks on advertisements? Can one fairly say that there are such things under the ASA? Do you need to have adequate procedures if you are going to make a system like the ASA work? And do not these demand that there should, for example, be an oral hearing for a member of the public who makes a complaint to the ASA?

Does the ASA provide this kind of hearing? Do you need to have a fairly large investigatory staff? Must there be power to fine or to blacklist offenders? Now, is the answer to any of these points 'Yes' in the case of the ASA? I doubt whether there is an unqualified 'Yes' to any of them.

It is because of this, that my own preference would be for something like the Federal Trade Commission in the United States. I think it has the following advantages.

1. It avoids all this business of local authority enforcement, which is subject to the criticisms I have made.
2. It is a great advantage to have all advertising controlled by one body. This is in contrast to the enormous overlapping and complexity of our present voluntary system. I welcome the idea of the same body framing the regulations for advertising standards, both with regard to what is prohibited and what is required and searching for violations and taking enforcement action.
3. I prefer the American system of cease and desist orders to our own approach of small fines in magistrates' courts. The order is made, if the advertisement is found after a hearing to be false and misleading, that the responsible body shall cease and desist from advertising in this way.
4. I like the idea of the regulations being expertly drafted and supervised rather than their being done by voluntary bodies. Although I would agree with what Mr Graham has said about how much better the ITA has regulated advertising than a vast majority of its critics expected it to in the beginning of Independent Television, I do not like the kind of solution which we have under the Television Act. My first objection to it is its enormous complexity. Anyone who wants to know what rules Mr Graham and his staff are working on, has a devil of a job to find out. He has to turn to Acts of Parliament; he has to turn to the ITA Code of Advertising Standards and Practice; he has to look through the annual reports of the ITA; he has to read the work *ITV 1965*; and unless he goes to all these different sources, he just has no means of knowing what the rules about television advertising are. I cannot think that that is a good thing. Nor do I feel entirely happy about the situation which allows, say, false advertising about 'Hello Dolly' to go through.

I do not think that this kind of quasi-legal organization allays such public disquiet as there is. I think it is unfortunate that this sort of system does not afford any machinery for hearing complaints.

To sum up my position, there is much in this Bill that I welcome in principle. I do not mind the tightening up on some of these matters. I think that the ordinary law of compensation through deceit, warranty and so on, needs extending but I do not like the present enforcement machinery. I would like to see something like the Federal Trade Commission experimented with, because of my doubts about whether a voluntary system of control will meet those objections to it which I have outlined.

Part four

The consumer interest

13

The role of the consumer organizations

Francis Noel-Baker

The interest which I represent is a very different one in this matter to that of Mr Braun. To use his slightly disparaging term, I represent the 'intellectual fringe' which does think that there is a very great deal wrong both specifically and generally about advertising in this country at the present time. May I start by getting an old chestnut out of the way. Politicians are often asked 'Who are you to talk about exaggerating and misleading because this is what you do all the time?' And the short answer to that is that *we* do not have any rules which prevent the disparagement of competing products.

On the contrary, we are so organized that we spend most of our time disparaging each other's products, or, to put it in another way, we do answer each other back and this is a very valuable corrective to any misleading or any exaggeration we may be tempted to do. This does not apply in the advertising industry.

To take a very simple example of this, you can spend, and indeed Guinness do spend, millions of pounds on saying that 'Guinness is good for you' which is by no means a proven point. It depends on who 'you' is. If you try to spend even a modest few shillings to put up a poster saying 'Guinness is bad for you' you get fetched up in the courts. So there is no answering back in the advertising business and this is very important to the ordinary person.

Now Mr Braun has mentioned three sides on a pyramid which represent different aspects of the advertising industry, but it seems to me that there is, in fact, a total of four quite separate interests in this matter. There are, as he has said, three of them on the advertising side: there is the advertiser himself, the advertising agent and the media-owner. The advertiser is the person who makes or produces the goods or services that are being advertised. His interest is in making money out of his product by selling more of it. Then there is the advertising agent who is paid to help sell the product or the service, and his interest is in making as much money as he can out of the process. Next there is the media-owner, the television network owner, the newspaper proprietor, the person who owns the hoarding, the mail order business owner, and his job is to make money out of his medium or media.

Then there is the consumer, and his interests are always quite different from those of the other three, and, in the nature of things, they are, from time to time, in direct conflict with them. One can sum up the consumer's interest in this matter of advertising by saying that he wants two things. He wants factual information which will help him first to learn about the availability of goods and services which he may need or want, to know that they exist, and, secondly, he wants to learn *about* them. He wants to know what their qualities and defects are. He wants to know what the relative merits of competing products are, and this is something which the advertising industry itself, to some extent, deliberately hampers because there are these rules against knocking copy. You may not say that your product is better than the other chap's, or that his is worse than yours, but this is something the consumer very much does want to know. He wants to know which electric kettle or which travel agency is best and why, and he wants to have information about prices. These are the real needs of the consumer, factual information, but this is not what the advertising industry is for. The advertising industry does not exist to provide factual information for the good of its own soul or for the convenience of the consumer. It exists to sell, to persuade people to buy goods and services which they would otherwise not buy, would not want, would not know they need. This is the purpose of advertising and, if it were not its effect, there would be no reason for it. If I were going to buy all the goods and services that are advertised anyway, then it would be a colossal waste of money, spending about £1,500,000 a day on persuading me to do so.

But, of course, there are a number of other aspects of this subject which interest the consumer. There is the very wide field, which is a matter of subjective judgement of the effects of advertising and the techniques it uses on the whole social and moral climate of the society we live in. The advertising industry is powerful, wealthy and all-pervading. It comes into our homes through the medium of the television screen. Nobody can escape it. It makes its impact on any member of a highly developed urbanized community and, indeed, when the citizen of the modern conurbation tries to get into the countryside, it makes its impact on him there too. It is extremely influential on the media themselves, including the main media of information. The press is dominated by the fact that in some cases two-thirds of its revenue depends on money made from advertisements. In some cases, a bit less. In some cases, a bit more. This is bound to have an effect, and, in fact, if there was not this revenue, with the present structure, all our existing newspapers would collapse.

The same thing, I think, applies to television. Clearly, the fact that commercial television depends for its existence on advertising, and that advertisers are interested almost exclusively in the TAM rating and the size of the audience they are going to catch with their commercial, this in turn affects the BBC. People often think that after all commercials on Independent Television cannot really affect the content of BBC programmes. On the contrary, they do. Because the BBC, perhaps unfairly, has found itself in competition with commercial television. It gets worried when it is told that its TAM ratings are very much lower than those of commercial television. And this means that it tends to produce the mass-audience programmes on about the same level as commercial television in order not to put itself in a position of numerical inferiority. The fact is that advertising does have a dominating influence on the climate in which we live, and this is a very important factor which worries a number of consumers.

Then there is the practical effect on the economy of the nation, and here we are, unfortunately, again in an area which is controversial and mysterious because there has been very inadequate, independent research into the economics of advertis-

Francis Noel-Baker

ing. Advertising agents and their market research organizations do a certain amount for their own purposes. And I suspect that sometimes when the results don't come out the way that would suit them in public, these results do not see the light of day. But there has been very little independent research into the real economic effects of advertising: the effect on the national economy as a whole, of the enormous sums of money that are being spent and, indeed, the actual effects of specific advertising campaigns. The only people who have really done research on a big scale on these, and who hitherto have been able to afford to do so, have been the advertising interests themselves.

The consumer is also concerned with the fact that his spending is being compulsorily distorted by advertising. We have been told that the *Daily Mirror* would cost 1s. (or was it 1s. 6d.?) if there were not any advertisements. But the difference in the price of the *Daily Mirror*, or any other newspapers, or commercial television for that matter, is being paid for by the consumer out of his pocket on other items. This is a point that is sometimes forgotten in discussions about advertising. What in fact is happening is that I, or my wife, or my friends and relations are being made to pay more for our cigarettes, for cosmetics, for confectionery and less for the *Daily Mirror*. Whether we want to spend our money in that way is not a question that Mr Cecil King has asked us.

The feeling that a number of advertising campaigns in the last few years have rather overdone it is probably shared by many of us. I think this is why the advertising industry gives the outsider the impression of being so very much on the defensive at present; because there has been a consumer reaction building up against the way in which the gullibility of the individual consumer and housewife has been exploited by the advertising industry. Archie Graham who, after all, is not one of the long-haired intellectual crack-pots who dare to criticize the advertising industry, started by saying that, of course, the advertising industry was not in the uplift business. He went on to say that some of the sentimental mumbo-jumbo that he had to deal with at ITA made his stomach turn. This is one of the things that has produced a consumer reaction and one of the reasons why the advertising industry has been put on the defensive.

Moreover, when advertising campaigns turn into advertising wars, the point about economic waste must be obvious. We have been hearing a good deal about detergents, and the Advertisement Director of the *Guardian* said that, after all, Levers aren't amateurs. It is reasonable to argue that when detergents were first put on the market and the campaign began to persuade the housewife to switch from soap to detergents, this was a new product on which big expenditures on advertising campaigns were justified. But the real fact behind the advertising war on detergents is now quite different, and everybody heard of detergents a good many years ago. I once went with some colleagues from the Advertising Inquiry Council to talk to one of the directors of a major British combine concerned with detergents. We said 'Surely it is a fact that you are wasting millions of pounds on your advertising campaign?' And he said, 'Yes, we certainly are. We would be glad to pull out. The trouble is that Procter & Gamble and other people won't, and we are in a race in which we are compelled to carry on although we know that it is inflating the price of the product and although we know that it is entirely wasteful.' I believe this to apply in a number of other fields, if you could really get the people in control of these big advertising budgets to take their hair down.

Another example, from the consumer's point of view, which is entirely unnecessary and wasteful is the advertising of motor fuel. It puts a small amount on the price of each gallon of the petrol I have to buy. There is no significant difference between any of the products. Until recently, when the independents started breaking in, there was no significant difference in the price. Very often, in fact, the product, although labelled differently, came out of the same barrel, or something so similar that it was of no interest to the consumer. My own personal interest as a consumer and indeed as a citizen, taking the national interest into account—on grounds of foreign exchange, traffic congestion, air pollution and economy, really can provide no justification whatsoever for persuading people to buy more petrol than they otherwise would. This

151

same rule applies to a number of other highly monopolized fields.

Indeed the argument that advertising is a vital element in the competitive go-ahead industrial and economic set-ups that advertising men love does not really stand up to the facts. What is happening in many spheres is that the enormous, inflated advertising budgets are making it impossible for smaller firms to break in. You are weighting the game very much in favour of the big outfit, with an established position and an established share of the market.

All this leads me to say that from the consumer's point of view I can perfectly well imagine the situation where we could do without advertising altogether, because there would be other ways in which the information, the factual information, about the existence of goods and services and their merits and qualities could be brought to the attention of the consumer. I am not arguing this as a matter of practical politics now, but the job could be done in other ways, and, indeed, for the small 'intellectual fringe', it is beginning to be done. It is beginning to be done by organizations like Consumer Association with its publication *Which?*, by consumer groups that are growing up all over the country, and to some extent by the Consumer Council which has been set up by the Government. These organizations are making it possible for the consumer to know about products and to get facts which he cannot get through the medium of advertising campaigns.

This brings me to the question of control. Here I do not deny that it is an excellent thing for the advertising interests to set up an internal organization to try to watch over standards and maintain their own code of practice. But I really cannot accept that these arrangements set up by the advertising industry are independent of it. I part company even with the title of 'Advertising Standards Authority'. Anybody from outside being asked what the Advertising Standards 'Authority' was would think it was some kind of official body. But, in fact, it isn't anything of the sort. It is a mechanism set up by the Advertising Industry itself, entirely paid for by the Advertising Industry, and really whether it moves its address out of the same building as the Advertising Association into another whose rent is going to be paid by the Advertising Association, or stays put, does not seem to me to be of any significance.

The chairman of ASA, Lord Drumalbyn, is a very nice man. I have known him for a number of years. But just to fish a well-known politician out of the House of Lords, pay him a salary or a retainer, and then say 'this is an independent outfit' really doesn't answer the case. This is *not* an independent outfit; it is part of the advertising industry, paid for, and set up and organized by the advertising industry. Quite frankly, some consumer organizations wonder whether its purpose isn't to be able to say, 'Well, we're doing it ourselves, and this is the reason why the Government need not step in.'

The fact that there is already a large number of Acts of Parliament, many of them obsolete, does not really meet the needs of the present situation. We have, in fact, a new Act of Parliament which has just got to the House of Lords, the Protection of Consumers (Trade Descriptions) Bill which goes some way in meeting some of the gaps in the existing legislation. Personally I believe that there is a very large field to be covered by legislation.

But making rules for advertising is extremely difficult. If you set down in black and white in an Act of Parliament what a television commercial may or may not do, or what a copywriter may or may not do, in practice it is very easy to run rings round it. Perhaps I might give one practical illustration of this which sticks in my mind. Some time ago there was a meat beverage which changed its advertising agency and started a new campaign. The thought of the executives handling this account was that it would be a good idea to sell this beverage as a bedtime drink. One or two people on their staff objected and said, 'On the contrary, if you drink a meat extract with a bit of water or milk poured on to it, if it does have any effect it is to wake you up and not to send you to sleep.' A discussion went on about this and in the end the advertisements appeared and I saw one or two of them. Nowhere in any of them was the fact mentioned that this drink was alleged to make you go to sleep. But there *was* a picture of a young woman with her head on a pillow, there *was* a graph showing that the protein content of the drink was less than that of a number of other drinks, A, B, C and D and the total effect of the picture and the copy was to make you think that this would make you go to sleep without actually saying so.

How an Act of Parliament could ever deal with that kind of situation I don't know, and I think that, in fact, complicated rules and regulations and, still more, complicated legislation are really not the way of dealing with this particular problem. Perhaps I may add in parenthesis, though it may be a legend, that I have been told that in parts of Africa Horlicks has been advertised as a drink that gives you energy, wakes you up and keeps you going all night if necessary.

I do not think that whatever steps the advertising industry itself has taken, or may take, are adequate to meet the situation. Nor are there many spheres of economic activity in which the business interests concerned are given a monopoly of policing themselves. After all, you could argue that British industrialists are, on the whole, benevolent, public-spirited people. But the inspection of factories is done by an outside body of inspectors appointed by the Government. Certainly I am not arguing that the Advertising Inquiry Council, or other bodies that take an interest in advertising, have an unbiased point of view either. They are trying to represent the interests of the consumer as they see them in the same way that the Advertising Association, the Institute of Practitioners in Advertising and the Advertising Standards 'Authority' are looking after the interests of their side of the question. What is needed is some kind of independent referee in the middle. This is why the Advertising Inquiry Council for several years, and the Consumer Council, since it came into existence, have been urging that there should be a body roughly on the lines of the Federal Trade Commission, about which we heard a good deal from Mr Braun, to do the job of policing, as an independent referee in the middle.

There may be other ways of doing this. It may be that the Consumer Council itself, and its department which takes an interest in advertising, could be expanded; that it could be given powers to look at complaints, to investigate and ask advertisers to produce evidence for the claims they were making, and, if not satisfied by the evidence produced, issue 'cease and desist' orders in the same way that the Federal Trade

Commission does. I must say that I have a slightly different picture from Mr Braun of the effectiveness of the Federal Trade Commission. My belief is that it is a very powerful institution which is respected and, to some extent, feared by the advertising industry. When it tells an advertiser to take an advertisement off, that advertisement comes off, and the onus is on the advertiser to prove his case. This is certainly something that the Advertising Inquiry Council would like to see here.

Finally I should like to look briefly at the points in the main Policy Statement of the Advertising Inquiry Council, a part of which has been implemented by the Government (see below— Appendix B).

On false and misleading claims, we should like to see a statutory body acting as an independent referee. I am glad to hear that the Advertising Standards Authority has gone through a major reorganization. Professor Plant has gone. Lord Drumalbyn has come, and there have been other changes. Yet our experience has been that the ASA since it started has not really been effective. We are not alone in this view. The Retail Trading Standards Association has stated its view that the ASA has been a total failure. One of the big defects of the ASA, it seems to me, is that if one took complaints up with it, any replies that were in the end received were always marked 'Confidential' and kept as secret documents. But, after all, there is a very great deal of public interest in the policing of advertising and to be effective anybody trying to do this job ought to be prepared to accept publicity.

I have already mentioned the point about monopolization. One of the things we hope the Government will do is to ask the Monopolies Commission to investigate the relationship between advertising and market control. I think a Monopolies Commission inquiry into the whole of the advertising industry would be extremely useful. If it did not turn up anything to the detriment of the advertising industry this would be very satisfactory to the advertising industry itself and it would allay public fears.

On the volume of advertising, frankly we feel that the tax arrangements should be looked at by the Government, and we took a deputation to the Board of Trade about this recently.

Another controversial point is the advertising of what we call 'Special Products', I think that my council can take part of the credit for getting cigarette advertising off television, and this was in the face of a very long battle with the tobacco industry, with the previous Government and to some extent with the present one until it did this. We take the view that there are some products which are either potentially so dangerous or sufficiently controversial to merit direct intervention by the Government which then simply says 'This may not be advertised.'

In our view, because of the medical evidence, we would apply this to cigarettes. A number of people would apply it to alcoholic beverages, not only hard liquor but other drink as well, and there are a number of television networks on the Continent which ban medical advertising altogether. I would like to refer you to the description by Archie Graham of the very complicated machinery the ITA has for vetting medical advertising and knowing what disquiet and complaints there still are about medical advertising, I personally believe that much the most satisfactory answer is for the Ministry of Health to say 'We will have all medical advertising off the television screen altogether.'

On outdoor advertising one is getting a bit technical, but we think it fair to say that the measures taken about 'clutter' have been sadly ineffective, and that it is time that the Government got on with its 'areas of special control'. As for the vital matter of advertising and editorial policy, we would like to see the Press Council empowered to investigate complaints about the effect of advertising pressure on the editorial columns and we would like to see them take more interest in this aspect of the Press.

14

Advertising and the consumer interest

Bruce McConnach

In the first section of my contribution, I shall try to explain the Consumer Association's relationship with advertising; on the one hand CA's own use of advertising and indeed its dependence on it, and on the other CA's official policy towards advertising. Up to that point, I shall be to some extent the official spokesman for CA as an organization. In the second section, where I shall be speaking entirely for myself, I shall try to examine the uses of advertising to the consumer. After explaining my basic assumptions, I shall try to examine how far the uses to which manufacturers put advertising are compatible with the consumer interest, and, in particular, its usefulness to consumers. In doing so, I shall look at such questions as: How well is advertising serving the consumer? What do consumers think of advertising? Do they think it's necessary? Can they believe it? and Do they believe it? In trying to answer these questions, I shall draw upon evidence from consumers, from advertisers and from the experience of CA during the past ten years of publishing *Which?*

Finally I shall try to answer the question: Is there a real conflict of interest? Can advertising really be expected to provide solutions to consumers' problems? If so, is it doing so, and if not, how can these solutions be provided?

What use has CA itself made of advertising?
In terms of the number of current subscribers, *Which?* is the second largest consumer testing magazine in the world, carrying out and publishing the results of research into branded goods and services.

Now this hasn't just happened. If CA had sat back and waited for members to apply for membership, *Which?* would have remained small in circulation and therefore very limited indeed in its resources, and therefore in the scope and effectiveness of its testing, unless it had charged £10 instead of 30s. for a year's subscription. *Which?* is, of course, totally dependent for finance upon its members' subscriptions and the sale of its publications. CA has no share capital, its financial reserves comprising the unexpired portion of its members' subscriptions which are paid in advance. *Which?* has grown in size because it has been reasonably priced, because it has been able to command very satisfactory renewal of subscriptions from its members and because CA has spent a realistic proportion of its budget on the promotion of new membership.

CA has made use of advertising to achieve growth of its membership and therefore of its income and potential. Advertising has in fact been and still is all the more important because of the fact that *Which?* is a subscription-only magazine and therefore the promotion of subscriptions ordered direct by mail represents virtually all of its selling effort—CA has no sales force, no display material, no circulation department, and with only a tiny proportion of its subscription circulation going through the retail trade, a low total cost of retailer discounts. CA's advertising costs are thus almost equal to its total sales costs.

So CA's full use of advertising has helped ensure that *Which?* is an economically viable publication. Which it is!

Now, what is CA's official policy towards advertising, other people's advertising? This can be stated very briefly indeed. CA is pro-consumer, and its attitude to advertising and manufacturers is entirely coloured by this fact. Its policy is neither for nor against advertising any more than it is for or against manufacturing.

If I may quote the Memorandum of Association of CA. 'The principal object for which the Association is established is to improve and maintain the standard of goods or commodities sold and services rendered to the public.' And the first four 'further objects' of CA are the following:

(a) To promote and advance public knowledge in all matters concerning users and consumers of materials, goods and services of all kinds . . .

Bruce McConnach

158

(b) To collect and diffuse information in all matters concerning the use, purchase, hire or hire-purchase, qualities, properties and prices of materials, goods, commodities and services of every description.
(c) To give advice to consumers on all matters concerning them in that capacity, and
(d) to conduct and maintain research whether by its own officers and servants or by the agency of others on all matters concerning consumers, and in particular on all aspects of the said materials, goods, commodities and services, and to encourage, promote and advise on the conduct of such research by others.

Thus, as CA is concerned principally about the 'standard of goods sold and services rendered to the public', advertising is only peripheral to this main concern; and it is only when there is a fairly obvious conflict of interest between consumers and an advertiser, for instance when a product perhaps doesn't quite match up in the laboratory or in user tests to what the advertiser leads the consumer to expect in his advertising for the product, that CA normally gets involved with advertising at all.

What do consumers think of advertising?
I should like to make it clear that what follows is an expression of my personal view and must not be taken as being an official statement of CA's views or policies.

I said that I was now going to examine the uses of advertising to the consumer, but first of all I'd like to make it clear that I recognize that the advertiser's viewpoint, the manufacturer's viewpoint, is a perfectly legitimate one.

Just as I say that CA's responsibility is to the consumer and only to the consumer, I recognize that the responsibility of a firm is to its shareholders. I also accept the respectability of the profit motive in business and accept profitability as a legitimate measure of business efficiency, not because private and corporate profits have any innate virtue but because they characterize a system which works, and is basic to the distributive system that we have.

One of the most important advantages of the profit system from the consumer's point of view is the fact that it leads to competition and competition means choice for the consumer.

At this point I'd like to quote from a recent speech on

Bruce McConnach

'Advertising and Productivity' by that champion of profits, competition and advertising, Sir Paul Chambers, former Chairman of ICI:[1]

... how do you find out what people want, and how do you get busy making it? You do it of course by marketing in one way or another, and one of the most important ways is by advertising what you have for sale and what service you can provide. People can then compare that with what other people can do; and, by their choice, you gradually find out what individuals want.

In all this, advertising not only stimulates competition but the customers as well. It stimulates them to choose; it stimulates them to find out what they really want. For many goods people want leading; they are not sure of their own wishes until they find themselves in front of the full range of what is available. This is one of the rules of advertising. If you say, 'Well, how can you say this? Is there any evidence in favour of it?', I would just say this: in general the highest standards of living are where the highest amount of advertising takes place.

Advertising fulfils another role, which is not always appreciated. It is not only advertising different brands of the same kind of product; it is advertising different ways in which you can spend your money. You may think that you want a new car, you may want to do some foreign travel; you may want to buy some pictures; you may want to buy furniture, or clothes. Your whole range of advertising gives you a chance of choosing not merely between one brand and another but of choosing whether you want to do this or do that, or to buy this or to buy that.

This, I think, can be regarded as the consumers' aspect of advertising.

Well, this is the manufacturer's *view* of the consumer's aspect of advertising. It tries to explain how advertising acts upon the consumer, but does it go any way towards describing how advertising looks from where the consumer is standing? The advertiser uses advertising to apply a stimulus to the prospective and existing users of his product.

Certainly, from the point of view of a large proportion of companies producing consumer goods and services, consumer-oriented marketing with its techniques of market research, product testing, test marketing and advertising research, are almost second nature.

But, however 'consumer-oriented' these companies are, their loyalties are firmly within the company and their dedication to

160

the consumer is quite understandably subservient to their dedication to company profitability.

So when Sir Paul Chambers says that advertising '. . . stimulates (people) to choose; it stimulates them to find out what they really want. For many goods people want leading; they are not sure of their own wishes until they find themselves in front of the full range of what is available . . .' he is stating a truth, but he is also implying that advertising gives people the information they want and the guidance they feel they need.

Well does it? How well is advertising serving consumers? Do they accept the necessity for it? Do they think that it gives them the information and guidance they need? Do they believe it? And indeed can they trust it?

About eighteen months ago, National Opinion Polls conducted what appears to have been a very respectable survey[2] among a representative sample of adults in Great Britain and 74 per cent of the sample thought that advertising was necessary. 65 per cent thought that advertising helped the public to make a better choice of things to buy, and when asked 'Do you think that, in general, advertisements present a true picture of the product advertised, or a false picture' over 53 per cent thought that a false picture is presented.

If I may dare to interpret these figures, it would appear that although most people accept that advertising is necessary, the business community has been less than wholly successful in convincing the public that what it chooses to say about its merchandise is altogether trustworthy.

Why is it then that over half of the population think that advertising in general presents a false picture of the product advertised? Is a large proportion of the advertising produced in this country downright untruthful? Of course not. It is undeniable that the vast majority of manufacturers recognize the need for putting into practice what Sir Frederic Hooper has expressed very clearly:[3]

Advertising is a guarantee of quality. A firm which has spent a substantial sum advocating the merits of a product and accustoming the consumer to expect a standard that is both high and uniform, dare not later reduce the quality of its goods. Sometimes the public is gullible, but not to the extent of continuing to buy a patently inferior article.

And of course the advertising industry has itself recognized the need to discipline would-be untruthful advertisers.

So how can we explain this awkward 53 per cent? Well, it might be useful to look at some products that *Which?* has tested to see whether the advertising industry has been entirely successful in controlling those advertisers who do not practise the gospel according to Sir Frederic.

The advertising for the 'Everlaster' torch, reported on in *Which?* in January 1966 (p. 32) and the 'Vent-o-Matic', reported on in *Which?* in March 1965 (p. 68), the pack copy for Farex cereal referred to in *Which?* in December 1965 (p. 351) and the BP Super Plus petrol advertisements referred to in *Which?* in September 1964 (p. 283) are just four instances that have emerged from CA's research which perhaps go a little way towards explaining why some people (53 per cent) think that advertising in general presents a false picture. Many members of the public have at some time bought goods and services which they have subsequently found did not live up to their advertising claims, and have as a result perhaps believed *all* advertising a little less.

Thus the untruthful advertiser is not just fooling the consumer. He is not just risking the loss of reputation and repeat business for himself. He is also eroding the confidence which consumers have in advertising in general.

So that when *Which?*, for instance, stumbles on discrepancies of this kind, it isn't merely protecting the consumer. It could be said that it is, in a sense, protecting the interests of all the other manufacturers of competing products whose advertising is truthful, whose products are good value for money and whose business ethics are not in conflict with the consumer interest.

This perhaps goes a long way to explain why CA has always enjoyed a very satisfactory relationship with the vast majority of manufacturers. In general, the more confident a manufacturer is of the quality of his product and the truthfulness of his advertising, the less afraid he is of *Which?* testing his products. In fact, it has not been unknown for a manufacturer actually to attempt to persuade *Which?* to test a particular product field where that manufacturer has an entry. (Needless to say, this kind of pressure has never been successful.)

But to return to my theme. We have established, I think, that people accept the need for advertising, but are not entirely convinced that they can trust it, and that it is seen by both advertising and consumer organizations that it is desirable for advertising both to be more trustworthy and to be thought so.

But is that all that needs to be said about the usefulness of advertising to the consumer? To go back to Sir Paul Chambers:[4]

In all this, advertising not only stimulates competition but the customers as well. It stimulates them to choose; it stimulates them to find out what they really want. For many goods people want leading; they are not sure of their own wishes until they find themselves in front of the full range of what is available. This is one of the rules of advertising.

This leads me to ask the question—'Is advertising, and by that I mean the generality of truthful advertising, sufficiently informative?'

Well some of it obviously is, but a great deal of it doesn't even try, and the marketing and advertising men present would no doubt be very quick to jump on me if I were to suggest that it should. For they would point out that their responsibility is primarily to produce advertising which works, which produces sales and therefore profits, and it is undeniable that many of the most successful advertising campaigns have been totally uninformative, relying upon the added value of a desirable image which has been superimposed on a product or some psychological satisfaction which the consumer derives from using a product advertised in a particular way.

Now I should not deny to an advertiser the right to advertise his product in this way, for it may well, as its apologists maintain, add to the colour, variety and richness of modern life.

However, advertisers should not be altogether surprised when certain sections of the public *want to know more*, because some people are quite understandably more concerned with the physical performance of the product and whether it constitutes good value for money, than with the psychological performance deriving from the pack design or the glamorous television commercial.

At least some practitioners recognize that advertising is often insufficiently informative. David Ogilvy, for instance, says that his experience at the working level leads him to agree that 'advertising does not give consumers sufficient information'.[5]

But Mr Ogilvy, who is not without influence in British advertising circles, goes even further. After quoting Dorothy Sayers, who he reminds us:

. . . . wrote advertisements before she wrote whodunits and Anglo-Catholic tracts, says: 'Plain lies are dangerous. The only weapons left are the *suggestio falsi* and the *suppressio veri*'. I plead guilty to one act of *suggestio falsi*—what Madison Avenue calls a 'weasel'. However, two years later a chemist rescued my conscience by discovering that what I had falsely suggested was actually true.

But I must confess that I am continuously guilty of *suppressio veri*. Surely it is asking too much to expect the advertiser to describe the shortcomings of his product? One must be forgiven for putting one's best foot forward.

So here we have it. The advertiser cannot be expected to tell the whole truth about his product, only that part of truth which is found to be effective in bringing him sales. Fair enough! But it is also true that it is frequently in the realms of what no advertiser will say about his product that the real differences lie between one brand and another, and although Sir Frederic Hooper is quite right in saying that the public is 'sometimes . . . gullible, but not to the extent of continuing to buy a patently inferior article', there are many fields, for instance, safety equipment, consumer durables, motor cars and indeed motor insurance, where by the time a consumer has discovered that he has bought an inferior article, *it's too late!*

This is quite clearly one of the main reasons why *Which?* and magazines like it in other countries exist. People want to know the snags as well as the selling points of the things they buy. And here I'd like to scotch a misconception about the readers of *Which?*—the idea which I have heard expressed that they're a herd of blind sheep who follow 'Auntie' *Which?* wheresoever she may lead. We have recently conducted a series of group discussions on 'The Problems of the Consumer' among CA members which quite clearly established that for most *Which?* readers, *Which?* is only one of many sources of information and guidance drawn upon in making buying decisions. These include past experience of brands, the reputation and standing of manufacturers, recommendations by retailers and friends, sales leaflets, design and, yes, *advertising!*

But perhaps there's another reason why people take *Which?*, and this brings me to my next point. When Sir Paul Chambers said 'In general, the highest standards of living are where the highest amount of advertising takes place' he implied a causal connection between these things. Whether one exists there or not, I should add a third element which is likely to result from both these things. It would appear that, along with high standards of living and high amounts of advertising, go consumer organizations. The countries where there are strong consumer organizations: the US, Norway, Sweden, Denmark, Holland, Austria, Australia, New Zealand and the UK, all have higher than average standards of living, quite high amounts of advertising expenditure, large numbers of competing brands in most fields of consumer expenditure and high educational standards. It seems to me quite clear that these organizations with their magazines, publishing independent reports on tests of branded goods and services have come into existence to compensate for the absence of something which advertising cannot provide, factual information which, taken together with the sum total of manufacturers marketing effort, provides consumers with a better chance of finding themselves, as Sir Paul Chambers puts it: '. . . in front of the full range of what is available.' Now this picture of the full range isn't perfect. The consumer testing magazines are not perfect. They are not rich organizations with large resources, their budgets being only a tiny fraction of the sums spent on advertising the products which they test. But then, as we've seen, advertising isn't perfect either and I think it's fair to say that when taken together, they reduce some of the confusion which consumers feel when confronted with the bewildering array of choice in the market place.

At this point I should like to make it clear that 'CA draws a clear distinction between legitimate methods of disseminating its views', for instance by means of 'the generous coverage CA receives in the press, . . . on radio and television' and CA's panel of forty lecturers, and 'the unauthorized exploitation of *Which?* recommendations by advertisers'.[6]

However, the vast majority of consumers do not see con-

Bruce McConnach

sumer testing magazines like *Which?* despite the fact that *Which?*, for instance, reaches an estimated 3 million readers, thanks to public libraries, pass-on readership and so on—quite apart from the mass audience for *Choice*—and draws about one third of its membership from the lower middle and skilled working classes and is certainly growing in this direction.

If I may quote from a recent article in the *Spectator* by Peter Goldman, the Director of CA, when he dealt with this problem:[7]

... it is precisely the educationally under-privileged who are most vulnerable to misinformation, least able to afford expensive mistakes, and therefore most in need of independent assessments and guidance. In Vienna, the *Verein für Konsumenteninformation* relies on a corps of highly trained personal advisers. The advisers are drawn from this consumer organisations' own testing and research staff and from independent experts in the physical and domestic sciences, economics and law. They take it in turn to be available for consultation in the afternoon and evening of most weekdays and every Saturday. Announcements are made by leaflet and advertisement and on the radio, indicating what demonstrations and buying advice will be given on specific days.

This advisory centre gives the Austrians the edge on consumer organisations that simply produce a magazine. Their programme of comparative testing may be less impressive than the American or the British or the German. But such guidance as they give is available at the time and in the place where most of the relevant shopping decisions are taken. Their advisory centre is, in fact, superbly located. It is plumb in the middle of Mariahilferstrasse, the Oxford Street of Vienna, where the large department stores are found and where all but the more moneyed Viennese appear to make their major purchases.

The accessibility of the advisory centre, however, would be of small account were it not for the acceptability of the advice given. Such verbal advice can often be more up-to-date than that in publications; It can be hand-tailored to the circumstances and requirements of the shoppers. It can get things clear by argument and counter-argument. Above all, it can be demonstrated, for the advisory centre's showrooms can house exhibitions of the competing brands of major consumer durable. In this way would-be purchasers are able to examine the available products (with their test ratings) in conditions free from sales pressure.

They come in droves. The advisory centre now has close on 250,000 inquirers yearly—a remarkable figure for a city whose population is well under two millions. Moreover, good verbal advice has not proved competitive with good published advice. The Austrian experience is that the advisory centre provides the best possible means of recruiting new readers for their test magazine. But *Konsument* is no exception to the rule that test magazines, being semi-technical, require efforts of critical concentration which large numbers of people are unable or unwilling to give. It is to such people—with their pre-shopping questions and their post-shopping complaints—that the advisory centre especially caters.

Can the Austrian example be followed in this country? It would be pleasant to think so, and proper to try.

Summary

So, if I may summarize. The advertiser who pursues a business policy based on fair dealing, producing a well-researched product which is good value for money and is advertised truthfully, is likely to be furthering both his own and the consumer's interest. And the untruthful advertisers, who still exist despite the efforts of the Advertising Standards Authority and the other control bodies, are doing harm to other advertisers as well as to the consumer, as there is certainly evidence to suggest that many consumers find it difficult to believe what advertisements tell them. But apart altogether from the question of downright untruths, advertising is limited in its usefulness to the consumer in three important ways. Firstly, the advertiser's interest in selling his product may require him to run advertising which is not informative and is not intended to be so, and here advertising is perhaps not serving consumers as effectively as *they* might wish.

Secondly, advertisers, quite understandably, do not see it as part of their function to inform the consumer of *all* the facts, even in informative advertising, only those facts which are found to be effective selling points.

Thirdly, the very large number of advertisers competing for the consumer's attention, reflecting the growing number of products and services competing for his money, can lead to confusion and even frustration, which consumer testing magazines can only partially alleviate, despite multiple readership and the existence of press publicity and linked television programmes like *Choice*.

There appears to exist a need for some kind of specific consumer advice beyond advertising, consumer testing magazines and television programmes. Perhaps the Austrian example indicates one useful line of development for the future.

Bruce McConnach

References

[1] Chambers, Sir P. *The Advertising Quarterly*. No. 10, Winter, 1966–1967. pp. 9–15.
[2] National Opinion Polls Ltd. *Advertising*. Report on a Survey. September 1965.
[3] Ogilvy, D. *Confessions of an Advertising Man*. Longmans, 1964. p. 154.
[4] Chambers, pp. 9–15.
[5] Ogilvy, pp. 155–6.
[6] 'This matter was referred to the Advertising Standards Authority in November 1965. The Authority declined to prohibit the kind of advertisements we complained about, but expressed the hope that advertisers would "respect Consumers' Association's wishes and refrain from such references from *Which?* in support of their products".' 1965–6 Annual Report of Chairman to the Ordinary Members of Consumers' Association.
[7] Goldman, P. 'Consuming Interest—Viennese Counter-Offensive.' *The Spectator*. 30 September 1966.

15

The proper functions of advertising
—is a balanced view possible?

Elizabeth Ackroyd

I would like to say as a preliminary that I know that eyebrows
have been raised because I was asked to talk on the subject of
'Is a Balanced View Possible about Advertising?' because it
seemed against nature, I gather, to quite a lot of people particularly those in the advertising industry, that what you might
call a professional consumer—of all people the most bigoted
example of the species of consumer—could be trusted with
surveying the field in a balanced way.

I think I will side-step that issue very promptly by saying that
I don't, in fact, propose to try to take a balanced view because
I do not believe, for quite profound reasons, that a balanced
view of advertising in the community is in fact possible. Perhaps I had better explain, therefore, what I understand by the
concept of a 'balanced view'. What I mean by that is a synthesis
of the views of all those concerned in and with advertising so
as to produce a general view between all the protagonists which
would be accepted, generally speaking, by all concerned. I do
not believe that this is, in fact, possible in the particular field of
advertising. Just saying 'on the one hand this' and 'on the other
hand that' is not, of course, producing a view. Some people
mistake analysis for opinion but, in fact, that is not a view. That
kind of balance one can make very well and we have had a
certain amount of interesting analysis in our proceedings. One
can also reach a *modus vivendi* between different parties by
saying that 'I do accept, we both accept, some part of the arguments in favour, say, of advertising or against advertising but
we disagree on other parts.' That again is not a balanced view.
Because of the parts where they disagree, the dichotomy be-

tween the two parties remains as acute even though they may have narrowed the area of disagreement. So what I had been seeking for was a synthesis of the different arguments taken by those approaching the subject from different angles.

I have not found that balanced view, and I am bound to say that I did not expect to find it. A great deal of what we have heard would demonstrate that my suspicions of the difficulty of finding a balanced view were justified. I think I need only point, on the one hand, to Mr Leask who has been perhaps the most vocal protagonist of one end of the argument, and to Mr Noel-Baker, on the other. Both these protagonists do, in fact, approach the subject of advertising from angles which are greatly influenced by general opinions, by general prejudices, if you like, deeply felt, genuinely felt, which have nothing to do with advertising at all. Mr Leask, in putting his point about the place of advertising in the community, laid a good deal of stress on its relevance to a free enterprise economy. He said, in effect, that if you believed in a free enterprise economy you believed in advertising; and I think that he would take also the opposite, converse proposition: that you cannot believe in advertising or think that advertising has a useful function to perform unless you believe in a free enterprise economy.

Mr Noel-Baker did not, overtly at any rate, approach his subject from such a political point of view. And when I say 'political', I am not talking in terms of party politics, but in terms of political science. What he did approach it from I think, was the ethical background of treating people as rational beings. 'Rational beings', in his sense, being perhaps more rational than many of us are or indeed many of us would want to be, or think it reasonable to be. So he also was influenced in his attitude to advertising by prejudices, or, if you prefer, by beliefs, or convictions, which cover a far wider range than advertising itself.

Against that background, to hope to get a synthesis of views so that you arrive at an agreed evaluation of advertising and its place in the community would really be too much to hope for. Indeed I do wonder whether we should want to get a balanced view in that sense, because, related as these respective views on advertising are to much wider considerations, political and ethical, I believe that probably a balanced view is not a thing to be desired. It would mean a uniformity about many basic beliefs which would not, in fact, be helpful to the progress of the human condition generally.

All this means that we are faced in dealing with advertising with the point which Professor Cohen made right at the beginning. It is very largely value judgements as well as facts which are involved in assessing the place of advertising in the community, and with that proposition I wholeheartedly agree. The value judgements which one must make about advertising are by definition subjective ones.

At this point, I should like to make a passing comment on what Mr Graham has said in connection with the ITA supervision of advertising. It may be that I am doing him some injustice here because I may be applying what he said to a rather wider field than he intended. What he said was that the advertising and the scrutiny of advertising with which ITA were concerned was simply a matter of selling goods and services, and not one of selling ideas. Certainly his comment arose in the context of religious and political ideas—that you cannot promote through television commercials any particular political party or any particular religious dogma—but I think that if anybody went away with the thought that ideas were not a very potent part of commercial advertising of goods and services, they would be greatly mistaken.

All the ideas which go into advertising whether on commercial television or in any other form are extremely potent ones. They are ideas which are part of the stock-in-trade of advertising techniques; ideas related to sex, to social status, indeed in some cases, although very deeply buried, to religious and political outlooks. Advertising without these underlying ideas would be advertising which was not very appealing.

This leads me on to what I regard as a rather sterile controversy between persuasive and informative advertising. It was pointed out that there is a field in which advertising is purely informative. If you want to buy a new lathe or something of that kind, what you look for is in the technical press. I don't think, however, that we need be deeply concerned with that kind of informative advertising. What we are really looking at is consumer goods and services advertising, and the place of persuasion and information in it. I really do not think you can generalize about this. It depends upon the product and the whole frame of reference.

In the case of cosmetics, which people constantly quote, persuasion rather than information is the stock-in-trade of the advertisers. I do not believe that this is a thing which we should condemn. The criticism was made that you could buy plain talcum powder very cheaply while the same thing, scented and rather agreeably packaged, was sold for a much higher price. A lot of people, Mr Leask maintained, would prefer to buy the expensive powder. So they would, and I do not see anything disreputable about that, with one qualification, and that is that there should be a choice.

I would apply the same thing in a slightly different context in the detergent field which is another very controversial field about the influence of advertising and the lack of information to help people's choice. In other words I think that you should be able to buy the loose talcum powder, smelling of nothing in particular, that you should be able to buy Square Deal Surf, and that you should not only have Omo, Dreft and the one accompanied by the plastic flower.

There has been a tendency to think, as I noticed the Prices and Incomes Board in their report recently on detergents evidently thinking, even if they did not explicitly say it, that the housewife was being a pretty poor sort of creature in preferring the packet with the plastic flower to the packet which, for the same money, had more detergent in it. It is a paradox that Square Deal Surf has not been a success. I believe that the powder may be disappearing off the market, and that Lever Brothers may now be promoting a Square Deal Liquid washing-up product. I suppose the answer to this very interesting paradox is partly that Square Deal Surf has not, by definition, been widely promoted. It has, of course, had some very worthy advertisements. If we toiled through what looked at first glance like an account of a social in the village hall, we eventually discovered at the end of the advertisement that it was about Square Deal Surf. This was a genuine attempt, I am sure, to give all the facts and information. The paradox is that people have not wanted Square Deal Surf, and have not bought it—probably largely because it has not been promoted and advertised in the same way as the other detergent powders have been, but also, I believe, because quite a lot of people do like getting a plastic flower. In some cases it may not be a positive pleasure to get it but it may be a consolation because a lot of household shopping is in fact rather dreary, and the plastic flower may bring a slight touch of brightness, or even soothe a fractious child for the time being.

So I would not at all subscribe to the theory which underlies Mr Noel-Baker's approach to the problem of advertising—that it is rational to buy the largest quantity for the least amount of money, or to buy something that is going to last longest for the cheapest amount of money. What I call rational is to buy something you want, and which you have the money to pay for. It is irrational to buy something which you cannot afford. And pure irrationality is when you buy something like an electric washing machine when in fact you are not plugged into the electricity. Curiously enough, you do meet such cases—a tribute perhaps to extremely high-pressure salesmanship. These are examples of really irrational consumers. Otherwise I never like to talk in terms of consumers being irrational. Quite often it is actually used as a term of abuse. Shopkeepers, for instance, often say to us: 'Oh, these ghastly irrational customers. How can you expect us to give them good service? They are so irrational they don't know what they want. They don't listen to what we have to say, and they don't ask the right questions.' I think that one can meet those arguments by saying that, short of the extremes of irrationality which I have mentioned, you should assume that consumers are in fact being rational when they buy something which, according to their own likes, meets their own wants and meets their purse.

This, of course, leads straight into the advertising field because you now run into value judgements about people's wants. And what they want, not from a commercial or economic view, but from the point of view of what really is pleasing and satisfying to some of their, in many cases, unexpressed and unacknowledged desires. Here you see an extremely subjective field where it is often very difficult for people outside the adver-

Elizabeth Ackroyd

tising world to be in sympathy with some of the ways, and with
some of the contexts, in which the advertising industry sets out
to appeal to the customer.

I noticed an advertisement in last week's *Sunday Times*
coloured magazine, which illustrates a number of these points.
It was for Embassy cigarettes. This, you see at once, is within
the whole ambit of what people feel about smoking cigarettes. I
don't smoke cigarettes and never have done. None the less I do
feel that there is a danger to health in the smoking of cigarettes,
and that it is wrong to persuade people to smoke cigarettes. I
therefore look at this advertisement against that background,
whereas lots of other people would look at it against a wholly
different background.

What it says is 'the accepted cigarette': that is the main bit at
the top. 'The accepted cigarette' appeals to what the trendsetters specify as social cachet, keeping up with the Joneses,
snobbery: very real motives in people's addictions. It then goes
on to say 'The best in smoking.' Well, of course, that is a claim,
which you could argue could be demonstrated objectively and,
indeed, the naïve seeing nothing but that particular advertisement might be prepared to take it on its merits—'The best in
smoking.' They may, however, get rather confused when they
turn over a page or two and see another advertisement: 'Robert
Nash', it says, 'smokes Perfectos.' And then: 'The best cigarettes
that money can buy.' So there you are, it is made apparent to you
at once if you press on from the one to the other that there is, in
fact, no objective criterion at all behind this statement about
'The best in smoking.'

Then, in the case of Embassy cigarettes, they go on to say
'with gifts for everyone'. This appeals to cupidity, which used
to be one of the seven vices, one of the ones from which most of
us suffer. It also has the additional connotation that in some
way you are getting it free, whatever the gift is. And, of course,
you are not. They wouldn't hand it to you if you did not buy
Embassy cigarettes. So there is also the kind of distortion of
phrasing which is now widespread in advertising and which
most of us take with a very substantial pinch of salt.

The point of taking you through that is to make clear that if I
saw that advertisement in the context of a face cream I should

feel far less critical of the slogans and the appeals to various hidden complexes than I do in reading it in the context of cigarettes. So I think it is extremely difficult for us, and we should not attempt, to generalize about persuasion and information. Nor can we really, as a generality, specify the criteria which are permissible in persuasion, to be applied uniformly. Again it is a subjective background conditioned by wholly different considerations from those relating simply to advertising.

Why is there such a defensive attitude in the advertising industry? Is it because quite a lot of people—perhaps more people than the advertising industry is willing to acknowledge— are uneasy about advertising? The evidence that people are generally rather suspicious of advertising can be drawn from a recent survey which National Opinion Polls did (and in so far as any market research is valid, I think this is reputable evidence).

One of the results was that 53 per cent of the people questioned said that they did not believe what they read in advertising. Now I am not saying, because it would obviously be a difficult thing to prove, that, if you faced these people with actual advertisements, 53 per cent would say that they didn't believe what they read in the case of these particular advertisements. What is interesting is that such a high proportion of people either did not believe what they read in advertising or felt that this was the right thing to say.

In all surveys of this kind, of course, you do not get an absolutely unprejudiced opinion when people are interviewed. But the fact that such a high proportion felt that they wanted to say that they didn't believe what they read in advertising does to me indicate that they felt there was some kind of insidious influence in advertising which they wanted to resist and be seen to resist. In the same sample, something like 75 per cent said that they had, in fact, bought things on the basis of the advertised claims for them. So there seems to be a very considerable schizophrenia.

The main point which I want to make, however, is not so much the discrepancy between the results, as that so many people said that they did not believe what they read in advertising. This result was spread pretty uniformly over all the A, B, C, D and E classes and over the age groups, except that, rather strikingly, the youngest age group interviewed were the most sceptical—or at any rate announced themselves as being the most sceptical. Yet one of the things in the code of advertising practice, which Mr Braun dealt with, is that advertisements, apart from a lot of other things, should not bring advertising into contempt. The survey indicates that this is one of the great problems for the advertising industry. It is one of the parts of the code that have not been observed. Obviously it is one of the most difficult ones to uphold because you cannot look at a particular advertisement and say this brings contempt. I do not know what the answer to this is.

There is, however, one solution which I suggest although this is something about which people in the advertising industry are sceptical. I believe that better awareness by consumers of the issues underlying the appeal of advertising to them would be a good thing. Critical, discerning, sceptical scrutiny of advertisements would be a valuable part of education, starting in the schools. This is something which the Consumer Council and other organizations have encouraged in quite a lot of secondary schools, as part of teaching English. I do not believe that this greater awareness by consumers of the limitations of advertising, in a more analytical way than just a general suspicion of advertising, would be damaging to the advertising industry.

Perhaps I might say now that I certainly don't accept that a modern industrial economy can function without advertising. I do believe the stock economic argument of mass production needing a mass market created by mass advertising in order to have the effect of reducing the cost of production. I accept that argument, and it would be madness to deny that in some things like detergents and washing machines, the result of this process has been an enormous boon to people in running their ordinary lives. Who wants to go back to hard soap and soda for washing clothes and for washing up the dishes?

Now I have been talking mainly on what you might call the upper level of justification for advertising and on the impossibility of a balanced view. But there is one area of advertising in which a balanced view is attainable, and that is on the much more down to earth, mundane area of factual claims in advertising. We have heard quite a lot about controls over advertising, and in particular the disciplinary machinery which Mr Braun described so clearly, and on which Professor Street has commented somewhat critically. On this the Consumer Council also has views.

It is, I think, possible to take a balanced view on factual claims about the performance of goods in a way which is not possible on these more general, ethical, value considerations which I have been talking about. A very good example of what I mean by taking a balanced view is advertising for toothpastes. Some toothpaste advertising, nowadays, stresses the prevention of decay. The proof of this is not positive. It would take a very long time, maybe a lifetime, or at least a generation to demonstrate that the use of this-or-that toothpaste does, in fact, prevent decay, because some of us in greater or less time may or may not have decay for other reasons. But undoubtedly, the toothpaste would in itself do people no harm, and advertising for toothpastes does encourage people to brush their teeth. Dentists would say that probably the best way of preventing decay is to brush your teeth. And there is a surprisingly large number of people in this country who are rather lax about brushing their teeth. So you can balance the exaggerated claim which does attract custom to the toothpaste against the fact that it is an inducement to people to brush their teeth, which they wouldn't otherwise do. Obviously there is an element of speculation about the extent to which the claim gets people to buy the toothpaste. However, I think that in this case you can obtain a balanced view about whether or not those advertisements are justified and there are other cases, no doubt, of the same kind. The Consumer Council would like to see, dealing with these claims, a greater statutory framework and, in some directions, a rather different one from the present.

May I say here that we have a lot to do with the Advertising Standards Authority and all the subsidiary machinery, and we find that a lot of the cases which we present to them are dealt with both sympathetically and efficiently, and very much from the same point of view as we ourselves would deal with them. But we also find, and I think Mr Braun would probably agree with this, an area in advertisements where there is just not a meeting of minds.

We maintain, in agreement here with Mr Noel-Baker, that the apex of the disciplinary machinery should be an independent body. By that I do not mean the Consumer Council, as some people have suggested, because we are, in our way, prejudiced and one-eyed, and are meant to be. I think that there should be something like, with all the necessary constitutional differences, the Federal Trade Commission. I share Mr Noel-Baker's view that the Advertising Standards Authority's independence does not fit in very well with its status. I think that the fact that it is the apex of the self-disciplinary machinery could be stressed in itself, and that the accent on the independence tends to confuse people about its real influence—which is considerable—within the self-disciplinary machinery.

In the same context, we have welcomed the Government's Protection of Consumers (Trade Descriptions) Bill. Like other people we recognize that there are certain drafting flaws in it. We should like, for instance, to see what I would describe as a general mis-description clause. That is to say that something that was misleading by impression or omission—not by something said, but by something not said—should be brought within the ambit of the legislation. The overall impression is just as important as any particular phrases or claims specifically spelt out or shown in a picture. This issue is a sort of nuts and bolts of consumer protection in relation to advertising, and in that area I think the famous balanced view might be possible. But over the field as a whole—No.

16

Advertisers and Educators

George Wedell

Advertisers and educators have a great deal in common. I suppose that is one of the reasons why they often do not get on well together. They are like different members of a family whose common idiosyncracies are obvious to all but themselves and who see the idiosyncracy which most irritates them only in their kinsmen, never in themselves.

I am always much struck by this family feeling when I read what the two tend to write and say about each other. They tend to have much the same objectives, at least of an avowed sort, and a similar strength of conviction about their ability single-handed to achieve them.

Persuasion and human frailty
One of a number of examples is the question of paternalism, or élitism, and its effect on the populace at large. Mr John Gloag, in his crusading book on *Advertising in Modern Life* quotes a speech of Lord Heyworth, a former chairman of Unilever, in which he 'demolished the assumption' that the public should be shielded from the temptation to choose what they want and buy what they like.

An idea appears to have grown up that people must be protected—though what they are to be protected from is not always clear. From making the wrong choice, I suppose, or what the benevolent and protective planner thinks is the wrong choice. I am sometimes tempted to wonder by what criterion those who think on these lines propose to divide the population into the select minority who are to have the right to pick and choose, and the remainder who are not considered fit to do so. Will provision be made for transfer rights from one group to the other—the time maybe of a provisional learner's licence to pick and choose for six months, pending passing the test?[1]

George Wedell

And he then goes on to quote Lord Heyworth on the ability of the common man to make up his own mind, given 'freedom of choice, including the right to make their choice, for whatever reasons seem best to them, whether they be emotional or icily rational'.

Now let us consider a quotation from Dr Daniel Jenkins' recent book, *The Educated Society*. Dr Jenkins is a minister and an educator.

When modern capitalistic society is left to its own devices, its inner logic drives it more and more in the direction of dividing itself into two categories of people, the providers and the consumers, the controllers and the controlled. The former may not be philistine in their private lives and indeed, for the sake of the rarer pleasures and joys of patronage they may seek to cultivate the company and talents of the representatives of high culture. But the very fact that their power depends on the trivialisation of mass desire means that they have an interest in keeping the world of high culture 'exclusive' . . . Establish a free flow between the world of high culture and the profitability of the latter are imperilled. The majority therefore must be made content with bread and circuses.[2]

We note that both writers, from diametrically opposed viewpoints, identify certain common elements in the socio-economic pattern of modern society:

(a) a division of the community into a minority group and a majority group;
(b) the pursuit by the minority group, composed, of course, of different people—the *guardians* on the one hand, and the *providers* on the other—of a course of action which they consider detrimental to the best interests of the majority;
(c) the identification of the majority group as the salt of the earth, or capable of so being if given a chance by the minority; and
(d) the placing of the writer firmly on the side of the oppressed majority, as whose champion he regards himself.

And here the two accounts come to the parting of the ways. Lord Heyworth's (and Mr Gloag's) adversaries are:

those who believe with Oliver Cromwell that the public should have 'not what they want but what is good for them'. Puritanism, that bitter stream which flows through our national life, sometimes rises to flood level and overflows into oppressive legislation . . .[3]

For Dr Jenkins the oppressive minority are the providers, those whose power 'depends on the trivialisation of mass desires' and whose 'pleasure derives from the unavailability of that which they enjoy to the majority'.[4]

We have seen how closely the psychological rationale of the two positions compares, although their objectives are opposed. If we now go on to look at the *means* by which they propagate their respective causes we find a further strong correspondence. This becomes apparent when we test their two statements against some of the specific techniques which are employed by propagandists and which are analysed by Dr J. A. C. Brown in his book *The Techniques of Persuasion*. Among the techniques described by Dr Brown are:

1. The use of stereotypes.
2. The substitution of names.
3. Selection.
4. Downright lying.
5. Repetition.
6. Assertion.
7. Pinpointing the enemy.
8. The appeal to authority.[5]

Let me hasten to say that Dr Brown's list was drawn up by reference to much more ruthless and totalitarian systems of propaganda than those with which we have to do.

But in the cause of persuasion, activities tend to be ranged in a continuum, from the mildest and unassertive at one end to the Inquisition and Dr Goebbels' methods in Nazi Germany at the other.

If we test the statements which I have just quoted against these techniques, we find that only the milder are used. Use is made of the *stereotype* in describing the majority; of the *substitution* of names in describing the minority; 'puritan' is an emotive term. (Jenkins, who incidentally pleads for a *new* puritanism, says that the word 'has now become one of the most loosely-used words in the English language, being used in the most general way as a synonym for austere self-discipline or a repressive hatred of all human enjoyment . . .')[6] Jenkins' description of the 'controllers' whose 'pleasure derives from the unavailability of that which they enjoy to the majority' falls into the category of the *substitution of names*, though in this case it is unfavourable terms with an emotional connotation, which are substituted for neutral ones unsuitable to the propagandist's purpose. Again, each author seems to me to make use of the device of *selection*: of selecting those facts only that are suitable to his purpose.

The question which we must ask ourselves is: given the universal use of techniques of propaganda, does this render *equivalent* their use, whatever the motive or whatever the ends to which these techniques are used? Or do the means so taint the ends that all ends pursued by them become equally obnoxious?

There are those who say, with Leonard Doob of Yale,[7] that sincerity or lack of it should be taken into consideration in deciding whether a piece of propaganda is legitimate.

In this view sincerity is to be defined as the state of affairs which exists when there is little or no discrepancy between the goals which an individual really seeks and the goals he publicly claims to be seeking.[8]

By this criterion both our authors can probably be acquitted. But, as Brown goes on to argue 'the issue is irrelevant, since the propagandist may be calculatingly deceitful or passionately sincere; it is the *method employed* which is deceitful, whether its operator is fully aware of the fact or not'. And that being so, I dare say we all find ourselves in very vulnerable glasshouses!

Social goals and social control

So both of us, advertisers and educators, are largely in the same boat when we come to pursue our concerns. There is an element of the propagandist in all of us which is liable to lead us into attempts to manipulate our fellow men. When we do so without knowing it, we become the more dangerous.

But it is also interesting to note that both our educator and our advertiser are concerned for social goals. Both claim to be concerned for human freedom. Mr Gloag for people 'to make their choice, for whatever reasons seem best to them, whether they be emotional or icily rational'. Dr Jenkins for freedom for ordinary people to express 'those convictions and loyalties to which, in their most responsible and clear-headed moments they wish to give their allegiance'.[9]

Both also recognize human frailty and unpredictability, and accept that people are at some times more emotional, at others more rational; that they have more responsible and clear-headed moments and those that are less so. And both writers, in consequence, accept the need for social controls of *some* kind, if the social goals of the community are to be achieved. Social controls are not necessarily external constraints and censorship. They include *conventions*; the public philosophy about which Walter Lippman has written; public *mores* inculcated by religion, education and social conditioning.

The difference in their attitudes arises at the point of definition of the nature of the social goals, and of the social controls needed to achieve them. In particular they concern the extent to which citizens should be protected against the consequences of their human frailty and unpredictability. Here Gloag would say, 'so be it: if X wants to smoke himself into an early grave, there is nothing that the community should do to make it more difficult for him. In particular there is no onus on the cigarette manufacturers to do so. If Y wants to restrict access to his hotels to white people, why should he not be able to do so? If Z wishes to import 50 per cent of his television shows from the USA, who has the right to stop him? Let the free flow of the market regulate supply and demand.'

Dr Jenkins, on the other hand, would argue that human frailty inhibits the free flow of the market and that society must not only provide a long stop for its inadequates but also aim at the improvement of the quality of life for the generality of citizens, and that this may involve curbing the freedom of action of the powerful minority.

The argument thus narrows down to one not about the existence of social goals, but about the extent and nature of these and of the social controls necessary to subserve them. And the crucial question is whether both groups, advertisers *and* educators, recognize this as an area of debate. It is the absence of such recognition that has all too often made any intelligent discourse on the subject impossible. People have assumed that to deny the existence of this area of debate would be enough to eliminate it. This obviously has not happened, nor is it likely to do so. Quite the contrary. Nor is it sufficient to devolve this job of creating the good society on to the educators alone. Mr Gloag writes:

Whether a consumer's world is a good thing or not, whether the people who inhabit it are pampered or degenerate, and whether they know, or can learn, how to use leisure gracefully, intelligently and creatively are matters which educationalists should ponder. Education in Britain is not yet objectively training people for an intelligent use of leisure, sharpening their critical powers, or improving their judgment.[10]

This may be, but social education does not go on in a vacuum: it consists of the whole of life. People are educated, for good or ill, by all the influences which are brought to bear on them in their setting—their families, the neighbours, the community in which they live, the press, radio, television, films. *If* people in the mass media *want* an intelligent use of leisure, a sharpening of critical powers, an informed judgement, not to mention the graceful, intelligent and creative use of leisure, then they must make their contribution. They must recognize that when it comes to the distinction between leaders and followers in any community, both they and the educators are on the side of the former, with all the uncomfortable responsibility which that implies. Not only must they not militate actively against these values; they have a duty to affirm them in their work.

Those in touch with the hard realities of the present mass media situation will recognize the need for the practical application of these simple principles. How can we set about this? What options are open to us?

Professionals and human beings
Firstly, integration of professional and personal roles. We all play a number of roles in the course of the day, in particular our professional and our personal ones. The geographical distance between home and office in modern societies means that these two roles are often played out in watertight compartments. At work we affirm one set of values; at home another; in the pub a third; and so on. It therefore comes naturally to compartmentalize our experience—it is to some extent a defensive mechanism, which helps to keep us sane. But at the cost of greater nervous strain, I think we must strive for a better integration of our several roles.

Next, because most of us see our professional contacts in only *one* of their roles, we see them as functionaries, not as people. Those concerned with advertising have a clear functional relationship one to another. The *advertiser* (whether he be producer or distributor) wants to move his stock and spends on advertising. The *medium owner* needs advertising to finance his operation, whether it is a newspaper, television or whatever. The *advertising agent* is the link between the two, the technical expert. The *consumer* is the fictitious composite personality whose function it is to buy the product made or distributed by the advertiser and which is brought to his notice by the intervention of the advertising agent through a medium of mass communication.

We tend to discuss these four partners separately and in the abstract, although in recent times we seem to come closer to developing an integrated view of these partners, as sharing in a human condition and each in his way labouring to make this condition more creative and free. I regard the nurturing and growth of this integrated view, this new ethos, as the most important development within the advertising profession in the next few years. The significant thing is that it is largely a process of self-education, in the last resort the only effective education. Those of us who are professional educators have, as I have shown, little to teach and can at best try to provide a setting within which this process can grow and develop.

Professional education
Out of this new *ethos* within the profession will come, secondly, a concern about the content of professional education. Education for advertising has followed that for other professions in being highly specialized. The problem is universal in the field of educational planning: how do we turn out the largest number of people best qualified in a particular field in the shortest time? More recently we have discovered two things:

(i) That a narrowly specialist education not only has educational drawbacks, but also fails to turn out really competent specialists, since no specialism exists in a vacuum. Hence the growth of *interdisciplinary* studies.

(ii) That a single 'bout' of education does not set up a man for a lifetime's effectiveness in his profession. The turnover of knowledge is such that education is coming to be seen as a life-long process, requiring intermittent periods of study throughout a professional career.

These discoveries have implications for Advertising as for other professions. They suggest, for instance, that the syllabus for the IPA examinations is too narrow. It includes only one paper at any stage which promotes thought on the setting within which the advertiser moves: this is the paper on Psychology in relation to Advertising in the Joint Intermediate Examination, and this is being discontinued. Surely this is inadequate, whatever the previous education of the candidates. The second discovery suggests that provision for professional development courses for people at different stages of their careers should increasingly be provided. I recognize that this cannot be done by the profession alone, and that the onus is to a large extent on the providing bodies.

Discrimination and commitment

Thirdly, there is the area of consumer education. A good deal has already been said and written about this. Hence it is merely necessary to emphasize that there is a substantial field for the development of the critical awareness of the consumer from a reasonably early age: the development of his powers of discrimination: and need for the study of ways and means of doing this without undermining, as Professor Hoggart so rightly points out in chapter 4, the emotional basis of the consumer's commitment to his own values. The erosion of this commitment in the face of the highly charged demands on it made by *all* aspects of modern society is a problem for the mass media as much as for advertising. Curiously enough, some education authorities are resistant to the systematic tackling of this task because they fear that yet another subject will be added to the syllabus. This resistance has substance, since the teaching of consumer education as a separate subject is likely to prove nugatory. Discrimination, like charity and honesty, is an *attitude* which must pervade the teaching and life of the school as a whole if it is to be taught effectively.

There is an exciting and challenging time ahead for both advertisers and educators. But only if both are willing to recognize the complexity of truth, to accept their own frailty as propagandists, and to treat their clients as human beings, will they do justice to their responsibilities in the affluent society.

References
1 Gloag, J. *Advertising in Modern Life*. Heinemann, 1959. p. 7.
2 Jenkins, D. *The Educated Society*. Faber and Faber, 1966. p. 53.
3 Gloag, p. 6.
4 Jenkins, p. 53.
5 Brown, J. A. C. *Techniques of Persuasion*. Penguin, 1966. pp. 25–7.
6 Jenkins, p. 82.
7 Doob, Leonard W. *Public Opinion and Propaganda*. Crescent Press.
8 Brown, p. 22.
9 Jenkins, pp. 53–4.
10 Gloag, p. 12.

17

Living with advertising

Alexander Wilson

Advertising has become part of our everyday life. We may not always like it. We may regard much of it as a calculated insult to our intelligence. Some of it may even make our stomachs turn. We may distrust its impact on our family spending pattern, and suspect that it uses us more than we use it. But it is here to stay for the foreseeable future. Modern economies cannot function without it, and even consumers' organizations rely on it. We have to learn to live with it, and need to come to terms with it on as satisfactory a basis as we can evolve.

The demand for advertising services has been growing steadily over the last two decades in the highly industrialized countries. In most cases, it has grown slightly faster than national income or consumer expenditure, but in Britain and the United States, in recent years, expenditure on advertising has been a constant or declining percentage of national income. In several European countries, the percentage is still rising towards the British figure.

Today Britain spends about £590 million on all forms of advertising. About two-thirds of this is channelled through the mass media, television, newspapers and magazines. The remainder includes promotions, direct mail, leaflets, catalogues, exhibitions and point-of-sale display materials. Much of this expenditure helps publishers to offer newspapers and magazines at a fraction of their cost, often less than half their economic cost. In 1966, for instance, 440 million copies of women's magazines carried approximately £25·7 million worth of advertising revenue, or about 1s. 3d. per copy. And, of course, viewers are not directly charged for their Independent Television programmes.

About 60 per cent of the total expenditure (£345 million in 1965) goes through the 275 agencies affiliated to the Institute of Practitioners in Advertising. These agencies made a net profit after tax of about £3·9 million in 1965, equivalent to about 16 per cent on capital resources. The top twenty of these agencies employed a total of about 8,300 people, with a salary total of around £12·5 million. 94 per cent of all advertising placed through agencies is handled by the IPA agencies.[1]

British advertising agencies have been severely affected in recent years by the economic recessions of 1961–2 and 1965–8, by Corporation Tax and the Selective Employment Tax (which costs them about £1 million a year). These factors have taken some of the bounce out of the agencies, which have found it difficult to keep up their profit ratios and employment figures. In 1961–2 about 1,000 people left the industry, which can economize mainly by cutting staff. But the calibre of its staff is perhaps the main factor in an agency's competitiveness, and clients are suspicious of constant changes among agency staff. In recent years, the number of trainees taken into the industry has been falling, despite the need to attract intelligent and lively-minded young men and women, if standards are to be maintained.

Meanwhile the healthy trend towards a marketing orientation throughout industry has had the consequence of making advertisers more concerned than ever with the return on their advertising expenditures. Their desire to optimize this increases the pressure on agency executives to find proven yardsticks of advertising effectiveness. This depends on adequate research into consumer motivation, communications, the efficiency of different media and methods, and measurements of sales efficiency. Demands for better or additional services become expensive for the agencies. This pressure seems to be associated with a readiness on the part of advertisers to switch their accounts. This is hardly a new feature in advertising, where a certain amount of poaching of accounts and executives has long been part of the game. Frequent changes of agency can hardly help the marketing of a product, while over-impatience for

results or exaggerated expectations may carry dangerous implications for the long-term improvement of ethical standards
within the industry, and for the development of mutual trust
and closer relationship between client and agent on which much
of the hoped-for improvement in advertising effectiveness
appears to depend.

Much of the advertising is aimed at the retailer as well as at
the final customer. Retailers tend to refuse to stock lines which
are neither brand leaders nor well supported by advertising.
Special offers and promotions are increasingly planned and
advertised in the trade journals months in advance of being set
before the public, and the retailer is given the assurance of
supporting advertising at the appropriate time. Mass product
manufacturers and mass retailers are both convinced of the
importance of good merchandising and display at store level,
but they are also convinced that this would not be so successful
without reliance on advertised products. Some advertising of
particular products will ensure that a whole range of associated
products will also be stocked.

Against this background, the advertising industry has been
subjected, probably more often than any other major industry,
to well-meaning but ill-informed criticism. This is hardly surprising since its practitioners earn a living by projecting their
output into the public eye. The more successfully they manage
to do this, the more they are at risk in inviting subjective
criticism. Nor is it surprising that advertising people who have
become extremely astute in associating particular emotions with
particular products, should arouse a good deal of reaction which
is itself charged with emotion. What is really surprising is that
advertising professionals who are so skilled in putting over their
clients' points of view, seldom seem capable of making coherent
and effective rejoinders to many of the unbalanced attacks made
upon them. Mild understatement and sweet reason would
normally make their critics look unrealistic, or silly, whereas
righteous fury tends to boomerang, and do their case little
good. The situation would seem to be that the advertising industry is riddled with decent and capable people who, despite
the basic conviction that they are devoting most of their energies
and abilities to exacting and useful activity, carry a chip on

their shoulders about criticism of their profession. Sometimes this is coupled with a slightly guilty conscience. Sometimes it tends to blind them to potentially constructive criticism. It is usually easier to be accommodating to criticism when one feels one's basic position to be sound and secure.

It is much to the credit of the advertising industry, that despite these pressures and criticisms, its practitioners have built up an impressive array of organizations to promote higher standards of behaviour, and uphold codes of practice which have been worked out in conjunction with other public watchdogs or self-determined. The work of the Code of Advertising Practice Committee, the Advertising Investigation Department, the Advertising Standards Authority and the Copy Committees of the media is obviously important and socially valuable. It may well be, as advertising people frequently claim, that advertising standards in Britain are significantly higher than they were fifteen years ago. Or even that they are probably the highest in the world.

Perhaps then we should come to terms with advertising; accept it for what it is, including the stomach-turning elements; note that it is in capable hands, and that its machinery of self-regulation is developing nicely; and worry about the many more important things which beset the world.

If, however, standards have been rising so satisfactorily since the advent of commercial television, this indicates that standards and practice are amenable to pressure, and that the limits to further improvement are probably not known. Here it seems fair to ask whether the perfecting of the ITA control system and the birth of the Advertising Standards Authority would have come about without some goading and encouragement from outside the industry? And if public suspicion and criticism were now to be stilled, could we be reasonably sure that the recent pace of improvement would be maintained?

Coming to terms with advertising on such a basis would not appear to be acceptable even to the representatives of the advertising industry, who all appear to accept the need for social control. The problem here which we have not managed to solve yet, despite the fifty or more statutory enactments and the codes of advertising practice, is largely over the form and extent of social control which is required, enforceable and acceptable.

Here the crucial questions which have emerged would seem to be:

1. Is the Advertising Standards Authority as weak as its critics suggest? Or, during its short life, has it been doing a reasonably good job? Could it do even better if it had more resources behind it, and more staff for monitoring? Should it look for offences against the Code of Advertising Practice, rather than await complaints? Should it be more ready to name offenders? Can a budget of about £30,000 possibly be adequate to operate a voluntary system of self-regulation effectively? Is compulsory, independent scrutiny, as with the ITA system of control, really needed for policing of standards? Would a body financially independent of the Advertising Association be at least as effective?

2. Why has the long list of existing legislation restraining advertising not been adequate? Is it mainly due to constantly changing conditions? Or does some fault lie with weak enforcement? Does the Board of Trade use its powers too sparingly? If so, has this been a matter of ministerial decision, or of economy of limited resources? Would its control function be better carried out by a fair trading control body set up on the lines of the US Federal Trade Commission? Or, as suggested by the Reith committee, by a National Consumer Board with powers to challenge false claims and initiate prosecutions?

3. If we do need more legislation, who is going to have responsibility for enforcement? The Board of Trade or Local Authorities? If the latter, how variable will enforcement be by authorities which may be enthusiastic, half-hearted or even sceptical?

The attraction of further legislation seems difficult to resist, especially perhaps if one is a politician or a lawyer, yet one must sympathize with the anxious advertising practitioner when one listens to a recital of all the bits and pieces of legislation which already exist to keep him on the straight and narrow path. If so much past legislation is already obsolescent, or has proved ineffectual, that new legislation is urgently needed, how can we expect it to be so much more helpful? Nevertheless, It is clearly the government's responsibility to ensure that the ordinary citizen is protected against practices which are both objectionable and can be clearly defined. Where this is not possible it is better to leave cases of dubious behaviour to be controlled by self-regulation. Since the law is concerned, in this context, merely with the maintenance of minimum standards, while most advertisers and agents will normally practise something better than this, it may be argued that the consumer stands to gain more from the development of high self-determined standards within the industry, than from the imposition of legal minima. Nevertheless, raising the level of the base can usually be relied upon to push up the general level.

The proposals in the Consumers Protection Bill for strengthening previous merchandising marks legislation and making false or misleading claims an actionable offence, appear to be widely welcomed. There may be some doubts about relying exclusively on criminal penalties for misleading advertising offences, but it seems to be accepted that the more responsible advertisers and agents stand to benefit from stricter control over fraudulent advertisements and unscrupulous characters. So the Bill, when it eventually gets passed, should bring benefits not merely to consumers. It should give better backing to the industry's voluntary system.

It is encouraging that the Bill intends to make prosecution by Local Authorities for alleged offences mandatory, and to provide grants to strengthen local Weights and Measures Inspectorates. This is long overdue. It is to be hoped that this new power will be effectively exercised without resulting in too many trivial prosecutions. It is interesting to find that members of the public may be able to complain to the Board of Trade if they feel enforcement by their local authority proves to be inadequate. It might be more desirable, however, to have complaints of this kind channelled through the Consumer Council and MP's.

The suggestion that Britain should set up a control body on the lines of the Federal Trade Commission has been mooted for a good many years, and obviously merits deeper study than it has so far received. It is by no means clear that the FTC, despite its right to protect consumers from deceptive advertising, has had conspicuous success in controlling misleading advertising in the United States. Its standards appear to be less stringent than the codes of advertising practice which are applied in Britain. Its machinery is rather ponderous and elaborate, and does not manage to obtain quick results. It has been said that it takes so long to deal with cases that advertising campaigns are normally completed before decisions are obtained. On the other hand, some aspects, such as the power to issue 'cease and desist' orders, might well be copied. Perhaps some variation of the system might operate well in Britain, but the Molony Committee was not impressed with its suitability.

The possibilities and weaknesses of the FTC can be seen in its recent victory over Procter & Gamble against which it brought a case concerning the acquisition of Clorox ten years ago. The Supreme Court has eventually ruled that this acquisition made its advertising power a threat to other much smaller producers of liquid bleach. The ruling implied that when a large advertiser entered a field occupied only by small advertisers, the market power of the large company creates a situation which tends towards monopoly and should therefore be forbidden.[2]

This, however, is perhaps of less concern to consumers than to controllers of monopolies and market power. More interesting and important for American, and British, consumers might be the recent criticism of consumer goods advertising by Mr Donald Turner, chief of the Anti-Trust Division of the Department of Justice. He feels that someone should be making objective tests of standard products such as aspirin, bread and petrol, and tell the consumer whether brand X is really better than brand Y. He proposes a government version of *Consumer Reports* (a magazine similar to *Which?*).[3]

This idea of government-sponsored appraisal and reporting services for consumer products could be a first step towards persuading governments and manufacturers' associations to adopt long-term policies which would deal with quality standards, guarantees and after-sales service. Ideally one would want to see much of the exaggerated advertising of today replaced by more informative advertising based on reliably conducted product tests, and to have products labelled on the basis of assessment in such tests. In fields such as medicines where public health and safety are concerned, there is an even stronger case for grants of public funds for the testing institutes.

With the tendency of British governments to interfere more in the description and sale of goods and in the determination of prices and incomes, it seems likely that the Board of Trade will begin to exercise more of its powers and influence over advertisers. The advertising world will have to learn to live with this. Efforts to make false or misleading claims less likely to occur will be fairly widely welcomed, though there is always the danger of over-protecting the consumer. Legislation, which is otherwise impeccable, may easily demand detail which increases the production, packaging, labelling or pricing operational costs beyond any likely benefit to the consumer in worthwhile protection.

There will also be some doubts about the wisdom of Board of Trade action to seek price reduction by forcing or encouraging reductions in advertising expenditure. This may be justified up to the hilt when both the Prices and Incomes Board and the Monopolies Commission have recommended such action. But it might be unhealthy to make frequent resort to such controls. Here it might be useful to remind ourselves of the caution, given by Professor Simmonds, that those interested in community values need to see advertising also in the context of its value to the profit-motivated firm, that it should be seen as part of the marketing mix, and to realize that trying to isolate the effects of advertising from that of the many other variables is a painstaking job.

If advertising is to be increasingly regulated in order to eliminate purely competitive padding, a good deal more thinking and research is needed about when and how to impose regulation . . . Advertising is not a homogeneous and separable element and to regulate it as such would be extremely ill-advised . . . Those concerned with advertising and community welfare, therefore, would be well-advised to adopt the approach of the marketer and to concentrate on developing tools and methods for situational decisions—rather than pursuing regulation aimed at advertising as a generic class.[4]

It is to be hoped that some of this thinking and research will emerge from the independent enquiry into the economic effects of advertising and its relationship to competition which is being instituted by the President of the Board of Trade. This may be greatly assisted by the results of the fascinating three-sided game of detergent chess which is being played by the Board of Trade along with Unilever and Procter & Gamble. Several intriguing moves have been made, with the Board of Trade virtually succeeding in carrying out the major recommendation of the Monopolies Commission by getting agreement from the big detergent companies to cut advertising and promotional costs heavily and reduce wholesale prices by 20 per cent on a range of products. The companies, having committed themselves to using their best efforts and marketing skills to launch the new brands as a commercial operation, have tried to minimize the extra cost by switching existing brands to the new price range, thereby capitalizing on years of heavy advertising in the case of 'Extra Value Tide' and 'Extra Value Oxydol'.[5]

This should provide an interesting and useful experiment, especially in relation to consumer reaction. Will housewives be sufficiently informed to take advantage of the opportunity offered them? Or are they not terribly interested even in a steady 20 per cent (or thereabouts) reduction? Will the assumption of many marketers that the housewife wants satisfactions which may be provided more readily by packaging, plastic daffodils and the occasional 4d. off coupon than by price reduction be substantiated? Will a steady 20 per cent differential be maintained by the retailers in the shops? Will they be offered the same volume discounts on the new range as on the old? Will there be rather more special offers of the heavily advertised range? Will the two companies gradually stop advertising the cheap range and increase advertising and promotion of 'new, improved' versions of the higher-margin range? Will price competition increase the monopoly position in the detergent market by eroding the present small shares of the other producers such as the CWS, Jeyes, Bibby? Obviously the Board of Trade had thought some of these out, in promising a review of the whole situation after the independent inquiry, and in extracting the undertaking that the prices of the detergents covered by the Monopolies Commission report would not be raised for two years.

The experiment would have been even more interesting if the cheap range had consisted of genuinely new brands, but this would obviously have involved the companies, initially at least, in heavier total expenditure, and the risk that the success of any of the new range would bring diseconomies of scale production and distribution for the established brand leaders. It is possible that big companies would be glad to be ordered to spend less on advertising some products, and it may be that the major contribution of the Prices and Incomes Board and the Board of Trade to the advertising scene may lie in their ability to help major advertisers to get gently off the hook when they find themselves committed to hopeless advertising wars.

In relation to voluntary controls within the advertising industry, an impressive case has been made out by Mr Braun for relying as far as possible on a system of self-regulation, and that the Advertising Standards Authority merits greater recognition as the apex of the system. It seems clear that legislation by itself would not be effective in developing high standards throughout the profession, and that without a substantial degree of co-operation on the part of advertising practitioners, advertisers and media owners, controls would not achieve their objectives. It is no doubt also true that the advertising world behaves more responsibly than ever before, and that advertisements are less sensational, vulgar, misleading and preposterous than they used to be.

If the system of self-regulation does not succeed in exercising a greater degree of control over provincial press advertising, classified advertisements and forms of advertising used by small advertisers and small agents, there will continue to be a chorus of critics demanding statutory controls. It will be difficult for the ASA on its present modest budget and staff even to give the impression of getting on with this job, apart from developing its activities in other, perhaps more useful, areas.

The annual reports of the ASA indicate that it has brought about notable improvements in the British Code of Advertising Practice, and has now overhauled it. Apparently it has been succeeding in enforcing the code more strictly, and that the Advertising Investigation Department is satisfied that about 95 per cent of advertising is blameless. With an industry such as advertising it is difficult to know how serious a failure rate of 5 per cent is.[6]

With regard to naming offenders, Lord Drumalbyn, the chairman of the ASA has stated:

It is not usual to make public the names of advertisers and advertising agencies who infringe the Code. The whole system depends on voluntary cooperation and the fullest cooperation is in all but a minute number of cases obtained. It could hardly be expected that advertisers against whom complaints are made would be so ready to cooperate if they knew that in the event of the case being decided against them they would be publicly 'named'.[7]

This is not entirely convincing. Presumably offenders would be named only if they persisted after the case had been decided against them, and not if they made amends. If advertisers and agencies were aware, moreover, that non-co-operation would be normally construed as confirmation of the complaint, it seems even less likely that they would refuse to co-operate.

A considerable bite comes in Lord Drumalbyn's further statement:

If, however, an advertiser or advertising agency were persistently to be in breach of the Code, media would be recommended not to accept any advertising from the advertiser or to withdraw recognition from the advertising agency. Withdrawal of recognition would mean that the agency would no longer be entitled to the customary commission and would virtually put it out of business ... The standard form of recognition between media and advertising agencies contains a term requiring the observance of the Code.

This is indeed strong medicine and should mean that there should be no great problem of enforcement of the Code, if the media sincerely accept the decisions of the Code of Advertising Practice Committee and the Advertising Standards Authority.

Many of these problems would be easier to solve if we could find that the effectiveness of advertising was enhanced rather than diminished by the adoption of higher standards of veracity, rationality, objectivity and visual beauty. But most advertising operates on the basis of accepting existing standards of taste, and following, rather than leading, any improvement in these. Yet here one is conscious of a gap between the best in advertising and the normal. Some advertising is so much more interesting, more attractive or more humorous than most. As for the worst it is steadily abysmal. This applies both to persuasive and informative advertising. This gap may be due to differences in ability and training, but it would seem largely due to different calculations about the effectiveness of different approaches in different markets. It would be delightful to discover that much advertising loses effectiveness if one adopts too pessimistic and cynical an assessment of public taste and consumer reaction to advertising. But until that can be proved, the challenge is at least as much to the educators as to the advertisers. Perhaps the first step might be for successful advertising men to persuade their colleagues, and competitors, that it does not really help effectiveness to push so many worn-out clichés, half-truths and flagrant fantasies. Obviously these do not help advertising as a whole, though they may temporarily help substandard products to obtain super sales.

Part of the answer may lie in closer collaboration between advertising practitioners and educators. Perhaps the latter have never quite accepted advertising as a proper subject of serious study. Why help the devil to do his job more efficiently? Despite the improvements in educational standards and professional training in recent years, it seems doubtful whether advertising people really know enough about psychology to fully understand the consumer. Do they know enough about the techniques of communication? Do they know enough about the technical qualities of the products they advertise? Do they really know how to measure the effects of particular advertising campaigns, or advertisements? Do they know which organizations under-use advertising and could with benefit add to their advertising budgets? Do they know how to make the best use of their computers?

No doubt within the next few years, advertisers and advertising executives will be able to look more confidently for answers to some of these problems and for indicators of effectiveness to the Business Schools and the University Departments of Marketing. Apart from their contribution to changing the traditionally unfavourable-to-business ethos of this country, they can be expected to build up a much more useful body of knowledge about advertising than exists at present in Britain.

Meanwhile the studies of advertising now being sponsored by the Advertising Association and the Board of Trade will probably throw a good deal of light usefully on certain aspects. The results are bound to have some effect on public opinion, though they will probably tend to reinforce existing attitudes. So much of the main debate about advertising is not about its cost to the nation in terms of economic resources otherwise available for the production of alternative goods and services. On the one side, it can be reasonably well demonstrated that advertising can be a very economical and efficient means of stimulating consumers into action. On the other side, this stimulation of the appetite to buy things can be shown to be an invasion of the private feelings and consciousness of need of the individual consumer. This will still be anathema to those who moralize against the cult of materialism, and many more will continue to object to the way in which the advertising results are achieved. The great majority of the British public will probably remain as unmoved as ever over the arguments.

It is obviously difficult to come to terms with advertising so that it helps in the progress towards the good society—in which enjoyment of life and delight in the aesthetic arts will seem more important than wise budgeting and material comfort, in which citizens will be well enough educated to be discerning in their spending of money and time, and well-enough-off to make ultra-careful discrimination in purchasing relatively unimportant. This may seem rather a tall order, but we are still so far from having achieved such a society that the possibilities must be considerable.

Perhaps as individuals, we might enhance our enjoyment of life by developing the ability, like Professor Street, of switching off subconsciously when one is being got at by advertising in newspapers, magazines, posters and television. One is at risk of seeing hundreds of commercial messages every day. Why do we watch, read or see ads unless we enjoy them or find them interesting? Millions of people obviously enjoy them as part of the evening's entertainment. Millions of others cheerfully accept TV commercials as the price they have to pay for otherwise free ITV programmes. Those who are not so keen on commercials might do rather more about switching off.

Yet it does not seem unreasonable that media should respect some civilized conventions, such as newspapers keeping most of their ads separate from the serious columns, magazines placing their ads mainly at the front and back pages and television showing ads only between programmes and not in the middle of them as we crassly do in Britain. One might also expect to be able to look round in one's urban and rural environment without distress to one's visual senses. Does it really help industry and commerce to befoul our surroundings with the hideous plastering of supermarket windows, the often unpleasing hoardings and the even more abominable clutter| of newsagents' forecourts? It is not that such advertising need be completely swept away. It is that the variation in appearance, and possibly in effectiveness, between well-dressed shop windows, well-appointed hoardings and forecourts and their miserable counterparts is enormous. This may be simply a reflection of the local social environment, and not the fault of commercial advertising. But too often there is a tendency to mutual degradation, which needs to be resisted by all who have the interests of the good society and good advertising at heart.

If we want a better advertising industry, then we need rather more rational and balanced criticism than the industry has had in the past. It would be useful to get beyond the usual confrontation between the critics and defenders of advertising to a situation in which all parties, including relatively uncommitted academics and realistically-minded representatives of consumer interests, could develop a more healthy and constructive dialogue. This might lead to a general improvement in the quality, and perhaps even the effectiveness of advertising, possibly moving a few steps away from the repetitious battering of the senses of the community towards the educator's dream of advertising which bases itself on high levels of intelligence and taste within a community of perceptive, discriminating, yet emotional, consumers.

References
[1] O'Connor, J. P. 'The Agency Role.' *Financial Times*, 26 June 1967.
[2] 'War on Advertising.' *The Economist*, 29 April 1967.
[3] Ibid.
[4] See above, pp. 47–8.

[5] *The Times*, 27 April 1967; 28 April 1967. *The Economist*, 29 April 1967. See above, pp. 61–2.
[6] *Annual Report of the Advertising Standards Authority*. May 1966. *The Times*, 8 May 1967. *The Guardian*, 8 October 1965; 3 May 1966.
[7] Lord Drumalbyn. 'Setting the Standards.' *Financial Times*, 26 April 1967.

Appendix A

The Independent Television Code of Advertising Standards and
Practice (July 1964, amended August 1965)

Foreword
Section 8(1) of the Television Act, 1964, states that it shall be the duty
of the Independent Television Authority—

(a) to draw up, and from time to time review, a code governing standards and practice in advertising and prescribing the advertisements
and methods of advertising to be prohibited, or prohibited in particular
circumstances; and
(b) to secure that the provisions of the code are complied with as
regards the advertisements included in the programmes broadcast by
the Authority.

The rules about advertising contained in this booklet govern all
advertising on Independent Television until further notice. In drawing
up this code the Authority has consulted the Advertising Advisory
Committee and the members of the Medical Advisory Panel appointed
in accordance with Section 9(5) of the Television Act, 1964.

Under Section 7(5) of the Television Act, 1964, the Authority must
consult the Postmaster-General about the classes and descriptions of
advertisements which must not be broadcast and the methods of advertising which must not be employed and to carry out any directions he
may give them in these respects. The Authority has consulted the
Postmaster-General on the rules here published and he has accepted
those to which Section 7(5) is applicable.

It should be noted that Section 8(2) of the Television Act, 1964,
expressly reserves the right of the Authority to impose requirements
as to advertisements and methods of advertising which go beyond the
requirements imposed by this code. The programme contractors, too,
may in certain circumstances impose stricter standards than those
here laid down—a right comparable to the recognized right of those
responsible for other advertising media to reject any advertisements
they wish.

Enquiries by advertisers and advertising agencies about the application
of the Independent Television Code of Advertising Standards and
Practice to individual advertisements should be directed to the Independent Television Companies Association Ltd, Knighton House,

52-66 Mortimer Street, London, W.1, or the programme contractor or contractors with whom it is proposed to place the advertisements.

Preamble

1 The general principle which will govern all television advertising is that it should be legal, clean, honest and truthful. It is recognized that this principle is not peculiar to the television medium, but is one which applies to all reputable advertising in other media in this country. Nevertheless, television, because of its greater intimacy within the home, gives rise to problems which do not necessarily occur in other media and it is essential to maintain a consistently high quality of television advertising.

2 Advertisements must comply in every respect with the law, common or statute. In the case of some Acts, notably the Merchandise Marks Acts, rules applicable to other forms of advertising may not, on a strict interpretation of the Acts, cover television advertising. Advertisments must, however, comply in all respects with the spirit of those Acts.

3 The detailed rules set out below are intended to be applied in the spirit as well as the letter and should be taken as laying down the minimum standards to be observed.

4 The word 'advertisement' has the meaning implicit in the Television Act, i.e. any item of publicity inserted in the programmes broadcast by the Authority in consideration of payment to a programme contractor or to the Authority.

Programme independence

5 No advertisement may include anything that states, suggests or implies, or could reasonably be taken to state, suggest or imply, that any part of any programme broadcast by the Authority has been supplied or suggested by any advertiser—Television Act, 1964, Section 7(6).

Identification of advertisements

6 An advertisement must be clearly distinguishable as such and recognizably separate from the programmes—Television Act, 1964, Schedule 2, paragraph 1(1).

'Subliminal' advertising

7 No advertisement may include any technical device which, by using images of very brief duration or by any other means, exploit the possibility of conveying a message to, or otherwise influencing the minds of, members of an audience without their being aware, or fully aware, of what has been done—Television Act, 1964, Section 3(3).

Good taste

8 No advertisement should offend against good taste or decency or be offensive to public feeling—Television Act, 1964, Section 3(1)(a).

Gifts or prizes
9 No advertisement may include an offer of any prize or gift of significant value, being a prize or gift which is available only to television viewers of the advertisement or in relation to which any advantage is given to viewers—Television Act, 1964, Section 3(4).

Stridency
10 Audible matter in advertisements must not be excessively noisy or strident—Television Act, 1964, Schedule 2, paragraph 1(4).

Charities
11 No advertisement may give publicity to the needs or objects of any association or organization conducted for charitable or benevolent purposes. (This does not preclude the advertising of 'flag days', fêtes or other events organized by charitable organizations or the advertising of publications of general interest.)

Religion and politics
12 No advertisements may be inserted by or on behalf of any body the objects whereof are wholly or mainly of a religious or political nature, and advertisements must not be directed towards any religious or political end or have any relation to any industrial dispute— Television Act, 1964, Schedule 2, paragraph 8.

Appeals to fear
13 Advertisements must not without justifiable reason play on fear.

Unacceptable products or services
14 Advertisements for products or services coming within the recognized character of, or specifically concerned with, the following are not acceptable:

(a) money-lenders
(b) matrimonial agencies and correspondence clubs
(c) fortune-tellers and the like
(d) undertakers or others associated with death or burial
(e) unlicensed employment services, registers or bureaux
(f) organizations/companies/persons seeking to advertise for the purpose of giving betting tips
(g) betting (including pools)
(h) cigarettes and cigarette tobacco

N.B. An advertiser who markets more than one product may not use advertising copy devoted to an acceptable product for purposes of publicizing the brand name or other identification of an unacceptable product. [See also Appendix 2(a)3].

Reproduction techniques

15 It is accepted that the technical limitations of photography can lead to difficulties in securing a faithful portrayal of a subject, and that the use of special techniques or substitute materials may be necessary to overcome these difficulties. These techniques must not be abused: no advertisement in which they have been used will be acceptable, unless the resultant picture presents a fair and reasonable impression of the product or its effects and is not such as to mislead. Unacceptable devices include, for example, the use of glass or plastic sheeting to simulate the effects of floor or furniture polishes.

Descriptions and claims

16 No advertisement may contain any descriptions, claims or illustrations which directly or by implication mislead about the product or service advertised or about its suitability for the purpose recommended. In particular:

(a) **Special claims**—No advertisement shall contain any reference which is likely to lead the public to assume that the product advertised, or an ingredient, has some special property or quality which is incapable of being established.

(b) **Scientific terms and statistics**—Scientific terms, statistics, quotations from technical literature and the like must be used with a proper sense of responsibility to the ordinary viewer. Irrelevant data and scientific jargon must not be used to make claims appear to have a scientific basis they do not possess. Statistics of limited validity should not be presented in such a way as to make it appear that they are universally true.

Advertisers and their agencies must be prepared to produce evidence to substantiate any descriptions, claims or illustrations.

Knocking copy

17 Advertisements should not discredit or attack unfairly other products, services or advertisements. In featuring product benefits, any comparison (either stated or implied) with other products or services must be fair, capable of substantiation and in no way misleading.

Imitation

18 Any imitation likely to mislead viewers, even though it is not of such a kind as to give rise to a legal action for infringement of copyright or for 'passing off', must be avoided.

Price claims

19 Visual and verbal presentations of actual and comparative prices and costs must be accurate and incapable of misleading by undue emphasis or distortion.

Testimonials

20 Testimonials must be genuine and must not be used in a manner likely to mislead. Advertisers and their agencies must be prepared to produce evidence in support of any testimonial and any claims therein.

Guarantees

21 No advertisement may contain the word 'guarantee' or 'guaranteed', 'warranty' or 'warranted' or words having the same meaning, unless the full terms of the guarantee are available for inspection by the Authority and are clearly set out in the advertisement or made available to the purchaser in writing at the point of sale or with the goods. In all cases, the terms must include details of the remedial action open to the purchaser. No advertisement may contain a direct or implied reference to a guarantee which purports to take away or diminish the statutory or common law rights of a purchaser.

Competitions

22 Advertisements inviting the public to take part in competitions where allowable under Section 3(4) of the Television Act, 1964, and the Betting, Gaming and Lotteries Act, 1963 (which requires the presence of an element of skill), should state clearly how prospective entrants may obtain the printed conditions including the arrangements for the announcement of results and for the distribution of prizes.

Homework schemes

23 Fullest particulars of any schemes must be supplied and where it is proposed to make a charge for the raw materials or components and where the advertiser offers to buy back the goods made by the home-worker, the advertisement is not acceptable.

Hire purchase

24 Advertisements relating to the sale of goods on hire-purchase or credit sale must comply with the provisions of the Advertisements (Hire-Purchase) Act, 1957, and from 1 January 1965, Part IV of the Hire-Purchase Act, 1964.

Instructional courses

25 Advertisements offering courses of instruction in trades or subjects leading up to professional or technical examinations must not imply the promise of employment or exaggerate the opportunity of employment or remuneration alleged to be open to those taking such courses; neither should they offer unrecognized 'degrees' or qualifications.

Mail order advertising

26 Advertisements for the sale of goods by mail order are unacceptable unless adequate stocks of the goods in question are carried and they correspond with the description given in the advertisement. Such advertisements are unacceptable where an accommodation address is given.

All advertisements should make it clear that the customer is entitled to return the goods within seven days if not satisfied and to obtain full refund of the purchase price.

Direct sale advertising

27 Direct sale advertising is that placed by the advertiser with the intention that the articles or services advertised, or some other articles or services, shall be sold or provided at the home of the person responding to the advertisement. Where it is the intention of the advertiser to send a representative to call on persons responding to the advertisement, such fact must be apparent from the advertisement or from the particulars subsequently supplied and the respondent must be given an adequate opportunity of refusing any call.

Direct sale advertisements are not acceptable without adequate assurances from the advertiser and his advertising agency (*a*) that the articles advertised will be supplied at the price stated in the advertisement within a reasonable time from stocks sufficient to meet potential demand and (*b*) that sales representatives when calling upon persons responding to the advertisement will demonstrate and make available for sale, the articles advertised.

It will be taken as prima facie evidence of misleading and unacceptable 'bait' advertising for the purpose of 'switch selling' if an advertiser's salesmen seriously disparage or belittle the cheaper article advertised or report unreasonable delays in obtaining delivery or otherwise put difficulties in the way of its purchase.

Financial advertising

28 In view of the importance of giving full information in connection with any offer to the public of debentures, bonds and shares and in view of the difficulty of ensuring that such information is given in the limited time of the normal television advertisement, invitations to invest are limited to the following:

(a) invitations to invest in British Government stocks (including National Savings Certificates), stocks of public boards and nationalized industries in the United Kingdom and Local Government stocks in the United Kingdom.
(b) invitations to place money on deposit or share account with building societies.
(c) invitations to place money on deposit with the Post Office or any Trustee Savings Bank, and, normally, banking companies which are recognized as such for the purposes of the Eighth Schedule to the Companies Act, 1948.

Advertisements by the Unit Trusts authorized as such by the Board of Trade may be accepted provided that these are strictly limited to the name and description of the Trust, the address of its manager, and an invitation to viewers to write to the manager for full particulars of the units available. No person may be shown on the screen during the course of the advertisement.

Advertisements announcing the publication in established national and provincial newspapers and journals of prospectuses offering shares or debentures to the public may be accepted provided that these are strictly limited to giving the name of the company whose shares or debentures are being offered, the amount of the offer and the names and dates of publication of the newspapers and journals in which a prospectus may be found. No person may be shown on the screen during the course of the advertisement.

No advertisement is acceptable which contains any review of or advice about the stock market or investment prospects, or which offers to advise on investments.

Advertising and children
29 Particular care should be taken over advertising that is likely to be seen by large numbers of children and advertisements in which children are to be employed. More detailed guidance is given in Appendix 1.

Advertising of medicines and treatments
30 Within the generality of the Independent Television Code the advertising of medicines and treatments is subject to the detailed rules given in Appendix 2.

Appendix 1 Advertising and children

The viewing child
1 No product or service may be advertised and no method of advertising may be used, in association with a programme intended for children or which large numbers of children are likely to see, which might result in harm to them physically, mentally or morally, and no method of advertising may be employed which takes advantage of the natural credulity and sense of loyalty of children.
In particular:

(a) No advertisement which encourages children to enter strange places or to converse with strangers in an effort to collect coupons, wrappers, labels, etc., is allowed. The details of any collecting scheme must be submitted for investigation to ensure that the scheme contains no element of danger to children.
(b) No advertisement for a commercial product or service is allowed if

it contains any appeal to children which suggests in any way that unless the children themselves buy or encourage other people to buy the product or service they will be failing in some duty or lacking in loyalty towards some person or organization whether that person or organization is the one making the appeal or not.

(c) No advertisement is allowed which leads children to believe that if they do not own the product advertised they will be inferior in some way to other children or that they are liable to be held in contempt or ridicule for not owning it.

(d) No advertisement dealing with the activities of a club is allowed without the submission of satisfactory evidence that the club is carefully supervised in the matter of the behaviour of the children and the company they keep and that there is no suggestion of the club being a secret society.

(e) While it is recognized that children are not the direct purchasers of many products over which they are naturally allowed to exercise preference, care should be taken that they are not encouraged to make themselves a nuisance to other people in the interests of any particular product or service. In an advertisement offering a free gift, a premium or a competition for children, the main emphasis of the advertisement must be on the product with which the offer is associated.

(f) If there is to be reference to a competition for children in an advertisement, the published rules must be submitted for approval before the advertisement can be accepted. The value of prizes and the chances of winning one must not be exaggerated.

(g) To help in the fair portrayal of free gifts for children, an advertisement should, where necessary, make it easy to see the true size of a gift by showing it in relation to some common object against which its scale can be judged.

The child in advertisements

2 The appearance of children in advertisements is subject to the following conditions:

(a) *Employment*
It should be noted that the conditions under which children are employed in the making of advertisements are governed by certain provisions of the Children and Young Persons Act, 1933 (Scotland 1937), and the Act of 1963; the Education Acts, 1944 to 1948; and the appropriate by-laws made by Local Authorities in pursuance of these Acts.

(b) *Contributions to safety*
Any situations in which children are to be seen in television advertisements should be carefully considered from the point of view of safety. *In particular:*
(i) children should not appear to be unattended in street scenes unless they are obviously old enough to be responsible for their own safety; should not be shown playing in the road, unless it is clearly shown to be a play-street or other safe area; should not be shown stepping care-

lessly off the pavement or crossing the road without due care; in busy street scenes should be seen to use zebra crossings in crossing the road; and should otherwise be seen in general, as pedestrians or cyclists, to behave in accordance with the Highway Code.

(ii) children should not be seen leaning dangerously out of windows or over bridges, or climbing dangerous cliffs.

(iii) small children should not be shown climbing up to high shelves or reaching up to take things from a table above their heads.

(iv) medicines, disinfectants, antiseptics and caustic substances must not be shown within reach of children without close parental supervision, nor should children be shown using these products in any way.

(v) children must not be shown using matches or any gas, paraffin, petrol, mechanical or mains-powered appliance which could lead to their suffering burns, electrical shock or other injury.

(vi) children must not be shown driving or riding on agricultural machines (including tractor-drawn carts or implements). Scenes of this kind could encourage contravention of the Agriculture (Safety, Health and Welfare Provisions) Act, 1956.

(vii) an open fire in a domestic scene in an advertisement must always have a fireguard clearly visible if a child is included in the scene.

(*c*) *Good Manners and Behaviour*
Children seen in advertisements should be reasonably well-mannered and well-behaved.

Appendix 2   The advertising of medicines and treatments

(A) Introductory
1   The rules contained in this Appendix have been adopted by the Independent Television Authority after due consultation under the terms of the Television Act with the Advertising Advisory Committee and the Medical Advisory Panel and with the Postmaster-General in so far as he is concerned with the classes and descriptions of advertisements which must not be broadcast and the methods of advertising which must not be employed.

The British Code of Advertising Practice
2   Within the generality of the Independent Television Code of Advertising Standards and Practice and subject to the additional rules below, the Authority's basic requirements in regard to the advertising of medicines and treatments are those laid down in Part B of the British Code of Advertising Practice which is reproduced as part B of this Appendix. The preamble to that Code states:

The harm to the individual that may result from exaggerated, misleading or unwarranted claims justifies the adoption of a very high standard and the inclusion of considerable detail in a Code designed to guide those who are concerned with this form of advertising.

Unacceptable products or services

3 Advertisements for products or services coming within the recognized character of, or specifically concerned with, the following are not acceptable:

(a) products or treatments for bust development or, except as permitted by the British Code of Advertising Practice, for slimming, weight reduction or limitation, or figure control
(b) contraceptives
(c) smoking cures
(d) products for the treatment of alcoholism
(e) contact or corneal lenses
(f) clinics for the treatment of hair and scalp
(g) products for the treatment of haemorrhoids

N.B. An advertiser who markets more than one product may not use advertising copy devoted to an acceptable product for the purposes of publicizing the brand name or other identification of an unacceptable product.

Avoidance of impression of professional advice

4 In advertisements for medicines, treatments and products which are claimed to promote health or be beneficial in illness, the following are not allowable:

(a) visual presentations of doctors, dentists, pharmaceutical chemists, nurses, midwives, etc., which give the impression of professional advice or recommendation, and
(b) statements giving the impression of professional advice or recommendation made by persons who appear in the advertisements and who are presented, either directly or by implication, as being qualified to give such advice or recommendation.

To avoid misunderstanding about the status of the presenter of a medicine or treatment, it may be necessary to establish positively in the course of an advertisement that the presenter is not a professionally qualified adviser.

Hospital tests

5 No reference may be made to a hospital test unless the Medical Committee of the hospital concerned is prepared to vouch for its validity.

Testimonials

6 No advertisement for a medicine or treatment may include a testimonial by a person well known in public life, sport, entertainment, etc.

Tonic
7 The use of this expression is not acceptable in advertisements for medicines or treatments or products for which medical or health claims are made.

Vitamins
8 No advertisement should state or imply that good health is likely to be endangered solely because people do not supplement their diets with vitamins.

(B) The British Code of Advertising Practice
This part of the Code deals with the Advertising of Medicines and Treatments and it is important that this should be regarded as setting forth the minimum standards to be observed by the parties concerned. The harm to the individual that may result from exaggerated, misleading or unwarranted claims justifies the adoption of a very high standard and the inclusion of considerable detail in a Code designed to guide those who are concerned with this form of advertising.

All advertising media are urged not to accept advertisements in respect of any product or treatment from any advertising agency or advertiser who disregards the provisions of this part of the Code in any form of advertising or publicity relating to that product or treatment.

The advance of medical science may influence the view to be taken of the efficacy of medicines, products, appliances or treatments and, therefore, this part of the Code will be subject to periodic review.

The provisions of this part of the Code do not apply to an advertisement published by or under the authority of a Government Ministry or Department, nor to an advertisement published only in so far as is reasonably necessary to bring it to the notice of registered medical or dental practitioners, registered pharmacists or registered nurses.

Section 1 General principles

Advertisements should not contain any of the following:

Cure
1 A claim to cure any ailment or symptoms of ill-health, nor should an advertisement contain a word or expression used in such a form or context as to mean in the positive sense the extirpation of any ailment, illness or disease.

Illnesses, etc., properly requiring medical attention
2 Any matter which can be regarded as an offer of a medicine or product for, or advice relating to the treatment of, serious diseases, complaints, conditions, indications or symptoms which should rightly receive the attention of a registered medical practitioner.

Misleading or exaggerated claims

3 Any matter which directly or by implication misleads or departs from the truth as to the composition, character or action of the medicine or treatment advertised or as to its suitability for the purpose for which it is recommended.

Appeals to fear

4 Any statement or illustration calculated to induce fear on the part of the reader that he is suffering, or may without treatment suffer, or suffer more severely, from an ailment, illness or disease.

Competitions

5 An offer of any prize competitions or similar schemes. It should be noted that such an advertisement may constitute an offence under Section 47 of the Betting, Gaming and Lotteries Act, 1963.

Diagnosis or treatment by correspondence

6 An offer to diagnose by correspondence diseases, conditions or any symptoms of ill-health in a human being or a request from any person for a statement of his or any other person's symptoms of ill-health with a view to advising as to or providing for treatment of such conditions of ill-health by correspondence or an offer to treat by correspondence any ailment, illness, disease or symptoms thereof in a human being.

Disparaging references

7 Any direct or implied disparagement of the products, medicines or treatments of another advertiser or manufacturer or registered medical practitioners or the medical profession.

Money-back offers

8 Offers to refund money to dissatisfied users.

College, clinic, institute, laboratory

9 The words 'College', 'Clinic', 'Institute', 'Laboratory', or similar terms unless an establishment corresponding to the description used does in fact exist.

Doctors, hospitals, etc.

10 Any reference to doctors, hospitals or hospital tests, whether British or foreign, unless such reference can be substantiated by independent evidence and can properly be used in the manner proposed; or the name of a product containing the term 'Doctor' or 'Dr' unless the product were so named prior to 1 January 1944.

Products offered particularly to women

11 Offers of products, medicines or treatments for disorders or

irregularities peculiar to women, which contain the following or similar expressions which may imply that the product, medicine or treatment advertised can be effective in inducing miscarriage: 'Female Pills', 'Not to be used in cases of pregnancy', 'The stronger the remedy the more effective it is', 'Never known to fail'.

Illustrations
12 Any illustration which by itself or in combination with words used in connection therewith is likely to convey a misleading impression, or any reasonable inference which can be drawn infringing the provisions of this Code.

Exaggerated copy
13 Copy which is exaggerated by reason of the improper use of words, phrases or methods of presentation, e.g. the use of the words 'magic', 'magical', 'miracle', 'miraculous'.

'Natural' remedies
14 A claim or suggestion, contrary to the fact that the article advertised is in the form in which it occurs in nature or that its value lies in its being a 'natural' product.

Special claims
15 Any reference which is calculated to lead the public to assume that the article, product, medicine or treatment advertised, or an ingredient has some special property or quality which is in fact unknown or unrecognized.

Sexual weakness, premature ageing, loss of virility
16 A claim that the product, medicine or treatment advertised will promote sexual virility or be effective in treating sexual weakness, or habits associated with sexual excess or indulgence, or any ailment, illness or disease associated with those habits.

In particular, such terms as 'premature ageing', 'loss of virility' will be regarded as conditions for which medicines, products, appliances or treatment may not be advertised.

Slimming, weight reduction or limitation, or figure control
17 An offer of any product or treatment for slimming, weight reduction or limitation or figure control, if the taking or using of the product or following the course of treatment is likely to lead to harmful effects.

Tonic
18 The expression 'tonic' if it implies that the product or medicine can be used in the treatment of sexual weakness.

Testimonials
19 Any testimonial containing a statement or implication which would not be permitted in the text of the advertisement, or any testimonial other than one limited to the actual views of the writer, or any testimonial given by a doctor other than a registered British medical practitioner unless it is obvious in the advertisement that the writer is not a registered British medical practitioner.

Hypnosis
20 Any offer to diagnose or treat complaints or conditions by hypnosis.

Hair and scalp products and treatments
21 (a) Any offer of diagnosis by post or telephone or any claim or implication that the product or treatment advertised will do more than arrest loss of hair.
(b) Any particulars of establishments administering treatments for the hair and scalp other than the name, address, telephone number and hours of attendance and the types of treatment available; any reference to specific conditions for which the treatment is intended.

Haemorrhoids
22 Any offer of products for the treatment of haemorrhoids unless the following warning notice appears with the directions for use on the container itself or its labels: 'Persons who suffer from haemorrhoids are advised to consult a doctor'.

Products offered for the relief of backache and rheumatic pains
23 Claims for the relief of backache and rheumatic pains based upon the urinary antiseptic properties of the products advertised.

Section II   Restrictions Imposed by Statute

Cancer
1 The Cancer Act, 1939, makes it an offence to take part in the publication of any advertisement which contains an offer to treat any person for cancer, to prescribe any remedy therefor, or to give any advice calculated to lead to its use in the treatment of cancer.

Abortion
2 The Pharmacy and Medicines Act, 1941, makes it an offence to take part in the publication of any advertisement referring to any article in terms which are calculated to lead to the use of the article for procuring the miscarriage of women.

Bright's disease, cataract, diabetes, epilepsy, fits, glaucoma, locomotor ataxy, paralysis, tuberculosis
3 The Pharmacy and Medicines Act, 1941, makes it an offence to

take part in the publication of an advertisement referring to any article in terms which are calculated to lead to the use of that article for the purpose of the treatment of these diseases.

(Note: Bright's Disease is sometimes referred to as 'Nephritis', Epilepsy as 'Falling Sickness', and Tuberculosis as 'Phthisis', 'Consumption' or 'Wasting Disease'.)

Venereal diseases

4 The Venereal Diseases Act, 1917, makes it an offence to advertise in any way any preparation or substance of any kind as a medicine for the prevention, cure or relief of venereal diseases.

The above prohibitions do not apply in the case of technical journals which circulate among persons of the classes mentioned in the respective Acts. It is permissible, for example, for advertisements to appear in technical journals intended for circulation mainly among registered medical practitioners, registered pharmacists and nurses (except in the cases of (4) above, where no provision is made in the Venereal Diseases Act, for advertising in journals circulating among nurses).

The foregoing is a very broad outline of the effects of the relevant sections of the respective Acts. For further and more detailed information, reference should be made to the Acts.

Section III   Examples of diseases, illnesses or conditions for which medicines, treatments, products or appliances may not be advertised

No advertisement should refer to any medicine, product, appliance or advice in terms calculated to lead to its use for the treatment of any of the following illnesses or conditions:

Amenorrhoea	Dermatitis
Anaemia (pernicious)	Diseased ankles
Ankles, diseased	Disseminated sclerosis
Arterio sclerosis	Ears (any structural or organic defect of the auditory system)
Artery troubles	
Arthritis	Enlarged glands
Asthma (a)	Erysipelas
Barber's rash	Eyes (any structural or organic defect of the optical system)
Bleeding disease	
Blood pressure	Fungus infections (b)
Breasts, diseases of the	Gallstones
Carbuncles	Glands, enlarged
Cardiac symptoms, heart troubles	Goitre
Convulsions	Heart troubles, cardiac symptoms

Impetigo
Indigestion, where the reference is to chronic or persistent
Insomnia, where the reference is to chronic or persistent
Itch
Kidneys, disorders or diseases of the
Lazy eye
Leg troubles
Lupus
Menopausal ailments
Obesity
Osteoarthritis
Pernicious anaemia
Phlebitis
Prolapse
Psoriasis—except where the reference is confined to relief from the effects of the complaint

Purpura
Pyorrhoea
Rheumatism, where the reference is to chronic or persistent
Rheumatoid arthritis
Ringworm
Scabies
Skin diseases, where the reference is to 'all or most' skin diseases, or skin ailments in general
Sleeplessness, where the reference is to chronic or persistent
Squint
Sycosis
Thrombosis
Ulcers: Duodenal, Gastric, Pyloric, Stomach
Urinary infections
Varicose veins (c)
Whooping cough (d)

Note:

(a) The restriction does not apply provided that:
(i) It is made clear in the advertisement that the medicine, treatment, product or appliance advertised is only for the alleviation of an attack of asthma.
(ii) The advertisement contains a recommendation that sufferers should seek medical advice.

(b) The prohibition does not apply to the advertisement of products for the treatment of athlete's foot.

(c) Advertisements for elastic hosiery are permissible provided that no claim is made that the product has any beneficial effect on the condition.

(d) This restriction does not apply where the reference to whooping cough appears only on labels or in literature issued with the product and is limited to offering the product for alleviating the symptoms of whooping cough.

Appendix 3   Statutes affecting television advertising

The following statutes may restrict, control or otherwise affect television advertising and should be noted:

Accommodation Agencies Act, 1953.
Adoption Act, 1958 (Section 51).
Advertisements (Hire Purchase) Act, 1957.

Betting, Gaming and Lotteries Act, 1963.
Building Societies Act, 1960 (Sections 5 and 7).
Cancer Act, 1939 (Section 4).
Children and Young Persons (Harmful Publications) Act, 1955.
Children's Act, 1958 (Section 37).
Children and Young Persons Act, 1933 (Scotland, 1937).
Children and Young Persons Act, 1963.
Copyright Act, 1956.
Defamation Act, 1952.
Education Acts, 1944 to 1948.
Food and Drugs Act, 1955, and the Labelling of Food Order (S.I. 1953, No. 536) as amended by the Labelling of Food (Amendment) Regulations.
Geneva Convention Act, 1957 (Section 6).
Hire-Purchase Act, 1964.
Larceny Act, 1861 (Section 102).
Merchandise Marks Acts, 1887–1953.
Opticians Act, 1958.
Pharmacy and Medicines Act, 1941 (Sections 8–13; 15–17).
Prevention of Fraud (Investments) Act, 1958 (Section 13).
Protection of Depositors Act, 1963.
Registered Designs Act, 1949.
Sale of Goods Act, 1893.
Television Act, 1964.
Trade Marks Act, 1938.
Venereal Diseases Act, 1917 (Sections 2 and 3).
Weights and Measures Act, 1963.

Appendix B

Summary of recommendations from the Statement of Policy of the Advertising Inquiry Council, July 1964

The principal recommendations for action by Government which AIC proposes may be summarized as follows:

1. On false and misleading claims
(a) That a body with powers similar to those of the Federal Trade Commission in the United States should be established to control the use of false and misleading claims in all types of advertisements and in all media.
(b) That the burden of substantiating all claims should rest with the advertisers.

2. On advertising and monopoly
(a) That the Monopolies Commission should be empowered to investigate the general relationship between advertising and control of the market.
(b) That the Commission should also investigate the trading practices of the advertising industry as soon as possible.

3. On the volume of advertising
(a) That the taxation of advertising should be seriously considered to encourage a stricter control of advertising expenditure, and limit the increase in the nation's advertising bill.

4. On advertising of 'special' products
(a) That legislation should be introduced to ban cigarette advertising on all media.
(b) That powers should be included in this legislation which could extend the ban to other 'special' products if advertisers failed to take voluntary action to remove features which were against the public interest.

5. On advertising and commercial television
(a) That the ITA should be asked to reduce the amount of advertising and to confine it to intervals between programmes at specific times during the day.
(b) That the ITA should reduce the tendency towards excessive and meaningless claims in television commercials.
(c) That where the ITA refuses to act, the Postmaster-General should use his existing or extended powers to the desired end.

6. On advertising and editorial policy
(a) That the Press Council, either on its own initiative or on receipt of a complaint, be empowered to investigate any case of advertising influencing editorial policy, and to publish its findings.

7. On the control of outdoor advertising
(a) That Government should review the effects of the advertising industry's voluntary code of standards for outside advertising, and accelerate the designation of areas of special control.

Appendix C

Advertising expenditure statistics

Table 1 *Advertising expenditure in Britain*

	1938	1960	1961	1962	1963	1964	1965	1966
Total expenditure (£million)	98	457	474	490	517	568	590	439*
as % of consumer expenditure	2·2	2·7	2·7	2·6	2·6	2·7	2·6	1·8*
as % of national income	2·0	2·2	2·1	2·1	2·1	2·1	2·1	1·5*
as % of gross national product	1·9	2·0	2·0	2·0	2·0	2·0	2·0	1·4*
Press advertising exp. on products (£million)	21	91	88	101	110	118	114	111·5
(of which) food & drink	5	22	20	22	24	22	20	18
(of which) tobacco & cigarettes	1·8	4	4	6	6	8	11	10·5
(of which) household stores & equipment	4·3			25·5	26·5	28	25·5	25·5
(of which) motors & cycles	2	9	9	9	10·5	12	11	11
Television advertising exp. on products		77	90	85	92·5	102	106	109
(of which) food & drink		31	37	38	41·5	45·5	52	56
(of which) tobacco & cigarettes		4·5	5	6	6	8	7	2·5
(of which) toiletries & cosmetics		8	8·5	9·5	10·5	10	11	12

* The estimates of total advertising expenditure published by the Advertising Association in 1967 exclude sales promotion expenditure which was previously included. The reasons for adopting the new basis are explained in *Advertising Expenditure 1960–66*.

	1938	1960	1961	1962	1963	1964	1965	1966
(of which) household stores & services	15	18	18	19	22	22·5	22	
(of which) motors & cycles	2	2	2	2·5	3	4	4	

Table II

	1960	1964	1965	1966
Total press advertising exp. (£million)	218	250	258	289
Total television advertising exp.	72	102	106	109
Total outdoor advertising exp.	25	33	34	32
Total film, radio & slide advertising exp.	6	8	8	9
Sales promotion	97	116	122·5	
(of which) window & interior display	26	37	39·5	
(of which) leaflets & catalogues	39	43	45	
(of which) exhibitions	16	18·5	19	
(of which) free samples, gift schemes	16	17·5	19	

(Sources: *Advertising Expenditure*, 1960–66; *Advertisers Weekly*, March 1966; 10 February 1967; *Business Man's Desk Book*, 1966, 1967)

Table III *Advertising expenditure in 5 countries*

	1956 % of NI	1962–5 % of NI	1965 % of consumer expenditure
United States	2·9	2·7	3·6
Britain	1·7	2·1	2·5
West Germany	1·5	1·8	2·3
Japan	1·0		2·3
France	0·6	0·8	0·9

(Sources: *Financial Times*, 26 June 1967; *Economist*, 17 July 1965, 20 August 1966)

223

Table IV *Display advertising expenditure in Britain (£million)*

Media	1960	1964	1965	1966
Press†	149	175	179	182
Television	72	102	106	109
Poster and transport	16	18	18	17
Outdoor signs	13	15	15	15
Cinema	5	6	6	6
Radio	1	2	2	3
Total	**256**	**318**	**326**	**332**

† excluding financial, classified and trade and technical advertising

Press classified advertising	34	51	56
(of which) national newspapers	8	14	15
(of which) regional newspapers	25	35	39
(of which) magazines & periodicals	1	2	2

(Source: *Financial Times*, 26 June 1967)

NB These estimates of expenditure tend to ignore the complicating factor of various kinds of discounts on published rate card prices. Estimates tend therefore to be somewhat excessive.

Table V *Consumer expenditure 1961–6 (£million at 1958 prices)*

	Total	Food	Alc. Drink	Tobacco
1961	17,113	4,838	1,080	1,101
1962	17,463	4,985	1,084	1,055
1963	18,282	4,961	1,115	1,084
1964	18,972	5,044	1,191	1,058
1965	19,292	5,059	1,169	1,012
1966	19,598	5,112	1,204	1,022

	Housing	Fuel & light	Clothing	Durable goods	Other goods
1961	1,566	758	1,667	1,419	2,166
1962	1,613	836	1,654	1,495	2,220
1963	1,667	904	1,712	1,814	2,308
1964	1,704	875	1,766	1,993	2,475
1965	1,767	936	1,833	1,954	2,599
1966	1,818	972	1,827	1,896	2,705

Source: *Financial Times*, 26 June 1967)

Bibliography

1. **The most useful of the books concerned with advertising are:**
Harris, R. & Seldon, A. *Advertising and the Public*. Deutsch, 1962.
Harris, R. & Seldon, A. *Advertising in Action*. Hutchinson, 1962.
Taplin, W. *Advertising—A New Approach*. Hutchinson, 1960.
Mayer, M. *Madison Avenue, U.S.A.* Penguin, 1961.
Pearson, J. & Turner, G. *The Persuasion Industry*. Eyre & Spottiswoode, 1965.
Wright, J. S. & Warner, D. S. *Advertising*. McGraw-Hill, 1962.

2. **Other books of interest include:**
Baster, A. S. J. *Advertising Reconsidered*. King, 1935.
Brown, J. A. C. *Techniques of Persuasion*. Penguin, 1966.
Birch, L. *The Advertising We Deserve?* Vista, 1962
Baynes, M. *Advertising on Trial*. Bow Group, 1956.
Corden, M. *A Tax on Advertising?* Fabian Society, 1961.
Dichter, E. *The Strategy of Desire*. Boardman, 1960.
Elliott, B. B. *A History of English Advertising*. Batsford, 1962.
Galbraith, J. K. *American Capitalism—The Concept of Countervailing Power*. Penguin, 1962.
Galbraith, J. K. *The Affluent Society*. Penguin, 1963.
Gloag, J. *Advertising in Modern Society*. Heinemann, 1959.
Harris, R. & Seldon, A. *Advertising in a Free Society*. IEA, 1959.
Henry, H. *Motivation Research: Its Practice and Uses*. Crosby Lockwood, 1958.
Heyworth, Lord & Tempel, F. J. *Advertising*. Unilever, 1958.
Hobson, J. W. *Selection of Advertising Media*. Business Publications, 1955.
Hoggart, R. *The Uses of Literacy*. Chatto & Windus, 1957.
Lees, D. S. *Economic Consequences of the Professions*. IEA, 1966.
McIver, C. *Marketing*. Business Publications, 1964.
Ogilvy, D. *Confessions of an Advertising Man*. Longmans, 1964.
Packard, V. *The Hidden Persuaders*. Penguin, 1960.
Packard, V. *The Waste Makers*. Penguin, 1963.
Silverman, R. *A Statistical Analysis of Advertising Expenditure*. Cambridge University Press, 1948.
Sutton, J. *Signs in Action*. Studio Vista, 1965.
Taplin, W. *The Origin of Television Advertising in the U.K.* Pitman, 1961.
Thompson, D. (ed) *Discrimination and Popular Culture*. Penguin, 1964.
Turner, E. S. *The Shocking History of Advertising*. Penguin, 1965.
Williams, F. *The American Invasion*. Blond, 1962.

3. **The most important reports have been:**
Report of the Committee on Broadcasting (Pilkington) (cmnd. 1753). HMSO, 1962.

Final Report of the Committee on Consumer Protection (Molony) (cmnd. 1781). HMSO, 1962.

Report No. 4 of the National Board for Prices and Incomes—Prices of Household and Toilet Soaps, Soap Powders and Soap Flakes, and Soapless Detergents. HMSO, 1965.

Report of the Monopolies Commission on the Supply of Household Detergents. HMSO, 1966.

Report of a Commission of Inquiry into Advertising (Reith). Labour Party, 1966.

Quadrennial Reports on Advertising Expenditure. Advertising Association, 1956, 1960, 1964

Advertising—Report on a Survey carried out by National Opinion Polls Ltd. 1965.

Index

Advertiser: brand loyalty, 21;
classified ads, 197; concern
with mass of public, 16; complaints handling, 112; crooked
advertisers, 104, 167; differentiation of products, 20; duty, 106-
107; economies of scale, 23-4;
emphasis on minor virtues, 35-
36; fear of losing competitive
advantage, 61; influence on
newspapers, 103; information
for consumers, 163; interests of
reputable advertisers, 148, 167,
185, 193; large expenditure to
catch national audience, 19;
limited choice advantages, 25;
manufacturer's role, interest
and methods, 15, 17, 24-7, 29-
33, 62, 112, 137-9, 160-2;
naming of Code offenders, 198;
pressure on agencies, 189; rate
of technical innovation, 22-3;
reflects standards of his society,
33-4; reluctance to knock competitors, 16; responsibility, 159;
self-regulation, 124-7; sex, 33-
34; small advertisers' danger,
194; social goals, 182; techniques of TV presentation, 89;
truth and exaggeration, 15, 38;
use of gimmicks, 18, 30-2; vulgarity, 36; wearisome repetition of message, 17
Advertisements: advertising features, 102, 130; classified, 102,
106, 123, 197, 224; direct sale,
72, 125, 208; financial, 208;
magazine, 124, 200; medical,
91-6, 125-6, 207, 211-18; mail
order, 125, 207; press, 72, 102-
106, 110, 123, 197, 200; television, 89-90, 93, 109, 121,
123, 141, 149, 200-1, 204-18;
unacceptable (products and
services), 92-3, 205, 212, 217-
218
Advertising abroad: Australia 123;
USA, 74, 76, 122, 132-3, 194,
223; USSR, 6-7, 113
Advertising agencies (and agents):
34, 96, 98, 114, 116-17, 120,
124, 126-7, 140, 148, 150, 153,
185, 189, 197-8
Advertising Association, 55, 70-1,
126, 128-9, 131, 152, 154, 200,
222; Advertising Investigation
Department, 126, 129, 191,
197; expenditure surveys, 200,
222; publicity clubs, 129
Advertising Inquiry Council, 151,
154-6, 220-1; policy statement, 155, 220-1
Advertising Standards Authority,
58, 71-2, 74-5, 83, 114, 124,
127-8, 139, 143-4, 152-5, 168,
177-8, 191-2, 197-8; budget,
128, 197; complaints, 75, 83,
143-4, 192; powers, 128, 130,
144, 198; relations with Advertising Association, xiii, 152,
192; with Consumer Council,
71-2, 177; with Consumer
Association, 168; self-regulation system, 71-2, 74-5, 120-
133, 139, 144, 178, 197-
198

খুলনা ৭৬২৭২৭

ঢাকা ৭৬৩ ১৭১০